The Spirit of the Book of Revelation

Journal of Pentecostal Theology Supplement Series

30

Editors

John Christopher Thomas
Rickie Moore
Steven J. Land

ISSN 0966 7393

Deo Publishing

The SPIRIT

of the Book of

REVELATION

Robby Waddell

deo
PUBLISHING

BLANDFORD FORUM

Journal of Pentecostal Theology Supplement Series, 30
ISSN 0966 7393

Published by Deo Publishing
P.O. Box 6284, Blandford Forum, Dorset DT11 1AQ, UK

The Odyssea Greek font used to publish this work is available from Linguist's Software, Inc., www.linguistsoftware.com, PO Box 580, Edmonds, WA 98020-0580 USA, tel. (425) 775-1130.

British Library Cataloguing-in-Publication data
A catalogue record for this book is available from the British Library

ISBN 90-5854-030-8

Contents

Chapter 3
Hearing What the Spirit Says to the Churches:
A Profile of a Pentecostal Reader of the Apocalypse

Chapter 4
The Faithful Witness of a Pneumatic Church:
The Spirit of Prophecy and the People of God

Preface

This book is a revision of my Ph.D. thesis written at the University of Sheffield. It could have never been brought to completion without the assistance and support of numerous people. First, I want to thank Jesus Christ, my savior, sanctifier, Spirit baptizer, healer, and coming king. In numerous ways, I have been sustained by His gracious hand and I will labor in His kingdom until He returns.

The thesis was jointly supervised by Professor Loveday C.A. Alexander and Professor John Christopher Thomas. Loveday supplied helpful guidance and encouragement during the research and writing process. She continues to be an example of first rate scholarship and stalwart commitment to the church. My debt to Chris is far too deep ever to repay. He is scholar, pastor, and friend. Indeed, the topic of the thesis was originally suggested by Chris and now he serves as the editor of the work in monograph form.

During my time in Sheffield, the post-graduate community offered me friendship and stimulation both academically and spiritually. I especially want to thank John (and Katie) Lyons, Mark (and Lisa) Blackwell, Peter Braunberger, and Carolyn Holding. Many nights discussing methodology, theology, and politics are remembered fondly. Although our time together was brief the relationships that were forged are deep and true, an authentic community of faith. I would also be remiss if I failed to thank Alison Bygrave and Gill Fogg, the departmental secretaries whose assistance was above and beyond the call of duty.

My development academically has been greatly influenced by the faculty at the Church of God Theological Seminary. My time at the seminary both as a student and as an Assistant Professor of New Testament has formed me in every aspect of my life. The friendship of Ken Archer has been especially helpful. I also would like to thank Rickie Moore who has mentored me in a variety of ways. His prophetic voice often rings in my ears and heart. Needed support was also offered by Jackie and Cheryl Bridges Johns, James Beaty, Steven Land, Oliver McMahan, and Hollis Gause.

My time spent in Sheffield would never have been possible without the prayers and financial support of my parents, Sue and the late Bob Waddell. I was reared in a Pentecostal home where I developed a passion for the Word and the Spirit. My interest in the Apocalypse can be traced back to my childhood when I would unroll my father's dispensational charts and try to decipher what the future would be. I would love to know his thoughts on this work. Generous support has also come in a number of ways from my in-laws, Jerry and Ann Patrick along with my siblings Suzanne and Greg, Chip and Sharon, and Stephen and Kelly.

Many friends in Cleveland have also been consistent dialog partners including: J.M. Creech, Keena Warren Cox, Lance Giannone, and Matt Boyd. I have taught a course on the book of Revelation in a variety of contexts including, Puerto Rico, North Carolina, Tennessee, and California. Students from my course have helped me clarify my position on the pneumatology of the Apocalypse as well as many other aspects of the text.

A fair amount of this book was written in San Just, Puerto Rico while I was on multiple teaching assignments. A special thank you goes to the hospitality of my host Ildefonso (and Maribell) Caraballo. Another significant portion was written in the wee hours of the morning in the basement of the North Cleveland Church of God. I offer my thanks to the many Master's Commission students who said a prayer for this project, and to Larry Wilson, a mentor and a friend. The final revision of this work took place in Oakland, California, on the campus of Patten University. The community at Patten was very supportive and I would like to make special mention of Ron Hooks, Gregg Moder and Gary Moncher, all who have inspired me in their own ways. I also want to thank Jennifer Hanson, Michael Johnson and David Bustos for help with preparing the indexes, and I especially want to thank David for proofreading the entire manuscript.

I must reserve my deepest gratitude for the church family at Woodward Avenue. The folks at Woodward offered constant support never felt more strongly than at the untimely death of my father. I thank Gail and Preston Moser for their prayers and support. Wanda Beck Norwood has been a spiritual companion whose friendship and encouragement remains invaluable.

My wife, Angela, along with my three daughters, Katie, Hannah, and Rebekah have certainly sacrificed the most. Katie and Hannah spent a large portion of their lives as the daughters of a Bible student and Angela has shared in every way the joy and the sufferings of bringing this work to completion. It is to them that I dedicate this monograph.

Abbreviations

APS	*Australasian Pentecostal Studies*
AUSS	*Andrews University Seminary Studies*
BAGD	W. Bauer, W.F. Arndt, W. Gingrich, and F.W. Danker, *A Greek-English Lexicon of the New Testament.* Chicago: University of Chicago Press, 1979.
Bib	*Biblica*
Bib Int	*Biblical Interpretation*
BibToday	*The Bible Today*
BJRLM	*Bulletin of the John Rylands Library of Manchester*
BR	*Biblical Research*
BTB	*Biblical Theology Bulletin*
CBQ	*Catholic Biblical Quarterly*
CGR	*The Conrad Grebel Review*
CR:BS	*Currents in Research: Biblical Studies*
CurrTheolMiss	*Currents in Theological Missions*
DPCM	*Dictionary of Pentecostal and Charismatic Movements,* Burgess, S.M. *et al.* Grand Rapids: Zondervan, 1988.
EPTA Bulletin	*European Pentecostal Theological Association Bulletin*
EQ	*Evangelical Quarterly*
EvT	*Evangelische Theologie*
ExpTim	*Expository Times*
HBT	*Horizons in Biblical Theology*
IBS	*Irish Biblical Studies*
ICC	International Critical Commentary
Int	*Interpretation*
ITQ	*Irish Theological Quarterly*
JAAR	*Journal of the American Academy of Religion*
JBL	*Journal of Biblical Literature*
JPT	*Journal of Pentecostal Theology*
JSNT	*Journal for the Study of the New Testament*
JTS	*Journal of Theological Studies*

KJV	King James Version
LXX	Septuagint
NASB	New American Standard Bible
Neot	*Neotestamentica*
NIV	New International Version
NKJV	New King James Version
NLT	New Living Translation
NovT	*Novum Testamentum*
NRSV	New Revised Standard Version
NTS	*New Testament Studies*
NZM	*Neue Zeitschrift für Missionwissenschaft*
Pneuma	*Pneuma: The Journal of the Society for Pentecostal Studies*
RB	*Revue Biblique*
REB	Revised English Bible
RevThom	*Revue thomiste*
RSR	*Revue de Sciences religieuses*
RSV	Revised Standard Version
SBL	Society of Biblical Literature
SPS	Society for Pentecostal Studies
StudP	*Studia Patristica*
Stud Theo	*Studia Theologica*
TDNT	*Theological Dictionary of the New Testament* I-X, ed. G. Kittel and G. Friedrich. Grand Rapids: Eerdmans, 1964-1976.
Theo Ed	*Theological Education*
Them	*Themelios*
TynBul	*Tyndale Bulletin*
WBC	Word Biblical Commentary
WTJ	*Wesleyan Theological Journal*
ZNW	*Zeitschrift für die Neutestamentliche Wissenschaft*

Introduction

The book is called Revelation, but much of it remains a mystery today.[1]

1. The Task

Apocalyptic literature is known for its cryptic language and equivocal symbols which have generated a plethora of esoteric interpretations. Accordingly, readers of the Apocalypse are often left with as many questions as answers. Who are the two witnesses? Who or what is the beast? What is the meaning of the numerology? Do the symbols of the Apocalypse refer solely to the lives of the original audience? Is the book a map of church history, or are the prophecies primarily concerned with current and future events?[2] Such questions have 'exercised the ingenuity of interpreters in the course of the centuries'.[3] I.T. Beckwith proposes that the various answers given to these questions have been influenced in each case by the interpreter's circumstances, either political or ecclesiastical, and by the methodology and hermeneutic applied to the text.[4] Despite the attention given to the Apoca-

[1] A.W. Wainwright, *Mysterious Apocalypse: Interpreting the Book of Revelation* (Nashville: Abingdon Press, 1993), p. 11. Jerome describes Revelation: *quot verba, tot mysteria,* 'as many mysteries as there are words', cited in F. van der Meer, *Apocalypse: Visions from the Book of Revelation in Western Art* (New York: Alpine Fine Arts Collection Ltd, 1978), p. 31.

[2] Various interpretative grids are used to understand Revelation. The four major views are the preterist, historicist, futurist, and idealist. The best approaches are those that realize these positions are not mutually exclusive. See G.K. Beale, *The Book of Revelation* (Grand Rapids: Eerdmans, 1999), pp. 44-49.

[3] I.T. Beckwith, *The Apocalypse of John* (Grand Rapids: Baker Book House, 1967, repr. of 1919 edition), p. 319.

[4] Beckwith notes the tacit subjectivism in his observation concerning the history of

lypse since 1919, when Beckwith's observation originally appeared, a consensus is far from being reached on most aspects of the text.

The pneumatology of the Apocalypse is one area that has received relatively little attention by comparison with other aspects of the text. In fact, some scholars suggest that the Apocalypse is completely devoid of a pneumatology because the text fails to make any explicit reference to the Holy Spirit, the Spirit of God, or the Spirit of Christ. In a treatment of the pneumatology of the Johannine community, Gary Burge allots only two paragraphs to the Apocalypse.[5] Burge does not exclude the Apocalypse as a legitimate portion of Johannine literature, but he fails to see any significant treatment of the Spirit in the text. He cites Eduard Schweizer's comment with approval that 'the decisive point' in understanding the pneumatology of the Apocalypse is to recognize that πνεῦμα is not the entity known as the 'Holy Spirit', but rather, πνεῦμα is 'no other than the exalted Lord Himself'.[6]

Part of the challenge of exploring the role of the Spirit in the Apocalypse is that John never uses the familiar New Testament designation πνεῦμα ἁγίον to describe the Spirit. However, it would be a mistake to assume that John never makes reference to the Spirit. Despite the fact that references to the Spirit, both explicit and implicit, are less numerous than references to Jesus or God the Father, the role of the Spirit is an intricate part of the message of Revelation. Although one cannot discern the Spirit's role merely by studying the explicit references to πνεῦμα, a survey of these does indicate the challenge facing an interpreter of this theme.

John uses πνεῦμα eighteen times to refer to the Spirit. These references can be divided into three major categories: (1) four references to the seven spirits, τὰ ἑπτὰ πνεύματα (1:4; 3:1; 4:5; 5:6); (2) four instances of the phrase, 'in the Spirit', ἐν πνεύματι (1:10; 4:2; 17:3; 21:10); and (3) ten references to the Spirit, τὸ πνεῦμα (2:7, 11, 17, 29; 3:6, 13, 22; 14:13; 19:10; 22:17).[7] The first seven references from the

interpretation of the Apocalypse, and he advises close attention to the historical situation of the author and his audience as well as attention to the literary influences of the text, primarily Jewish Apocalypses and Old Testament scriptures.

[5] G. Burge, *The Anointed Community* (Grand Rapids: Eerdmans, 1987), pp. 176-177.

[6] E. Schweizer, 'Πνεῦμα', *TDNT* 6 (1968), p. 449.

[7] John uses πνεῦμα four other times, where the reference is not to the Spirit (13:15; 16:13, 14; 18:2). Three times πνεῦμα refers to foul spirits (16:13, 14; 18:2). Once πνεῦμα means 'breath' (13:15: the second beast gives 'breath' to the image of the first beast). The remaining two uses of πνεῦμα represent a *double-entendre* (11:11; 22:6).

final category fall into a single group with the repetitive phrase, ὁ ἔχων οὖς ἀκουσάτω τί τὸ πνεῦμα λέγει ταῖς ἐκκλησίαις, placed before the admonition to conquer in the first three letters to the Asian churches and after the admonition in the final four letters. On two occasions John records the direct discourse of the Spirit (14:13; 22:17). The reference to the Spirit in 19:10 is somewhat disputed as is evidenced in the English translations. Some translations use a lower case 's' when translating πνεῦμα in 19:10, suggesting that the reference is not to the Holy Spirit.[8]

2. The Methodological Preliminaries

While focusing on the pneumatology of Revelation, this study also gives special attention to a pair of hermeneutical matters, namely methodology and location of the interpreter. In investigating the role of the Spirit in the Apocalypse a method is employed that contains two primary foci. The method has been dubbed 'intertextuality'. Utilized primarily within biblical studies in relation to the 'Use of the Old Testament in the New', intertextuality approaches the issue of allusions from a literary perspective as opposed to the more traditional historical perspective. Historical approaches to Old Testament allusions are primarily concerned with identifying sources and establishing the extent to which a prior text exerts influence on a later text. Notwithstanding the value of a literary approach to the allusions within the text, intertextuality in its native discipline of literary studies refers to more than the effect of chronologically earlier texts on a later text. An intertextual analysis is also concerned with the effect that chronologically later texts have on the interpretation of earlier texts. In other words, the interpreter must read in two directions. Not only does the old affect the new but the new affects the way in which one reads the old. In the intertextual approach, then, the reader also plays a significant part in the process of understanding.

As with other aspects of the text, comprehending allusions to the Old Testament is essential in regard to the role of the Spirit in the Apocalypse. In addition to the literary allusions, the context of the

See the argument in Chapter 4 below.

[8] Cf. M.W. Wilson, 'Revelation 19:10 and Contemporary Interpretation', in *Spirit and Renewal: Essays in Honor of J. Rodman Williams,* ed. M.W. Wilson (Sheffield: Sheffield Academic Press, 1994), 191-202.

reader also intersects with the text of Revelation as well as the texts to which Revelation alludes. In this work I seek to delineate an interpretation of the role of the Spirit which integrates the text of Revelation, allusions within the text, and my own religious context of Pentecostalism. Partially owing to the influence of Dispensationalism upon Pentecostalism, the majority of attention allotted to the Apocalypse of John by Pentecostals has been reserved categorically for eschatology.[9] It is my hope that Pentecostals and others alike may find in the following pages an avenue which may be used to approach other theological aspects of the book.[10]

3. The Flow of the Argument

The study begins with a survey of literature on the pneumatology of the Apocalypse. Although significant contributions have been offered on the pneumatology of Matthew,[11] Luke-Acts,[12] and Paul,[13] no monographs have been devoted entirely to the role of the Spirit in the Apocalypse. Thus, this survey focuses on periodicals, book chapters, theological dictionaries and excerpts from commentaries. The survey of scholarship in Chapter 1 provides more than an overview of previous work on the role of the Spirit in the Apocalypse as it also unveils the presuppositional stance of the interpreters.

On the basis of the observation that the Apocalypse is replete with allusions to the Old Testament, Chapter 2 investigates intertextuality

[9] A noted exception is R.H. Gause, *Revelation: God's Stamp of Sovereignty on History* (Cleveland, TN: Pathway Press, 1983).

[10] Beyond its value as a work of eschatology, the Apocalypse has significant contributions to make to Christian theology in the areas of ecclesiology, missiology, Christology, the trinity, theodicy, and more.

[11] B. Charette, *Restoring Presence: The Spirit in Matthew's Gospel* (Sheffield: Sheffield Academic Press, 2000).

[12] R. Stronstad, *The Charismatic Theology of St. Luke* (Peabody: Hendrickson, 1984); idem, *The Prophethood of All Believers: A Study in Luke's Charismatic Theology* (Sheffield: Sheffield Academic Press, 1999); R.P. Menzies, *The Development of Early Christian Pneumatology with special reference to Luke-Acts* (Sheffield: Sheffield Academic Press, 1991); idem, *Empowered for Witness: The Spirit in Luke-Acts* (Sheffield: Sheffield Academic Press, 1994); J.B. Shelton, *Mighty in Word and Deed: The Role of the Holy Spirit in Luke-Acts* (Peabody: Hendrickson, 1991); M. Turner, *Power from on High: The Spirit in Israel's Restoration and Witness in Luke-Acts* (Sheffield: Sheffield Academic Press, 1996).

[13] G.D. Fee, *God's Empowering Presence: The Holy Spirit in the Letters of Paul* (Peabody: Hendrickson, 1994).

both in theory and in practice as it relates to previous Revelation studies. As a method intertextuality has several benefits which commend it as a helpful tool for interpreting the Apocalypse. Unlike other New Testament books which use clear references to the Old Testament, John avoids the use of introductory formulae and direct citations. The use of the Old Testament in Revelation is more subtle. Intertextuality offers a middle pathway between limitation to the clearest allusions and the relegation of allusions to unintentional coincidences in language.

Contrary to those who argue that the Old Testament has no real effect on the New, many scholars have demonstrated that new and convincing insights occur when a reader is aware of particular literary allusions. Thus, the role of the interpreter includes identifying allusions and echoes for others. Nevertheless, awareness of an allusion does not guarantee interpretative unity. As R.B. Hays observes, 'No longer can we think of meaning as something contained by a text; texts have meaning only as they are read and used by communities of readers'.[14]

Given that intertextuality places an emphasis on the role of the reader's context, Chapter 3 focuses on my religious context, namely Pentecostalism. With an awareness that not all Pentecostals read alike, I seek to describe a possible Pentecostal hermeneutic that is faithful to the ethos of the movement. This chapter also contains an assessment of the previous work by Pentecostals on the role of the Spirit in the Apocalypse. Chapter 3 ends with a turn toward the Apocalypse to see what additional insights the book might contain toward further development of the hermeneutic.

Chapter 4 contains the exegetical focus of the study, concentrating on the prophecy concerning the temple and the two witnesses in Rev. 11:1-13. The chapter includes a discussion of the literary contextualization of this key passage, which sits at the center of the book in theological as well as literary terms, forming the intertextual center of the role of the Spirit in the Apocalypse. While the three major rubrics mentioned above (the seven spirits, in the Spirit, and the Spirit) are certainly helpful, bringing to light the repetitive nature of John's use of πνεῦμα, this chapter ventures in more of an intertextual direction. Given the multiple allusions to the Old Testament which can be found in this passage, coupled with the cross-references to other sections of the Apocalypse, this passage provides avenues of investigation into

[14] R.B. Hays, *Echoes of Scripture in the Letters of Paul* (New Haven: Yale University Press, 1989), p. 189.

every aspect of the Spirit in Revelation. The study concludes with a delineation of its contributions and their implications.

1

Interpretations of the Role of the Spirit in the Apocalypse: A Survey of Modern Scholarship

1. Introduction

The pneumatology of the Apocalypse has received relatively little attention in comparison to other aspects of the book of Revelation.[1] The majority of commentators reserve no room for a discussion on the Spirit, only noting the role of the Spirit in specific references in the verse-by-verse manner. A few commentaries allot room for an excursus or short discussion of the role of the Spirit.[2] The most substantial work has been offered in periodicals,[3] book chapters,[4] and theological

[1] For broader investigations of the history of interpretation of the Apocalypse see A.W. Wainwright, *Mysterious Apocalypse* and R.H. Charles, *Studies in the Apocalypse* (Edinburgh: T & T Clark, 1913; repr. Wipf & Stock, 1996). For a survey of scholarship up to 1980 see the bibliographical essay by U. Vanni, 'L'Apocalypse johannique: Etat de la question', pp. 21-46 in *L'Apocalypse johannique et l'Apocalyptique dans le Nouveau Testament,* ed. J. Lambrecht (Leuven: Leuven University Press, 1980). The recent scholarship in French has been reviewed in L. Devillers, 'L'Apocalypse', *RevThom* 95 (4, 95), pp. 689-699. Historical commentaries that provide a brief history of interpretation include E.B. Allo, *Saint Jean: L'Apocalypse* (Paris: Lecoffe, 1921); I.T. Beckwith, *The Apocalypse of John* (Grand Rapids: Baker Book House, 1967, repr. of 1919 edition); W. Bousset, *Die Offenbarung Johannes* (Göttingen: Vandenhoeck & Ruprecht, 1906); R.H. Charles, *A Critical and Exegetical Commentary on the Revelation of St John,* 2 vols. (Edinburgh: T. & T. Clark, 1920); H. Kraft, *Die Offenbarung des Johannes* (Tübingen: Mohr, 1974); H.B. Swete, *The Apocalypse of St John* (London: Macmillan, 1907).

[2] D. Aune, *Revelation 1–5,* vol. 1 (Waco: Word, 1997), pp. 36-37; I.T. Beckwith, *The Apocalypse of John,* pp. 316-317; Charles, *A Critical and Exegetical Commentary on the Revelation of St John,* vol. 1 pp. cxiv-cxv; J.M. Ford, *Revelation* (Garden City, New York: Doubleday, 1975), pp. 19-20.

[3] R.J. Bauckham, 'The Role of the Spirit in the Apocalypse', *EQ* 52 (1980), pp. 66-83; G. Dix, 'The Seven Archangels and the Seven Spirits', *JTS* 28 (1926), pp. 233-250; J.M. Ford, 'For the Testimony of Jesus is the Spirit of Prophecy', *ITQ* 42.4 (October 1975), pp. 285-292; R.L. Jeske, 'Spirit and Community in the Johannine

dictionaries.[5] No monographs have been devoted entirely to the role of the Spirit in the Apocalypse.

Although the Apocalypse contains numerous mysteries, the focus of this chapter will be limited to a survey of the modern scholarship that has attempted to answer a singular question, 'What is the role of the Spirit in the Apocalypse?' Answers to this question vary. In fact, some scholars suggest that there is no pneumatology because the text is completely devoid of references to the Spirit, while other scholars claim that the role of the Spirit, providing John his visionary experience, is an integral part of the message of Revelation, despite the fact that the references to the Spirit are fewer in number than the references to Christ and God. According to these scholars, the role of the Spirit should not be limited to the explicit references that use πνεῦμα.

Surveys of scholarship are inevitably selective, but this study seeks to cover the major contributions. The organization of the following material is typological.[6] The survey begins by examining the symbol of 'the seven spirits'. The history of interpretation of the seven spirits is divided into two main categories, namely Jewish Angelology and the

Apocalypse', *NTS* 31 (1985), pp. 452-466; P. Joüon, 'Apocalypse, 1:4', *RSR* 21 (1931), pp. 486-487; E. Schweizer, 'Die sieben Geister in der Apokalypse', *EvT* 6 (1951-52), pp. 502-512; A. Skrinjar, 'Les sept Esprits (Apoc. 1:4; 3:1; 4:5; 5:6)', *Bib* 16 (1935), pp. 1-25, 113-140; J.C. de Smidt, 'Die Oë van die Gees in die boek Openbaring – 'n teologiese perspektief', *Scriptura* 54 (1995), pp. 159-176; idem, 'Hermeneutical Perspectives on the Spirit in the Book of Revelation', *JPT* 14 (1999), pp. 27-47; idem, 'The Holy Spirit in the Book of Revelation-Nomenclature', *Neot* 28 (1, 1994), pp. 229-244.

[4] R.J. Bauckham, 'The Role of the Spirit', in *The Climax of Prophecy: Studies on the Book of Revelation* (Edinburgh: T. & T. Clark, 1992), pp. 150-173; idem, 'The Spirit of Prophecy', in *The Theology of the Book of Revelation* (Cambridge: Cambridge University Press, 1993), pp. 109-125; F.F. Bruce, 'The Spirit in the Apocalypse', in *Christ and Spirit in the New Testament: In Honour of Charles Francis Digby Moule,* eds. B. Lindars and S.S. Smalley (Cambridge: Cambridge University Press, 1973), pp. 333-344; M.W. Wilson, 'Revelation 19.10 and Contemporary Interpretation', in *Spirit and Renewal: Essays in Honor of J. Rodman Williams,* ed. M.W. Wilson (Sheffield: Sheffield Academic Press, 1994), pp. 191-202.

[5] E. Schweizer, 'Πνεῦμα', *TDNT* 6 (1968), pp. 396-455; R.F. Martin, 'Apocalypse, Book of the', *DPCM* pp. 11-13.

[6] The difficulty with typological surveys is that they often overlook the finer nuances of smaller contributions in favor of more substantial material. As with any work of art, it is often the subtle nuances of the Apocalypse that distinguish it from other voices in the New Testament or other apocalyptic literature. One would not expect an art critic to limit his or her comments to the largest paintings or sculptures; due attention is also given to quantitatively smaller works that I would classify as major contributions to the recent history of the interpretation.

Spirit of God. The seven spirits as a symbol for the Spirit of God is subdivided into two sections based on the possibility of textual influence, Isaiah 11 and Zechariah 4, respectively. The next major category comprises references to the Spirit, and is subdivided into two sections, those who claim the references to the Spirit are secondary because they are principally due to interpolations and glosses and those who claim the Spirit's role is to enable John's prophetic visionary experience. The prophetic visionary interpretation is further divided between those who focus on John's prophetic role and those who focus on the role of the Spirit in the prophetic community. In addition to the passages which contain the word πνεῦμα, attention is also given to the pericope concerning the two witnesses (11:1-13). Although few scholars identify a reference to the Spirit in this passage, the prophecy of the two witnesses is vital for an understanding of the pneumatology of the apocalypse because of its intertextual relationship with Zech. 4. The survey of scholarship will elucidate the attention which the role of the Spirit in Revelation has received, and reveal an area in which a new pneumatology of the Apocalypse might be offered.

2. The Seven Spirits

The seven spirits are interpreted by the majority of scholars to be either a reference to the seven principal angels of Jewish and Christian angelology[7] or a reference to the Spirit of God.[8] First, consideration will be given to the former possibility followed by two possible interpretations of the latter (i.e. allusions to Isa. 11:2 or Zech. 4:1-13). The comments of R.H. Mounce in his commentary on Revelation illustrate the extent to which the meaning of the symbol of the seven

[7] Arguing in favor of an angelic interpretation of the symbolism are G.R. Beasley-Murray, *The Book of Revelation* (London: Marshall, Morgan & Scott, 1974), p. 55; G. Dix, 'The Seven Archangels and the Seven Spirits', pp. 233-250; C.H. Giblin, *The Book of Revelation: The Open Book of Prophecy* (Collegeville, Minnesota: Liturgical Press, 1991), pp. 71-72; R.H. Mounce, *The Book of Revelation* (Grand Rapids: Eerdmans, 1977), pp. 69-70; E. Schweizer, 'Die sieben Geister in der Apokalypse', pp. 502-512; and A. Skrinjar, 'Les sept Esprits', pp. 1-25, 113-140.

[8] Bauckham, *The Climax of Prophecy,* p. 164; Beckwith, *The Apocalypse of John,* pp. 424-427; Bousset, *Die Offenbarung Johannes,* pp. 184-187; Bruce, 'The Spirit in the Apocalypse', pp. 333-337; C.J. Hemer, *The Letters to the Seven Churches of Asia in their Local Setting* (Sheffield: Sheffield Academic Press, 1986), p. 142; de Smidt, 'Die Oë van die Gees in die Boek Openbaring', pp. 159-176; idem, 'The Holy Spirit in the Book of Revelation-Nomenclature', pp. 229-244; J.P.M. Sweet, *Revelation* (London: SCM Press, 1979), p. 65.

spirits has evaded scholarly consensus. As possible sources for the symbol of the seven spirits, Mounce lists Isa. 11:2, Zech. 4:1-13, and Jewish angelology, but he concludes that the phrase remains enigmatic because 'a survey of the four occurrences of the phrase fails to provide sufficient information to arrive at a certain understanding'.[9] Hence, Mounce concludes tentatively with the conjecture that the seven spirits are part of a heavenly entourage that has a special ministry with the lamb.[10]

The traditional argument against the interpretation of angelic symbolism hinges on Rev. 1:4b, where the seven spirits are placed between God and Jesus Christ. The argument presupposes that nothing less than the divine Spirit would be placed between God and Jesus Christ.[11] This interpretation has been challenged by a comparison of the similar terminology used of the seven spirits in 1:4b (ἅ ἐνώπιον τοῦ θρόνου αὐτοῦ) and of the seven angels in 8:2 (οἵ ἐνώπιον τοῦ θεοῦ).[12] The challenge operates with the assumption that the identity of the seven spirits and the seven angels should be equated because of their shared location before God. Mounce offers two references from other New Testament texts in support of his theory that the placement of the seven spirits between God and Jesus Christ does not preclude the interpretation that the seven spirits are a symbol for the seven archangels. He cites Luke 9:26, 'For whoever is ashamed of me and my works, of him will the Son of Man be ashamed when he comes in his glory and the glory of the Father and the holy angels'; and 1 Tim. 5:21, 'In the presence of God and of Christ and of the elect holy angels'. Despite the close proximity of angels in these passages to Christ

[9] R.H. Mounce, *The Book of Revelation* (Grand Rapids: Eerdmans, 1977), pp. 69-70.

[10] Other possible interpretations include that of J.M. Ford, who suggests that the seven spirits may be a metaphor for the 'Lord of the Spirits, i.e., God, found frequently in 1 Enoch'. According to Ford, the idea of the Lord of the Spirits is even more primitive than the concept of the spirit as an angel or the confusion between the Son and the Spirit which is found in the *Shepherd of Hermas*, Similitudes 9.1.1 (cf. 2 Macc 3:24) (Ford, *Revelation,* p. 19). See also Swete, who suggests that 'the spirits are seven because the churches are seven' (H.B. Swete, *The Apocalypse of St. John* [London: Macmillan, 1906], p. 274).

[11] The traditional argument suggests the high Christology of the interpreters, or rather their low angelology. An objection to placing 'the seven angels of the presence' between God the Father and Christ would not have disturbed authors of other apocalyptic texts, where ideas of Christology, pneumatology, and angelology are not rigidly defined. Note the confusion of the Spirit and the Son in *Hermas*, Similitudes 9.1.1. Cf. also *2 Clement* 14:4; Justin's *First Apology* 33.

[12] Mounce, *Revelation,* p. 69.

and the Father, Mounce fails to recognize that the angels are not placed between Jesus Christ and God in Rev. 8:2 as they are in Rev. 1:4.

2.1. The Seven Spirits and Jewish Angelology

R.H. Charles. Charles denies that there is a definite doctrine of the Spirit in the author of Revelation and concludes that the limited references to the Spirit were additions inserted into the text by later editors.[13] In reference to the seven spirits, Charles's argument focuses chiefly on the first occurrence of the phrase. The book of Revelation is written in the form of a letter,[14] with a standard salutation (1:4-6) and a closing farewell (22:21). The first reference to the seven spirits comes in the middle of the threefold greeting (1:4), where John addresses his audience, 'the seven churches that are in Asia', in a standard fashion that is reminiscent, according to Charles, of the Pauline epistles, 'Grace to you and peace from God our Father and the Lord Jesus Christ'.[15] John's greeting differs from Paul's in two ways. First, the salutary offerings of grace and peace come from three entities instead of two[16] and second, the description of the entities is thoroughly symbolic. The salutation in Revelation is the most elaborate in the New Testament. John's offering of grace and peace come 'from the one who is and who was and who is to come,[17] and from the seven spirits

[13] For a fuller explanation of Charles's understanding of the pneumatology of the Apocalypse see below section 3.1.

[14] John expects his prophetic letter to be read aloud in the congregations. Included in the introduction of the book is a blessing for 'the one who reads aloud and those who hear the words of the prophecy and keep what is written therein' (Rev. 1:3). The intended oral transmission of the prophecy heightens the value and necessity of special consideration of repetitions and allusions used to communicate the message. See D.L. Barr, 'The Apocalypse as a Symbolic Transformation of the World: A Literary Analysis', *Int* 38 (1984), pp. 39-50; idem, 'The Apocalypse of John as Oral Enactment', *Int* 38 (1984), pp. 243-256; A.M. Enroth, 'The Hearing Formula in the Book of Revelation', *NTS* 36 (1990), pp. 598-608.

[15] E.g. Rom. 1:7; 1 Cor. 1:3; 2 Cor. 1:2; Gal. 1:3; Eph. 1:2; Phil. 1:2; 1 Thess. 1:1; 2 Thess. 1:2. A parallel may also be drawn between Rev. 1:4-5 and 2 John 3, where the Elder writes χάρις ἔλεος εἰρήνη παρὰ θεοῦ πατρός, καὶ παρὰ Ἰησοῦ Χριστοῦ τοῦ υἱοῦ τοῦ πατρὸς ἐν ἀληθείᾳ καὶ ἀγάπῃ.

[16] The only other NT letter to use a threefold greeting is 1 Peter. 'Peter, an apostle of Jesus Christ, to ... [those] who have been chosen and destined by God the Father and sanctified by the Spirit to be obedient to Jesus Christ... May grace and peace be yours in abundance' (1 Pet. 1:1-2, NRSV).

[17] This description of God is in the nominative case although it is the object of ἀπό, which takes its object in the genitive case.

who are before his throne, and from Jesus Christ the faithful witness, the firstborn of the dead and the ruler of the kings of the earth' (1:4b-5a).

Charles suggests, 'without hesitation',[18] that the reference to the seven spirits in Rev. 1:4b is an early interpolation. His decision to classify the reference to the seven spirits in Rev. 1:4b as an interpolation is based on the assumption that the seven spirits are angelic beings and therefore could not be located in a place of worship between God and Christ. Charles suggests that the interpolation may have been added by an editor, who was influenced by the later doctrine of the trinity and misinterpreted the seven spirits to be a reference to the Spirit of God. Charles offers further argumentation with an analysis of Rev. 3:1, where Christ has the seven spirits of God and the seven stars (ὁ ἔχων τὰ ἑπτὰ πνεύματα τοῦ θεοῦ καὶ τοὺς ἑπτὰ ἀστέρας). He suggests the καί be understood as a copulative, differentiating the seven spirits from the seven stars, which had been identified in Rev. 1:20 as the angels of the seven churches. It is probable, according to Charles, that the seven spirits represent the seven archangels. He cites Zech. 4:10 as a source for the symbol in Rev. 4:5; 5:6 but offers no further explanation in his examination of the final two references.

Charles's argument that the first reference to the seven spirits is an interpolation has often been rejected by subsequent scholars arguing that the utter lack of textual support refutes the notion that the phrase is an interpolation. Nevertheless, Charles represents the quintessential historical critic and his contribution to the enigma of the seven spirits sets the standard to which subsequent scholarship must refer, either in acceptance or rebuttal.

E. Schweizer. Schweizer argues that 'from a religio-historical standpoint' the seven spirits 'are simply the seven archangels'.[19] Schweizer, not unlike many other New Testament scholars, attributes the historical background of Jewish and Christian angelology to Babylonian planetary speculation and/or Zoroastrianism (cf. Ezek. 9:1-11); and therefore, he interprets the seven spirits in Revelation to be nothing more than a reference to the seven principal angels of Jewish and

[18] Charles, *A Critical and Exegetical Commentary on the Revelation of St. John*, p. 11.

[19] E. Schweizer, 'Πνεῦμα', *TDNT* 6 (1968), p. 450; idem, 'Die sieben Geister in der Apokalypse', pp. 502-512. Bruce agrees that from a religio-historical standpoint the seven spirits may well be a symbol for the seven archangels, but he continues by insisting that John is not bound by any religio-historical roots (F.F. Bruce, 'The Spirit', p. 334).

Christian angelology. Examples of this popular angelology appear in the New Testament and the Apocrypha. In Luke 1:19, Gabriel, one of the seven archangels, declares that he stands before God. Raphael, another one of the seven, describes the group of angels as 'the seven holy angels who present the prayers of the saints[20] and stand before the presence of the Holy One' (Tobit 12:15). The seven archangels are also described in *1 Enoch* 20:2-8, 'seven names of archangels'.[21] The existence of the seven archangels in the literary world which Revelation shares is evident; this helps to explain the popularity of the interpretation that the seven spirits may simply be a particular nomenclature for the seven archangels. In addition to his comments on the seven spirits, Schweizer is often cited for his interpretation that the identity of the Spirit in the Apocalypse is confused with the identity of Christ. Schweizer classifies the Apocalypse as a form of primitive pneumatology.[22]

D. Aune. Aune begins his discussion of the identity of the seven spirits with a brief taxonomy of 'spirit' in the Old and New Testaments.[23] Aune highlights that the symbol, 'the seven spirits', which occurs four times in the Apocalypse, is unique to Revelation among the books of the New Testament. He is correct that Revelation never uses the familiar adjective, ἅγιος, in relation to the Spirit, nor does Revelation contain the phrase 'spirit of God'; however, it does contain the phrase 'seven spirits of God' (Rev. 3:1; 5:6). Furthermore, the phrase 'spirits of God' never occurs in the Old Testament, though the singular, 'spirit of God', occurs ninety-four times. In the Old Testament, the plural, 'spirits', is never used in reference to angels. The number seven is first used in the Apocalypse with the symbol of the seven spirits, which are also related to the seven stars (3:1), the seven torches of fire (4:5, 'where it is probably', according to Aune, 'an explanatory gloss'),[24] and the seven horns and seven eyes (5:6).

Aune dismisses the notion that the seven spirits are a reference to the singular divine Spirit as an unfortunate anachronism, as the mod-

[20] Cf. Rev. 5:8; 8:3-4, John describes the prayers of the saints as incense which is offered to God.

[21] The names of the angels are: Uriel, Raphael, Raguel, Michael, Saraqael, Gabriel, and Remiel.

[22] This aspect of Schweizer's scholarship will be explored in more detail under his contribution to the understanding of the references to the Spirit (cf. 3.1).

[23] Aune, *Revelation 1–5,* p. 36.

[24] Aune, *Revelation 1–5,* p. 33.

ern interpreter is reading his or her own trinitarian concept back onto the text of Revelation. Despite the relatively rare occasions in Jewish literature where the word 'spirits' is used as a synonym for 'angels',[25] Aune supports the interpretation that the seven spirits are a reference to the seven archangels of Jewish literature. He is persuaded by the frequent use of the phrase 'spirits of God', which is used in the Dead Sea Scrolls as a designation for angels.[26] Aune attempts to reconstruct the historical *Sitz im Leben* of the Apocalypse, and he offers an elaborate theory of the original composition and subsequent redactions of the text.[27] The composition history which Aune presupposes provides a delimiting range of meaning through which the definition of the Spirit, he would suggest, has evolved.

2.2. The Seven Spirits as the Spirit of God

The second major interpretation of the seven spirits is that they represent the singular Spirit of God. This interpretation has been supported by multiple allusions to Old Testament texts within the text of Revelation. The Apocalypse contains more allusions to the Old Testament than any other New Testament book.[28] The passages which have been proposed to be sources for the imagery of the seven spirits are Isa. 11:2 and Zech. 4:1-13.

2.2.1. *The Sevenfold Spirit of God from Isaiah 11:2*

Early Interpreters. Early interpreters have suggested that John is making an allusion to Isa. 11:2, where the prophet supposedly names seven attributes of the Spirit of Yahweh, which are to rest on the Davidic Messiah denoting seven gifts of the one Spirit. Justin Martyr († 165) attests to this sevenfold interpretation of Isa. 11:2 but does not mention any relationship to Revelation nor does he stress the number seven. Justin seems more concerned that Christ possessed all the characteristics of the Messiah and not merely one or two as did other kings.[29] Victorinus of Pettau († 304) represents the earliest commenta-

[25] Cf. *Jub.* 1:25; 2:2; 15:31-32; *1 Enoch* 61:12, 'spirit of light', cited in Aune, *Revelation 1–5,* p. 34.

[26] Cf. 4Q403 1 i 43; 1 ii 8,9; 4Q404 5.5; 4Q405 20 ii 21-22 11; 4Q405 23 i 9-10, cited in Aune, *Revelation 1-5,* p. 35.

[27] See Chapter 4 below for a review of Aune's composition theory.

[28] See S. Moyise, *The Old Testament in the Book of Revelation* (Sheffield: Sheffield Academic Press, 1995), pp. 13-14 for a list of works on the relationship between the Old Testament and Revelation.

[29] Dial. c. Tryph. 87.2.

tor to make the connection between Isa. 11:2 and the seven spirits in Revelation,[30] an interpretation that continues to be offered.[31]

J. Fekkes. According to Fekkes, the problematic nature of interpreting Isa. 11:2 as the textual source for the symbol of the seven spirits has been compounded by the majority of scholarship that has addressed it.[32] The difficulty lies in the debatable assumption that the LXX and later Jewish and Christian interpreters make reference to seven features of the Spirit of Yahweh in Isa. 11:2, while the MT contains only six features. Fekkes offers a systematic treatment of all the allusions to Isaiah in Revelation and ranks each allusion as being Certain/Virtually Certain, Probable/Possible, or Unlikely/Doubtful. According to Fekkes, this classification of allusions is helpful in two ways: classification of doubtful allusions prevents undue attention being paid to these texts; and the classification of certain allusions lends more credence to the identification of Isaianic texts at the heart of the Apocalypse.

Fekkes categorizes Isa. 11:2 as 'Unlikely/Doubtful'.[33] Fekkes's comparison of the texts of Isa. 11:2 in the MT, LXX, and Targum reveals that the texts are remarkably similar. The three texts each include 'an introductory clause, three couplets of two spiritual gifts, and a final clause'.[34] Some interpreters have offered καὶ εὐσεβείας ('and of piety') as the seventh feature,[35] but this may be an interpretive substitution for יראת יהוה, rather than an addition to the Hebrew list. Other interpreters have argued that the phrase πνεῦμα φόβου θεοῦ (Isa. 11:3a) defines the seventh feature.[36] This second interpretation falters at two points. The phrase πνεῦμα φόβου θεοῦ is governed by a new verb (ἐμπλήσει) and should not be included with the characteristics modifying ἀνα-

[30] Victorinus, *Commentarius in Apocalypsin,* ed. J. Haussleiter (Vienna, 1916), pp. 16-18. Previously cited in Bruce, 'The Spirit', p. 334.

[31] Caird also connects the possible allusion to Isaiah but does not mention the LXX (G.B. Caird, *A Commentary on the Revelation of St. John the Divine* [London: A. & C. Black, 1966], p. 15).

[32] J. Fekkes, *Isaiah and Prophetic Tradition in the Book of Revelation. Visionary Antecedents and their Development* (Sheffield: Sheffield Academic Press, 1994), p. 17.

[33] Fekkes, *Isaiah and Prophetic Tradition in the Book of Revelation,* pp. 107-110. Fekkes notes the problematic interpretational history of Isa. 11:2 and the faulty assumption that the LXX contains seven features of the Spirit of Yahweh.

[34] Fekkes, *Isaiah and Prophetic Tradition in the Book of Revelation,* p. 109. Fekkes provides the three texts in a parallel format.

[35] Bruce, 'The Spirit', p. 334; Mounce, *Revelation,* p. 70.

[36] Hemer, *The Letters to the Seven Churches,* p. 261; E.J. Kissane, *The Book of Isaiah* (Dublin: Veritas, 1941), p. 142.

παύσεται ἐπ' αὐτὸν πνεῦμα τοῦ θεοῦ. Moreover, the etymology of πνεῦμα φόβου θεοῦ may be a translator's attempt to deal with the tautology in 2b and 3a.[37]

Clearly, the texts of the LXX and the Targum are easier to interpret as sevenfold than the MT, as was most likely the case with Justin, the early apologist who interpreted Isaiah in this manner. Nevertheless, Fekkes closes his argument by appealing to some early Jewish exegetical traditions which 'consistently interpret Is. 11:2 of the Messiah, who is endowed with six qualities rather than seven'.[38] Fekkes's work, albeit thorough and helpful, has recently been critiqued as being useful but antiquated,[39] owing to its attempt to follow the guidelines of source criticism and thereby not taking advantage of more recent literary forms of inquiry.

2.2.2. *The Seven Lamps and the Seven Eyes from Zechariah 4:1-14*

The seven spirits have been interpreted as a symbol for the singular Spirit of God based on the literary relationship between Rev. 4:5; 5:6 and Zech. 4:2; 10b. In Rev. 4:5 John identifies the seven spirits as ἑπτὰ λαμπάδες πυρὸς καιόμεναι ἐνώπιον τοῦ θρόνου. This has been taken as a possible allusion to the seven lamps, which are on the golden lampstand in Zech. 4:2 (LXX: ἑπτὰ λυχνία). The seven lamps from Zech. 4:2 are depicted as the eyes of the Lord which range throughout the whole earth in Zech. 4:10b (LXX: ἑπτὰ οὗτοι ὀφθαλμοὶ κυρίου εἰσὶν οἱ ἐπιβλέποντες ἐπὶ πᾶσαν τὴν γῆν). Zech. 4:10b seems to be alluded to in Rev. 5:6, where John describes the seven spirits of God as the seven horns and seven eyes of the Lamb (κέρατα ἑπτὰ καὶ ὀφθαλμοὺς ἑπτὰ οἵ εἰσιν τὰ [ἑπτὰ][40] πνεύματα τοῦ θεοῦ

[37] Isa. 11:2 ends with the words ויראת יהוה, and Isa. 11:3 begins: והריחו ביראת יהוה.

[38] Fekkes, *Isaiah and Prophetic Tradition in the Book of Revelation*, 109. Fekkes cites *Num. R.* 13:11, *Gen. R.* 2.4.97, and *Ruth R.* 7:2 as examples of the Jewish exegetical tradition.

[39] Moyise, *The Old Testament in the Book of Revelation*, p. 18.

[40] An interesting variant occurs here with the omission of ἑπτά in A P^{vid} 1 1006 1611 it^{61} vg eth Irenaeus^{arm} *al.* The inclusion of ἑπτά is supported by $\mathfrak{p}^{24}$ x 046 1854 2053 2344 2432 it^{gig} vg^{cl} syr^{ph,h} cop^{sa,bo} arm Hippolytus *al.* The external evidence is rather evenly balanced between those in favor of inclusion and those in favor of omission. On the one hand, the word may have been omitted owing to confusion with the prior two uses of the word in the preceding phrase. On the other hand, the word may be an addition by a copyist imitating 1:4; 3:1; 4:5. The editors of the UBS Fourth Revised Edition rate the probability of ἑπτά low with a [C]. The omission of the numerical description of the spirits leaves the ambiguity concerning their identity intact because πνευμάτα is still plural.

ἀπεσταλμένοι εἰς πᾶσαν τὴν γῆν). Although many scholars have identified Zech. 4:2-14 as a possible source for the seven spirits in the Apocalypse, the primary contributions have been offered by F.F. Bruce,[41] R.J. Bauckham,[42] and J.C. de Smidt.[43]

F.F. Bruce. Bruce's contribution to the present topic, published as a chapter in a Festschrift for C.F.D. Moule, is divided into four sections: (1) the Seven Spirits, (2) the Spirit of Prophecy, (3) What the Spirit Says to the Churches, and (4) the Responsive Spirit. Bruce begins with an analysis of the initial occurrence of the seven spirits in the salutation, noting the surprising placement of the seven spirits between the eternal God and Jesus Christ. He dismisses R.H. Charles's proposal that Rev. 1:4c is an interpolation as a 'precarious course in default of textual support'.[44] Bruce notes the historical interpretation relating the seven spirits to Isa. 11:2 and the difficult numeration of the spiritual gifts, which the Davidic prince is to possess; however, Bruce is not convinced that the Apocalypse is dependent on the LXX text.

Recognizing the placement of the seven spirits 'before the throne' in Rev. 1:4c, Bruce suggests that an analysis of the vision of the throne room in Rev. 4-5 elucidates the reasoning behind the placement of the seven spirits in the salutation between God and Jesus. The first occurrence of the seven spirits in the vision of heaven appears in Rev. 4:5, where the seven spirits are depicted as seven torches of fire burning before the throne. In the following chapter the seven spirits are depicted as the seven horns and seven eyes of the Lamb.[45] According to Bruce, 'the Old Testament background to Rev. 5:6 is clearly to be discerned in Zech. 4:2, 10b'.[46] Although he fails to elaborate on the transfer of the eyes of Yahweh in Zechariah 4 to the Lamb in Rev. 5:6, Bruce comments that this transfer of symbolism is relevant to the Christology of the Apocalypse.

41 Bruce, 'The Spirit in the Apocalypse', pp. 333-344.

42 Bauckham, 'The Role of the Spirit', pp. 150-173; idem, 'The Role of the Spirit in the Apocalypse, pp. 66-83; idem, 'The Spirit of Prophecy', pp. 109-125.

43 de Smidt, 'Die Oë van die Gees in die boek Openbaring', pp. 159-176; idem, 'Hermeneutical Perspectives on the Spirit in the Book of Revelation', pp. 27-47; idem, 'The Holy Spirit in the Book of Revelation', pp. 229-244.

44 Bruce, 'The Spirit', p. 334.

45 The description of the seven spirits may include only the seven eyes. Although the relative pronoun οἵ agrees with ὀφθαλμούς, Bruce suggests that κέρατα need not be excluded from the total antecedent.

46 Bruce, 'The Spirit', p. 335.

Bruce acknowledges the possible interpretation of the seven spirits as the seven principal angels of Jewish angelology. The letter to Sardis is addressed from the one who has the seven spirits of God and the seven stars (Rev. 3:1). Bruce notes the identity of the seven stars as the angels of the seven churches. He insists the angels of the seven churches are not to be confused with the seven chief angels who stand before God (Rev. 8:2). Bruce comments on the possible connection of the seven angels of Judeo-Christian angelology with Zoroastrian theology. He suggests that the Amesha Spentas of the Gathas only number seven when Ahura Mazdah, the supreme lord, is included as one of them; however, Ahura Mazdah may have been included in the number by the time that Zoroastrianism influenced Judaism, if he was ever distinct from them.[47]

After dismissing Isa. 11:2 as a source for the symbolism of the seven spirits and suggesting that something more than angels is implied by the fuller description of the seven spirits in Rev. 4-5, Bruce concludes in agreement with Beckwith that the seven spirits are best understood as a symbol for the Holy Spirit in light of the dual symbolism from Zechariah. Furthermore, Bruce proposes that the order of the three entities in the salutation is based on the order of appearances in the vision of heaven, as in the program for a play where the cast are listed in order of appearance. God sits on the heavenly throne (4:2) before whom burn the seven torches of fire (4:5), which are subsequently ascribed to the Lamb (5:6). Although Isa. 11:2 is most likely not the source for the number 'seven', the text may still serve as a source for the idea that Jesus Christ (i.e. the Davidic king) is endowed with the Spirit of Yahweh, as the allusion in Rev. 5:6 to Zech. 4:10b suggests. Bruce's contribution to the understanding of the symbolism of the seven spirits has been endorsed and utilized by the subsequent scholarship of R.J. Bauckham and J.C. de Smidt.

R.J. Bauckham. In agreement with Bruce, Bauckham identifies the seven spirits as a symbol for the Spirit of God and not as a reference to the seven principal angels. Bauckham includes a discussion of possible meanings of the numerology in relation to the seven spirits. There are four references to the seven spirits. Four represents the number of the world and seven is the number of completeness. The seven spirits are the fullness of God's power sent out into all the earth (5:6), and they

[47] Bruce, 'The Spirit', p. 335. See J.H. Moulton, *Early Religious Poetry of Persia* (Cambridge: Cambridge University Press, 1911), p. 58.

are closely related to the Lamb (5:6). Moreover, the Lamb is mentioned twenty-eight times (7 x 4).[48]

Bauckham is convinced that the symbolism in the Apocalypse can only be properly understood when sufficient attention is given to the influence of John's allusions to the Old Testament. According to Bauckham, the seven spirits (i.e. the Spirit of God) have a vital role to play in the central message of the Apocalypse. In his larger work, *The Climax of Prophecy,* Bauckham proposes that the center of John's prophetic message is the conversion of the nations via the prophetic witness of the faithful churches, which are symbolized in Revelation 11 as the two witnesses.[49] Although the seven spirits are not explicitly mentioned in the passage concerning the two witnesses, an intertextual relationship exists due to their shared allusions to Zechariah 4. In Revelation 11 the two witnesses are identified as olive trees and lampstands. The olive trees in Zechariah's vision were called the sons of oil who stand before the whole earth. In the vision of Zechariah, the lampstand contained seven torches of fire. John expands the symbol of the two olive trees by equating them with two lampstands (Rev. 11:4). The two witnesses occupy the identical position of the olive trees (αἱ ἐνώπιον τοῦ κυρίου τῆς γῆς ἑστῶτες Rev. 11:4b). Slightly modifying Zechariah's symbolism, John uses the symbol of the lampstands to represent the churches in Rev. 1:12-20. In the vision of the two witnesses John integrates the symbolism of the lampstands (i.e. the faithful church) and the olive trees (i.e. the sons of oil), thereby prophesying that the church would receive the oil of the Spirit in order to proclaim a faithful witness to Jesus Christ. According to Bauckham, the role of the church in the conversion of the nations is the *climax* of biblical prophecy. The churches' role as faithful witnesses to Jesus is only possible by the anointing of the Spirit. Bauckham suggests that John may have chosen Zechariah 4 because of its central message found in 4:6b, 'not by might nor by power but by my spirit says the Lord of hosts', which is the answer to the question of the seven Asian churches, 'How are we to be faithful witnesses to Jesus Christ in a world controlled by the beast?'

The universal language of the Spirit as being sent out into the whole world adumbrates the unanimous response to the prophecy of the two witnesses in Rev. 11:13, where a tenth of the city and seven thousand people are destroyed in an earthquake. John inverts the imagery of the

[48] For a fuller explanation and defense that the numerology is too intricate to be accidental see Bauckham, *The Climax of Prophecy,* pp. 29-37.

[49] See Bauckham, *The Climax of Prophecy,* pp. 238-337.

faithful remnant in the Old Testament where the symbols of 'a tenth of the city' (Isa. 6:13; Amos 5:3) and 'seven thousand people' (1 Kgs 19:18) represent the minority that will be saved. However, in the Apocalypse the imagery of a remnant, represented by 'a tenth of the city and seven thousand people', do not form the minority that are saved but rather the minority that are damned. The majority respond positively to the message of the witnesses. The universal response to the prophecy of the witnesses is contrasted with the lack of response to the judgment of the sixth trumpet (Rev. 9:20, Καὶ οἱ λοιποὶ τῶν ἀνθρώπων, οἵ οὐκ ἀπεκτάνθησαν ἐν ταῖς πληγαῖς ταύταις, οὐδὲ μετενόησαν).[50]

Bauckham suggests that the role of the seven spirits in the Apocalypse is twofold. First, 'the seven spirits are the presence and power of God on earth, bringing about God's kingdom by implementing the Lamb's victory throughout the earth'.[51] Secondly, the seven spirits empower the churches to be faithful witnesses to Jesus Christ. The role of the Spirit as the presence and power of Jesus is illustrated in the symbolism of Rev. 5:6, where the seven spirits are described as the seven horns and the seven eyes of the Lamb which are sent out into the whole earth. The horns are a symbol of Christ's power and the eyes are a symbol of Christ's knowledge. The dispersal of the seven spirits into all the earth takes place through the spiritually enabled proclamation of the churches concerning the true identity of Jesus Christ. Additional attention will be given to Bauckham's conception of the climax of prophecy as the witnessing of the churches in section 3.2.2 (i.e. Bauckham's contribution to the understanding of the Spirit in the Apocalypse).

J.C. de Smidt. In agreement with Bruce and Bauckham, de Smidt identifies the seven spirits as the singular Spirit of God and agrees that the symbolism most likely is derived from Zechariah 4; however, de Smidt's principal goal is not to identify the seven spirits, but rather to focus on the theological significance of the symbolism of the seven eyes.[52] According to de Smidt, the symbolism of the seven eyes of the Lamb serves the seven Asian churches as a source of comfort. Despite their difficult socio-economic and political circumstances, the early

[50] *Contra* G.K. Beale, *The Book of Revelation* (Grand Rapids: Eerdmans, 1999), pp. 602-608; G.R. Osborne, *Revelation* (Grand Rapids: Baker Academic, 2002), p. 435.

[51] Bauckham, 'The Spirit of Prophecy', p. 113.

[52] De Smidt, 'Hermeneutical Perspectives on the Spirit in the Book of Revelation', pp. 27-47.

Christians could be comforted by the fact that God was in control and was seeing the events of the world. Furthermore, the Spirit provides the church and each believer with the heavenly perspective of the present and the future. De Smidt identifies the Spirit as the Spirit of perception, who perceives both the positive aspects in the church and the negative forces in the world.

The imagery of the eyes of Yahweh which range through the entire world connotes more than merely a passive viewing of human events but also evokes the capable action of the divinity. Citing Bauckham, de Smidt offers 2 Chron. 16:9 as support that the sight of God is a symbol for provision. In 2 Chron. 16:9, the prophet Hanani makes an allusion to Zech. 4:10b, 'the eyes of the Lord range throughout the entire earth'. Hanani rebukes king Asa for relying on his own power instead of the eyes which range throughout the whole earth. De Smidt concludes with an admonition for the contemporary church to rely on the perception of the Spirit in the manner of the seven churches of Asia.[53]

3. The Spirit

As mentioned above, the references to the Spirit in the Apocalypse fall into two major categories: (1) the Seven Spirits and (2) the Spirit. The following material surveys the references to the Spirit. Excluding the references to the seven spirits, the use of the word 'πνεῦμα' and its cognates occurs in six categories: (1) the repeated phrase ἐν πνεύματι (1:10; 4:2; 17:3; 21:10), (2) the repetitive phrase, ὁ ἔχων οὖς ἀκουσάτω τί τὸ πνεῦμα λέγει ταῖς ἐκκλησίαις (2:7, 11, 17, 29; 3:6, 13, 22), (3) the phrase πνεῦμα τῆς προφητείας (19:10), (4) direct discourse of the Spirit, (14:13; 22:17), (5) the breath of life (11:11; 13:15), and (6) demonic spirits (16:13f; 18:2). All of the scholars surveyed will refer to at least one of these categories. The two major subdivisions of scholarship may be divided between those scholars who believe that the author of Revelation identifies the person and work of the Holy Spirit and those scholars who believe that the identity of the Spirit in the Apocalypse is confused with Jesus, therefore suggesting a more primitive pneumatology. The scholars who propose that the Apocalypse is an example of primitive pneumatology believe the con-

[53] De Smidt, 'Hermeneutical Perspectives on the Spirit in the Book of Revelation', pp. 39-40.

fusion of identity has been augmented by interpolations and glosses added by editors and/or scribes.

3.1. Interpolations, Marginal Glosses, and Pre-Gnostic Judaism

R.H. Charles. Charles's two-volume commentary in the ICC series continues to serve scholars as a valuable resource for the study of the Apocalypse, particularly in relation to its historical context, yet in his 141-page introduction, Charles only offers a single paragraph on the doctrine of the Spirit.[54] He insists that the reference to the Spirit in the letters to the seven churches is the Spirit of Christ for Christ is the speaker. Likewise, Charles proposes that the same is true for the responsive Spirit in 14:13 and 22:17, which leads him to conclude that the personhood of the Spirit, which becomes so popular in the third century, is a concept totally absent from Revelation as it was originally penned by its author.

As for the phrase ἐγενόμην ἐν πνεύματι, Charles suggests that the meaning is nothing more than falling into a trance; however, this causes him difficulty when the phrase gets repeated in 4:2. The seer, as Charles refers to the author, is already in a trance as 1:10 reveals. In fact, the seer had to fall into the trance before he could hear the revelation from Jesus. In the second occurrence of the phrase, the seer sees first and then falls into a trance. Charles suggests that the difficulty can be explained best by adopting an interpretation that the author is combining visions which he received on different occasions. Thus, the seer inserted ἐγενόμην ἐν πνεύματι in order to connect Rev. 1–3 with Rev. 4–9.[55] The other occurrences of the phrase ἐν πνεύματι (17:3; 21:10) refer to a bodily translation and are not difficult.

According to Charles, the phrase in 19:10c, ἡ γὰρ μαρτυρία Ἰησους ἐστιν τὸ πνεῦμα τῆς προφητείας, has a precarious existence. This clause is part of a larger doublet (Rev. 19:9b-10 || Rev. 22:8-9), which prompts Charles to deem 19:9b-10 to be an interpolation. The exact parallelism of the doublet is destroyed by the clause, ἡ γὰρ μαρτυρία Ἰησους ἐστιν τὸ πνεῦμα τῆς προφητείας, which Charles judges to be a marginal gloss because it changes the meaning of the preceding clause, τῶν ἐχόντων τὴν μαρτυρίαν Ἰησου. According to Charles, the angel in 19:10 claims to be a fellow servant with the prophets or those with a prophetic gift alone; however, this is a differ-

[54] Charles, *Revelation,* vol. 1, pp. cxiv-cxv.

[55] Swete describes the second occurrence of the phrase ἐν πνεύματι as '[t]he state of spiritual exaltation which preceded the first vision ... has returned, but in greater force' (H.B. Swete, *The Apocalypse of St John,* p. 284).

ent meaning from the second half of the doublet in 22:8-9 where the angel is a fellow servant with all Christians. Charles explains the gloss as an addition of a later editor/disciple of the seer who misuses the 'diction'[56] of the author and supplements the writing of the Seer with his own comments.

E. Schweizer. Schweizer proposes that the understanding of the Spirit in the Apocalypse is unique in the New Testament, displaying similarities to pre-Gnostic Judaism. Schweizer notes that demonic spirits are called πνεύματα (Rev. 16:13f, 18:2), and that πνεῦμα as life-giving force is given by both God and the beast (11:11; 13:15). According to Schweizer, the dominant role of the Spirit is the idea of the πνεῦμα τῆς προφητείας (Rev. 19:10). Moreover, he suggests that according to Rev. 19:10 all members of the community (at least potentially) are prophets.[57] The πνεῦμα is the power which gives visions to ordinary persons and the reception of the vision is ἐν πνεύματι, which Schweizer equates with being ἐν ἐκστάσει (cf. Acts 11:5). The prophetic visionary understanding of the role of the Spirit can be seen in Rev. 11:8, where πνευματικῶς should be translated 'prophetically' as opposed to ordinary speech. The Spirit spoke in the past but continues to speak today, recalling the promises of Scripture and formulating those promises afresh (Rev. 14:13).

Since the publication of his article on πνεῦμα in *TDNT*, Schweizer has often been cited as an authority, both by those who agree with him and by those who disagree with him. Schweizer denies that the book of Revelation makes a reference to the Spirit. He insists that 'the decisive point'[58] in understanding the pneumatology of the Apocalypse is to recognize that πνεῦμα is not the entity known as the 'Holy Spirit', but rather, πνεῦμα is 'no other than the exalted Lord Himself'.[59] According to Schweizer, the repeated phrase, 'let anyone who has an ear listen to what the Spirit is saying to the churches', identifies

[56] In 19:10, Charles suggests that προσκυνῆσαι αὐτῷ is only used by the Seer to describe divine worship and that he would expect προσκυνῆσαι αὐτόν if this passage was from the hand of the seer (Charles, *Revelation,* vol. 2, pp. 128-129).

[57] Schweizer, 'Πνεῦμα', p. 449. Cf. Charles, *Revelation*, vol. 2, pp. 128-129. In support of this interpretation, Schweizer cites E. Lohmeyer, *Kommentar zur Apokalypse,* 1926.

[58] Schweizer, 'Πνεῦμα', p. 449.

[59] Schweizer, 'Πνεῦμα', p. 449.

the Spirit with the speaker of the address (i.e. Jesus Christ). 'Only as πνεῦμα is [Christ] with His own'.[60]

Schweizer perceives the role of the Spirit to be communal and not individual. The Spirit is the presence of Christ on earth that speaks to the community. On the one hand, in Rev. 22:17, when the Spirit and the bride say, 'Come', it is ultimately Jesus who calls to himself. On the other hand, Schweizer claims that the Spirit can be differentiated from Christ as the power which goes forth from him. He seems to equate Christ and the Spirit, and yet claim that they can be differentiated with no attempt to resolve this apparent contradiction in his understanding of the pneumatology of the Apocalypse. He concludes with an apology as to why the doctrine of the Spirit is so 'primitive', asking, 'is not the absence of a doctrine of the Spirit here due to the fact that in this book, as in primitive Christianity, the whole emphasis lies on the future, not on the presence of the Spirit?'[61]

J.M. Ford. In her commentary on the Apocalypse, Ford begins a brief discussion on pneumatology with the declaration that 'Revelation exhibits almost complete absence of Christian pneumatology in even its primitive development'.[62] Ford proposes that the Apocalypse does not contain a theology which distinguishes between the 'person' of Jesus and the 'person' of the Spirit. She identifies the seven repeated references to the Spirit in the letters to the seven churches as the chief mentions of the Spirit; however, Ford suggests that these references do not seem to describe the distinct 'person' of the Spirit. Her conclusion is based on the following two points: (1) the absence of the adjective ἅγιον to qualify the noun πνεῦμα, and (2) the identification of the Spirit with the speaker of the exhortations (i.e. 'one like the son of man'). In agreement with E. Schweizer, Ford concludes that the references to the Spirit in Rev. 2–3 are 'probably not the distinct entity known as the Holy Spirit'.[63] In reference to Rev. 19:10d and in agreement with R.H. Charles (who calls it v. 10c), Ford believes the phrase 'the testimony of Jesus is the Spirit of prophecy', to be an editorial gloss, and she concludes that the editor expected the readers to 'make an association with Pentecost and/or the re-introduction of

[60] Schweizer, 'Πνεῦμα', p. 449.

[61] Schweizer, 'Πνεῦμα', p. 449, n. 815.

[62] Ford, *Revelation,* p. 19.

[63] Ford, *Revelation,* p. 19. Ford concludes that Revelation 1-3 does not exhibit Christian pneumatology despite the fact that she believes Revelation 1–3 is a Christian addition to an otherwise Jewish document.

prophecy on that occasion'.[64] In addition to explaining the purpose of the gloss, Ford intimates that the meaning of the gloss could mean that 'the Spirit of prophecy (the subject of the sentence) is [ἐστιν] the witness to the authenticity of Jesus (the predicate of the sentence), with "Jesus" as the objective genitive'.[65]

Ford supports her position by a comparison of Revelation with other Christian apocalyptic texts which identify more explicitly the Holy Spirit. Ford claims that the Spirit in the Apocalypse fails to inspire confession of the Christian who is facing persecution, contrary to the account of the Markan apocalypse (and parallels). An example of an early Christian apocalyptic text in which the Spirit inspires confession can be found in the *Ascension of Isaiah* 3:19, 'the Holy Spirit gives people the power to speak'. Further, she notes that Revelation does not have a developed doctrine of the trinity as does the *Shepherd of Hermas* and the *Ascension of Isaiah*; Ford concludes that Revelation is more primitive than these writings.

Ford's conclusions are partially shaped by her unique supposition that the author of Revelation is none other than John the Baptist. Ford deems that the first three chapters are a later Christian addition to an otherwise Jewish document, which has been edited by a Christian disciple of John the Baptist.

D. Aune. In his recent commentary on Revelation in the WBC series, Aune includes a one-page excursus on the Spirit in Revelation. The contribution of Aune serves as a transition from the scholars who attribute the role of the Spirit to interpolations and glosses to the scholars who attribute the role of the Spirit to the original author. Although Aune argues for multiple editions and interpolations, he sees in the final form of the text the notion of the Spirit being associated with both a prophetic motif and an apocalyptic understanding of inspiration. Critiquing some of the previous scholarship on the pneumatology of the Apocalypse as being anachronistic, Aune claims that

[64] Ford, 'For the Testimony of Jesus is the Spirit of Prophecy', p. 291. The textual evidence does not warrant the conclusion that 10d is a gloss; however, the association with Pentecost is right on the mark.

[65] Ford, 'For the Testimony of Jesus is the Spirit of Prophecy', p. 289. Wilson refutes Ford's explanation of the grammatical construction by examining the uses of the third person singular form of εἰμί. Wilson shows that of the twenty-seven times this form of the verb occurs in Revelation, twenty-five times the copulative interpretation is preferred over the epexegetical, which would be required in order to follow Ford's explanation (M.W. Wilson, 'Revelation 19:10 and Contemporary Interpretation', p. 197).

discussions on the Spirit in Revelation have frequently relied on concepts of the Spirit that are extraneous to Revelation.[66] Aune is quick to point out that the phrases 'the Spirit of God' and 'the Holy Spirit' never occur in Revelation.[67] In the critical tradition of R.H. Charles, Aune divides the references to the Spirit into a final stage of composition and the earlier layers of composition.

To the final stage of composition, Aune assigns all references which indicate that the Spirit may be conceived in personal terms or as a means of prophetic inspiration. Often in 'the Second Edition', as Aune defines the later additions, the Spirit is the subject of the verb λέγει. In Rev. 2-3, the Spirit speaks the words of Christ to the seven churches, suggesting a close relationship between the Spirit and Christ. Aune does not support the idea that Revelation confuses the identity of the Spirit and Christ. Aune describes the words of the Spirit in Rev. 14:13 as having features of a prophetic oracle. He suggests that this verse is an interpolation added by the author-editor in the final stage of composition. Aune also assigns Rev. 22:17, where the Spirit and the Bride speak together, to the final stage of composition. In Rev. 19:10, Aune sees a similar association of witnessing to Jesus and the Spirit of prophecy which is also implicit in Rev. 2–3.

References to the Spirit which indicated a role or function related to an apocalyptic understanding of inspiration have been categorized as being a part of the early stage of composition. This would include the references to being ἐν πνεύματι, where the Spirit is the divine agent who mediates apocalyptic visions as opposed to the notion of the Spirit inspiring the mediation of the word of God through the seer. In line with his contribution to the understanding of the seven spirits, Aune's somewhat hypothetical history of composition prescribes the possibilities of the role the Spirit can play in the Apocalypse.

[66] Aune is in agreement with Beckwith, who suggests that the author of the Apocalypse did not possess a fully developed third century notion of the Spirit's place in a trinitarian doctrine which later became so prevalent and has been solidified in ecclesiastical history by the creeds. However, contrary to Aune, Beckwith claims that the less distinct personality of the Spirit as compared to Christ is to be expected. The apocalyptic role of the Spirit (Beckwith calls it the 'office' of the Spirit) is that of revealer and inspirer. Beckwith concludes that the doctrine of the Spirit in Revelation does not differ from the Pauline Epistles or the Gospel of John. The Spirit has unity with both God (Rev. 3:1; 4:5) and Christ (Rev. 3:1; 5:6). The Spirit is the organ of Christ's message to the churches in the seven letters, 'Hear what the Spirit is saying to the Churches', Rev. 2-3 *passim* (Beckwith, *The Apocalypse,* pp. 316-317).

[67] Aune, *Revelation,* p. 36.

3.2. Christian Pneumatology: The Prophetic Visionary Spirit

The contributions of three of the five scholars discussed below (Bruce, Bauckham and de Smidt) have been partially surveyed above in relation to their work on the symbolism of 'the seven spirits'. To this list of scholars, R.L. Jeske and M.W. Wilson are added. All of these scholars agree that the Apocalypse assigns a prophetic visionary role to the Holy Spirit, but the scholars are categorized according to their interpretation of the location of the Spirit's activity either in John and the prophets (Bruce and Bauckham) or in the entire Christian community (Jeske, de Smidt, and Wilson). Bruce acknowledges the possibility that all true believers may be referred to as prophets (Rev. 19:10) and, therefore, possess an indwelling of the Spirit. However, according to Bruce, no other text supports the probability of individual community members possessing an indwelling of the Spirit. Bauckham exclusively reserves the role of the Spirit's inspiration for John as the apocalyptic seer and for those whom John would designate as 'his brothers the prophets'. Jeske, de Smidt, and Wilson interpret the role of the Spirit as having a more communal dimension.

3.2.1. *John the Prophet*

F.F. Bruce. Bruce identifies the central role of the Spirit in Revelation to be 'the Spirit of prophecy', a phrase found only once in the Apocalypse (Rev. 19:10, 'the testimony of Jesus is the Spirit of prophecy'); however, he notes that 'the Spirit of prophecy' often occurs in post-biblical Jewish literature as a circumlocution for the Spirit of Yahweh.[68] An example of this kind of circumlocution can be found in the translation of Isa. 61:1 in the Targum of Jonathan, 'The Spirit of prophecy from before the Lord God is upon me'. Bruce also compares the similarities between 1 Pet. 1:11 and Rev. 19:10. In 1 Pet. 1:11, 'the Spirit of the Messiah' spoke through the Old Testament prophets, foretelling the events which would come to pass in the suffering of Christ and his glorification that would follow. Bruce proposes that 'the Spirit of the Messiah' may refer to 'the Spirit of messianic prophecy'.[69] Furthermore, he additionally cites *1 Clement* 22:1 as an example where the words of the Old Testament are offered to the Christian church as an exhortation by means of appealing to the authority of Jesus Christ

[68] Cf. also D. Hill, *Greek Words and Hebrew Meanings* (Cambridge: Cambridge University Press, 1967), pp. 227-228; E. Sjöberg, 'רוח in Palestinian Judaism', *TDNT* 6 (1968), pp. 375-389.

[69] Bruce, 'The Spirit', p. 337.

and the role of the Holy Spirit through whom the words of Christ (i.e. the Old Testament text) are communicated.[70]

Bruce concludes that the genitive,'Ἰησοῦ, in Rev. 19:10c, ἡ μαρτυρία'Ἰησοῦ, is probably objective, which is supported contextually by the earlier use of the objective genitive where the angel refuses to receive praise from John because, as the angel claims, 'I am a fellow-servant with you and your brothers who have the testimony of/to Jesus ('Ἰησοῦ)'. Bruce acknowledges the ambiguity in the recurrent phrase 'the testimony of Jesus'. He suggests that the subjective genitive is, at times, a better interpretation. On the one hand, Jesus is the 'faithful witness' (Rev. 1:5), and the entire Apocalypse is his testimony to the people (Rev. 22:16, 20). On the other hand, certain members of the Christian churches serve as witnesses to him. For example, Antipas from the church at Pergamum, is called 'my faithful witness' (Rev. 2:13),[71] and John had been exiled to the island of Patmos for 'the word of God and the testimony of Jesus' (Rev. 1:9). Furthermore, the followers of Jesus who were being assaulted by the dragon were able to 'conqueror him by the blood of the Lamb and by the word of their testimony, for they loved not their lives even unto death' (Rev. 12:11). Bruce writes, 'No doubt their Lord was bearing *his* testimony in theirs, and suffering in them, but it is through their own testimony that they conquer, and their own testimony is that which they bear to Jesus and his redeeming power'.[72]

To define the role of the Spirit of prophecy, Bruce offers a comparison with 1 Cor. 12:3, 1 John 4:2f., and John 15:26. The recurrent theme in these passages is that a genuine expression of the Spirit will always testify to Jesus. This test of legitimacy requires that the prophecy of the Spirit affirm the lordship of Jesus (according to 1 Cor. 12:3) or the incarnation of Jesus (according to 1 John 4:2f.). Further, in John 15:26, the disciples are told that the Spirit will bear witness to Jesus with the disciples, who are also witnesses. Bruce interprets this passage to mean that the witness of the Spirit was to be borne in the disciples. The idea that the disciples embody the witness of the Spirit may also be supported by Acts 5:32, where the disciples defend their actions

[70] *1 Clement* 22:1, 'Ταῦτα δὲ πάντα βεβαιοῖ ἡ ἐν Χριστῷ πίστιν καὶ γὰρ αὐτὸν διὰ τοῦ πνεύματον τοῦ ἁγίου οὔ των προσκαλεῖται ἡμας', which is followed by a quotation from Ps. 34 (LXX 33).

[71] According to Bruce's assessment, 'μάρτυς has clearly begun its transition from "witness" to "martyr"' (Bruce, 'The Spirit', p. 338).

[72] Bruce, 'The Spirit', p. 338.

before the Sanhedrin by saying, 'we are witnesses to these things, and so is the Holy Spirit whom God has given to those who obey him'.

Bruce suggests that a similar idea is proposed in the Apocalypse with the unique difference that the Spirit who bears witness to Jesus is the 'spirit of prophecy'. Despite the fact that the Spirit of prophecy is not explicitly mentioned in the pericope of the two witnesses in Rev. 11:3-14, Bruce believes the Spirit of prophecy is implied by the phraseology of the pericope and the description of the prophetic actions of the witnesses.[73] In Rev. 11:8, the city of Jerusalem is spiritually (πνευματικῶς) identified as Sodom and Egypt.[74] The description of the ministry of the witnesses places them in continuity with Moses and Elijah; furthermore, the witnesses are described using symbolism borrowed from Zech. 4:1-14, to which there was a previous allusion in Rev. 4:5; 5:6. Thus, Bruce defines the ministry of the two witnesses as being empowered by the Spirit of prophecy.

When John uses the terminology ἐν πνεύματι to describe his visionary experience, Bruce holds that John is describing an experience where the Spirit of prophecy has come upon him. Bruce notes that the final two occurrences of ἐν πνεύματι describe a transportation in the Spirit via an angel. This terminology, suggests Bruce, is reminiscent of Ezekiel's, 'although Ezekiel uses other expressions than "in Spirit".'[75] He highlights Ezek. 37:1 as the closest approach to the phraseology of John, 'the hand of Yahweh was upon me and carried me out in the Spirit of Yahweh'. Ezekiel also writes, 'the Spirit lifted me up and took me away' (Ezek. 3:14). Although it is the Spirit which transports Ezekiel and the angel that transports John, Bruce suggests that the 'same type of ecstasy is described under the variant terminology'.[76]

After discussing the Spirit of prophecy, Bruce turns his attention to the repeated phrase in the seven letters to the churches: 'let anyone who has an ear listen to what the Spirit is saying to the churches'. He warns that the repeated phrase should give the reader 'pause', because the speaker of the seven letters is designated as the 'exalted Lord'. Ac-

[73] Bruce deems the reference in Rev. 11:11 to πνεῦμα ζωῆς to be 'the "breath of life", as in Gen. 2:7 and not the prophetic Spirit'. Likewise, the reference in Rev. 22:6 to τῶν πνευμάτων τῶν προφητῶν is understood not as the Spirit of prophecy but the individual human spirits of the prophets (Bruce, 'The Spirit', p. 339). In contrast, Swete claims, in reference to πνεῦμα ζωῆς, '[t]he oil of the Spirit ... keeps alive the light of life' (H.B. Swete, *The Apocalypse of St John,* p. 135).

[74] As mentioned above, Schweizer understands πνευματικῶς to mean 'in prophetic rather than ordinary speech' (Schweizer, 'Πνεῦμα', p. 449).

[75] Bruce, 'The Spirit', p. 340.

[76] Bruce, 'The Spirit', p. 340.

cording to Bruce, the conclusion to this conundrum, 'is plain: it is not that the Spirit is identical with the exalted Lord, but that the exalted Lord speaks to the churches by the Spirit',[77] who is none other than the Spirit of prophecy. Bruce continues by asserting that all the words of the exalted Lord are spoken by the Spirit. He cites the declaration in Rev. 16:15 where Christ offers the beatitude for those who are ready when Christ returns as a thief. The simile of a thief had already been used by John in Rev. 3:3, echoing the words of Jesus in Matt. 24:43 and Luke 12:39.

Bruce closes with a discussion of the two instances of direct discourse by the Spirit in Rev. 14:13 and 22:17. In Rev. 14:13, the Spirit affirms the words of blessing of the heavenly voices that those who lose their lives may rest from the turmoil of the earth. In the final reference to the Spirit, John records the response of the Spirit and the Bride to the words of Christ in Rev. 22:12, 'Behold, I am coming soon'. Bruce suggests that the Spirit may be understood as dwelling in the community and prompting the response; or rather, 'more probably', according to Bruce, 'the Spirit is the Spirit of Prophecy, who takes the initiative in making the response, and is seconded by the community'.[78] The coming of Christ entails both blessing and cursing. Between the invitation of the Spirit and the Bride for Christ to come and the acceptance of the invitation by Christ is the warning to those who would take away or add to the words of the book. The promise that Christ is coming provokes Bruce to conclude that the eucharist may be an appropriate time and place to read the Apocalypse because of the manifested presence of Christ. According to Bruce, '[t]he Lord's coming in the Apocalypse is more than his eucharistic presence, but it is anticipated in his eucharistic presence'.[79] The eucharist contains the same twofold blessing and cursing as the Apocalypse. Those who partake of the elements with a forgiven heart are blessed but those who partake unworthily will suffer with those who take away or add to the words of the Apocalypse.

R.J. Bauckham. Bauckham first contributed to the topic in a journal article published in 1980.[80] That contribution was later revised and

[77] Bruce, 'The Spirit', p. 340.

[78] Bruce, 'The Spirit', p. 343. Bruce cites the words of H.B. Swete who writes, 'the Spirit and the Bride', is 'practically equivalent to "the Prophets and the Saints"' (H.B. Swete, *The Apocalypse of St John,* p. 306).

[79] Bruce, 'The Spirit', p. 344.

[80] Bauckham, 'The Role of the Spirit in the Apocalypse', pp. 66-83.

republished in 1993 as a chapter in *The Climax of Prophecy: Studies on the Book of Revelation.* He offers a less detailed and perhaps more apologetic version in *The Theology of the Book of Revelation,* also published in 1993. The following summary of his contribution essentially follows his most extensive treatment of the topic which is in Chapter 5 of *The Climax of Prophecy.* Bauckham divides his treatment of the role of the Spirit into four categories, (1) the Spirit of vision, (2) the Spirit of prophecy, (3) the seven Spirits, which has been discussed above, and (4) the Spirit and the eschatological perspective.

Under the heading 'the Spirit of vision', Bauckham offers an analysis of the phrase ἐν πνεύματι. He suggests that the phrase is predominantly a theological statement. Contrary to interpreters who wish to focus on John's psychological experience of ecstasy, Bauckham proposes that John is making a claim of authenticity when he declares that his prophecy was received when he was in the Spirit. Beyond the theological significance of the phrase, ἐν πνεύματι serves as a literary marker signifying the beginning of a new vision in the prophecy. The first two references come at the beginning of the vision, first on the earth with the seven churches (Rev. 1:10) and then in heaven (Rev. 4:2). The phrase also introduces the parallel visions of Babylon and the new Jerusalem (Rev. 17:3; 21:10).

Bauckham offers several parallel examples of being in the Spirit from Christian and Jewish literature. The history of the phrase reveals various usages. The phrase can mean 'in the Spirit's control' (cf. Matt. 22:43; Luke 1:7; Acts 19:21; 1 Cor. 12:3). Polycrates writes of people living in the Spirit suggesting that the phrase does not refer to a punctiliar experience but rather a way of life.[81] For the author of the *Didache,* the phrase was apparently theologically neutral, for a prophet speaking in the Spirit would have to be tested according to his or her own behavior.[82] Contrary to the interpretation that supposes John to be in a trance and thereby acting only as a passive mouthpiece, Bauckham suggests that John never completely loses his volition though his normal consciousness is suspended and replaced by visions given by the Spirit.

Like Bruce, Bauckham deems the primary role of the Spirit to be the 'spirit of prophecy'. The Spirit performs a role distinct from the

[81] Eusebius, *Ecclesiastical History 5:24:2-5.* Polycrates writes that a daughter of the apostle Philip lived in the Holy Spirit (ἐν ἁγίῳ πνεύματι πολιτευσαμένη), and he writes of Melito, the eunuch, of whom it is said he 'lived entirely in the Holy Spirit' (τὸν ἐν ἁγίῳ πνεύματι πάντα πολιτευσάμενον).

[82] *Didache* 11:7-9.

chain of revelation, God-Christ-angel-John (Rev. 1:1-3). The Spirit does not give the content of the revelation, but rather enables John to receive the revelation. Yet this revelation is not merely a transcription of the visionary experience but a complex literary composition. The prophecy inspired by God includes the content and reception of the revelation as well as the literary composition and the transmission of the composition to the churches.

Besides the Spirit's role as an agent of visionary experience, the Spirit inspires prophetic oracles (cf. Mark 4:9-23). In the letters to the seven churches the hearers are encouraged to hear what the Spirit is saying to the churches. Although Christ is the speaker, Bauckham does not equate Christ and the Spirit. Instead, he deduces that the Spirit speaks the words of Christ to the churches, thereby being the immanent presence of Christ on earth. Christ also speaks in Rev. 16:15; 22:7, 12-13, 16, 20, which would be spoken by the Spirit as well. However, the Spirit says more than the words of Christ (cf. Rev. 14:13; 22:17). In Rev. 14.13, the Spirit adds an emphatic endorsement to the words of the heavenly voice. The Spirit inspires the prayer in Rev. 22:17 when the Spirit and the Bride say, 'Come'. Accordingly, Bauckham argues that the Spirit is the agency of Christ's words to the church via the prophets. He denies that the pneumatology of the Apocalypse is deficient, lacking the concept of the Spirit of life or the concept of the Spirit as power that enables morality in the Christian life. Although he defines the primary role of the Spirit to be the Spirit of prophecy, the Spirit, according to Bauckham, has life-giving and life-changing effects by bringing the words of Christ to the churches vis-à-vis Spirit-inspired response to prophecy and Spirit-inspired prayer. In summary, the Spirit of prophecy, to use Bauckham's words,

> indicates the inspired utterance of Christian prophets (principally, in this context, John) [by bringing] the words of the exalted Christ to his people on earth [thereby endorsing] on earth the words of heavenly revelations [and directing] the prayers of the churches to their heavenly Lord. The Spirit is the divine presence on earth not in heaven, but unlike the seven Spirits which are 'sent out into the whole earth', the Spirit's sphere is the churches.[83]

Bauckham turns his attention to the question of prophetic participation. In other words, he asks if Spirit-inspired prophecy was a function which the Apocalypse confines to the Christian prophets, or if there is a sense in which each individual member of the church fulfills the role

[83] Bauckham, *The Theology of the Book of Revelation*, p. 118.

of a prophet.[84] Bauckham is willing to agree that prophecy in the Apocalypse is equivalent with the testimony of Jesus and that the churches function prophetically in their witness to Jesus. However, he disagrees that every believer can therefore be identified as a prophet. In Rev. 19:10, Bauckham interprets the genitive to be subjective, thus indicating that the testimony Jesus bore is the Spirit-inspired prophecy. It is therefore also the content of John's prophecy (Rev. 1:2), for Jesus is the one who attests to the prophecy (Rev. 22:20). In essence, this word of God is also that to which Jesus bore witness in his earthly life (Rev. 1:5) and to which his followers bear witness in the world (Rev. 1:9). In Revelation witnessing is a verbal activity (cf. Rev. 11:7; 12:11), but it is strongly linked to obedience to God's commandments (Rev. 12:17; 14:12). All Christians must bear witness to Jesus, not merely the prophets, a fact which (as I shall argue below) is revealed in the vision of the two witnesses in Rev. 11:3, thus equating prophecy and witnessing. The function of the churches as a witness attributes the prophetic role to the whole church. As a result of the Spirit-inspired witnessing the nations are converted. The idea of the conversion of the nations is unique to Bauckham's interpretation of the content of the prophecy (i.e. the Apocalypse). Bauckham distinguishes between the role of the prophet in the community and the role of general Christians in public. The prophets speak the word of God to the churches by the Spirit and by the Spirit the churches speak to the world (i.e. special vocation vs. general vocation).

Bauckham concludes with a discussion of the eschatological perspective of the Spirit. He writes, 'The spirit mediates the activity of the exalted Christ in and through his church, declaring Christ's word to his people in vision and prophetic oracle, leading in the prayers of his people and inspiring his people's missionary witness to the world'.[85] The Spirit provides an eschatological perspective which enables the Christian churches to see the age to come. 'Not simply predicting the events of the end, the purpose of John's prophecy was to enable the Christians of the seven churches to bear witness to Jesus, and this could only be done by directing their sight and their lives toward the coming of the Lord, not so much seeing the future as seeing the present from the perspective of the future'.[86]

[84] Cf. D. Hill, 'Prophecy and Prophets in the Revelation of St John', *NTS* 18 (1972), pp. 401-414. See also D. Aune, *Prophecy in Early Christianity and the Ancient Mediterranean World* (Grand Rapids: Eerdmans, 1983), pp. 206-208.

[85] Bauckham, *The Climax of Prophecy,* p. 166.

[86] Bauckham, *The Climax of Prophecy,* p. 166. Cf. E. Schüssler Fiorenza, *The Book of*

In Rev. 22:17, the bride, suggests Bauckham, is the eschatological church and not the seven churches. 'The bride is the church seen from the perspective of the parousia',[87] arrayed in righteous deeds (Rev. 19:7-8). Bauckham contrasts the 'unpreparedness' of the seven churches with the Bride's 'ardent prayer' for the parousia (Rev. 22:17). The eschatological prayer of the churches is the voice of the Spirit speaking through the prophets, 'for the function of the Spirit is to direct the churches towards their eschatological reality'.[88]

3.2.2. *The Prophetic Community*

R.L. Jeske. Contrary to F.F. Bruce and R.J. Bauckham, Jeske does not attempt to offer a full pneumatology of the Apocalypse. Instead, he focuses on the phrase ἐν πνεύματι. Jeske critiques the history of interpretation of ἐν πνεύματι for being too narrowly defined as simply a phenomenological trope for ecstasy.[89] He insists that ἐν πνεύματι is not a technical term in the New Testament. Arguing that John uses the phrase as a literary device to connect with the experience of his audience, Jeske proposes that the role of the Spirit is to provide a common spiritual community or ethos in which the churches can experience life in the Spirit. John's claim to be in the Spirit served as more than ecclesial authenticity because the community could identify with the experience that John was describing. The message of John carried authority not because it was from a prophet but rather because it was from the Spirit of prophecy. The shared experience of being in the Spirit, according to Jeske, served as the bond of communal fellowship, which carried with it the responsibility to be sensitive to the Spirit. Jeske concludes that the interpretation of ἐν πνεύματι as a private experience needs to be discarded in favor of an understanding that entails the relational aspect of the role of the Spirit in the churches.

J.C. de Smidt. The work of de Smidt, a South African scholar, some of which is published in Afrikaans,[90] has not received much attention in

Revelation: Justice and Judgment (Philadelphia: Fortress, 1985), pp. 46-51.

[87] Bauckham, *The Climax of Prophecy,* p. 167.

[88] Bauckham, *The Climax of Prophecy,* p. 167.

[89] For a description of the visionary experience of the early church see J. Dunn, Jesus and the Spirit, A Study of the Religious and Charismatic Experience of Jesus and the First Christians as Reflected in the New Testament (Philadelphia: Westminster, 1975), pp. 177-179; 213-216.

[90] De Smidt, 'Die Oë van die Gees in die boek Openbaring', pp. 159-176, has been addressed above because it deals with the symbol of the seven eyes which is closely related to the seven spirits.

the English-speaking world.[91] De Smidt discusses the nomenclature of the Spirit used in Revelation and concludes, in agreement with Bruce and Bauckham, that the Holy Spirit is to be inferred from the references to the Spirit in the seven letters, the repeated phrase ἐν πνεύματι, and the direct discourse of the Spirit in Rev. 14:13; 22:17. De Smidt attempts a brief discussion of the Spirit in the New Testament before spending the majority of his time on the concept of ἐν πνεύματι, which he deems to be both a literary sign and a theological claim possessing eschatological significance. In a *JPT* article de Smidt focuses on what he calls the hermeneutical perspectives of the Spirit.[92] De Smidt finds common ground between Bauckham, who insists that John's experience of being in the Spirit is unique to prophets, and Jeske's argument that being in the Spirit is solely a communal experience. He discusses the phenomenological experience of John being in the Spirit, but he includes the congregational perspective of the seven churches, a perspective which is only possible because the Spirit is active in the community. De Smidt concludes with the identical admonition as in his contribution to the meaning of the symbol of the seven eyes, viz. the Spirit, provides a new perception of the present from the perspective of the future.

M.W. Wilson. Wilson's contribution to the scholarship of the Spirit in the Apocalypse focuses primarily on the phrase in Rev. 19:10 (ἡ γὰρ μαρτυρία Ἰησοῦ ἐστιν τὸ πνεῦμα τῆς προφητείας).[93] Wilson acknowledges the traditional interpretation of the role of the Spirit to be prophetically pointing to Christ; however, he argues that Rev. 19:10 has been misinterpreted.[94] He agrees that the Spirit is an active character in the narrative of Revelation but denies that there is a reference to the Spirit in this passage. Wilson's argument can be summarized as follows: (1) he agrees with Bruce that 19:10c begins with an objective genitive (i.e. for the witness *to* Jesus); (2) Wilson notes that each of the ten occurrences of the construction τὸ πνεῦμα (except for 19:10) takes

[91] The exception is the reference to de Smidt in the excursus in Aune's WBC commentary on Revelation (Aune, *Revelation 1–5,* pp. 36-37).

[92] De Smidt, 'Hermeneutical Perspectives on the Spirit in the Book of Revelation', pp. 27-47.

[93] M.W. Wilson, 'Revelation 19:10 and Contemporary Interpretation', pp. 191-202. See also Wilson's discussion of the prophetic ministry of John in idem, 'A Pie in a Very Bleak Sky: Analysis and Appropriation of the Promise Sayings in the Seven Letters to the Churches in Revelation 2-3', Ph.D. thesis (University of South Africa).

[94] Wilson, 'Revelation 19:10 and Contemporary Interpretation', pp. 191-202.

the present tense of λέγω as its verb; furthermore, 'spirit' is capitalized in each of these nine cases in the KJV, NIV and NSAB, which is contrary to Rev. 19:10, where 'spirit' is not capitalized;[95] (3) he proposes the uncapitalized 'spirit' refers to an abstraction such as 'the essence', an interpretation, Wilson suggests, which makes more sense out of the grammatical construction of the sentence; and (4) Wilson opposes the unanimous decision of the English translations to omit the definite article in the final phase of the sentence (τῆς προφητείας). He suggests that the article be translated, thereby inferring a reference not to prophecy in general but rather to *the* prophecy (i.e. the Book of Revelation), which John designates five times as 'prophecy'. Wilson proposes that the meaning of Rev. 19:10 is that the testimony to Jesus (objective genitive) is the spirit (or essence) of *the* prophecy (i.e. the book of Revelation).

Wilson's denial that πνεῦμα in Rev. 19:10 refers to the Holy Spirit should not be interpreted to intimate that he denies the presence of the Spirit in the entire Apocalypse. Wilson's overall understanding of the pneumatology of the Apocalypse includes a role for the Spirit that is vital to the existence of the church and its proclamation. According to Wilson, '[t]he "witness to Jesus" that John and the saints are holding is identical with the prophecy the Spirit is speaking to the seven churches. It is this same message that the saints are declaring during the time of tribulation'.[96] Wilson concludes with an explanation of the beatitudes as 'prophetic paraenesis urging [the church] to faithfulness and endurance'.[97] Thus, Rev. 19:9-10 (the fourth beatitude) promises the eschatological blessing of dining with the Lamb for those who hold the testimony of Jesus and worship God, for the testimony *to* Jesus is the spirit of *the* Prophecy.[98]

4. Conclusion

The survey has shown that a consensus has yet to be reached on a definition of the role of the Spirit in Revelation, so that the question,

[95] Wilson notes that contrary to these English translations, Ford, Bauckham and Bruce all choose to capitalize 'spirit' in their discussion of Rev. 19:10 (Wilson, 'Revelation 19.10 and Contemporary Interpretation', p. 198).

[96] Wilson, 'Revelation 19:10 and Contemporary Interpretation', p. 201.

[97] Wilson, 'Revelation 19:10 and Contemporary Interpretation', p. 202.

[98] Wilson proposes that 'the Prophecy' may be capitalized as the title of John's work in the manner of 'the Revelation', or 'the Apocalypse' (Wilson, 'Revelation 19:10 and Contemporary Interpretation', p. 201, n. 39).

'What is the role of the Spirit in the Apocalypse?' remains open. Although an exact consensus does not exist, there are a few common threads which seem to be shared by the majority of scholars. The most common thread appears to be the notion of the Spirit of prophecy. The scholars who ascribe the references to the Spirit to editors and the scholars who credit John with the references to the Spirit seem to agree that the primary role of the Spirit (at least in the canonical version of the text) is the Spirit of prophecy. Likewise, the majority of scholars (excluding Jeske, de Smidt and Wilson) also agree that the Apocalypse is devoid of the notion of the Spirit who indwells the believers in general (cf. John 14:17; 1 John 2:20, 27; 3:24).[99] The scholarship seems to be divided rather evenly on the topic of the identity of the seven spirits. Those who identify the seven spirits as the seven archangels attach more importance to the religio-historical setting of the Apocalypse. Conversely, the scholars who identify the seven spirits as a symbol for the divine Spirit, while acknowledging the existence of the seven archangels in the literary world of the Apocalypse, propose that the allusions in Revelation to Zechariah 4 signal John's intended meaning of the symbolism of the seven spirits.

As mentioned above, I.T. Beckwith proposes that questions like, 'What is the role of the Spirit in the Apocalypse?' have 'exercised the ingenuity of interpreters in the course of the centuries'.[100] He suggests that the various answers given for these questions have been influenced by the interpreter's circumstances, either political or ecclesiastical, and by the methodology and hermeneutic applied to the text. Like interpreters before me, I too have been influenced by my circumstances along with my presuppositions concerning the text of the Apocalypse. In this study, I seek to offer a new contribution to the understanding of the role of the Spirit in the Apocalypse, a *pro nobis* understanding which acknowledges the influences of my own cultural and spiritual context. The goal is to inquire into the intertextual relationship between my own confessional context in a Pentecostal interpretative community and the literary references to the Spirit in the Apocalypse.

[99] Schweizer's proposal that all believers may be prophets (cf. his comments on Rev. 19:10) would suggest that he could be included in the list with Jeske, de Smidt and Wilson who understand the Spirit to be active within the individual members of the churches.

[100] Beckwith, *The Apocalypse of John,* p. 319. Despite the attention given to the Apocalypse since 1919, when Beckwith originally made this observation, a consensus is far from being reached on almost every aspect of the text.

The survey of scholarship in this chapter provides more than an overview of the previous work on the role of the Spirit in the Apocalypse because it also unveils the presuppositional stance of the interpreters. While the methods applied to the text by the various scholars have not been monolithic, the worldview of modernity has prevailed. In an attempt to produce neutral acultural interpretations, modernity has encouraged scholars to renounce their cultural or religious contexts when engaging in academic pursuits, thereby avoiding distortion or coloration of their work. Nevertheless, with the rise of post-modernity, the context of the interpreter has become one of the primary intertexts with which to pursue academic inquiry.[101] What follows is an exploration into the theory and practice of 'intertextuality', a notion which maintains a focus on the Old Testament in Revelation without losing sight of the role of the reader in the interpretative process.

[101] For the relationship between post-modernity and biblical studies see E.V. McKnight, *Post-Modern Use of the Bible: The Emergence of Reader-Oriented Criticism* (Nashville: Abingdon, 1988); W. Brueggemann, *Texts under Negotiation: The Bible and Postmodern Imagination* (Minneapolis: Fortress, 1993). The paradigm shifts which mark the fissure between modernity and post-modernity are in no way limited to the discipline of biblical studies. Cf. T.S. Kuhn, *The Structure of Scientific Revolutions* (2nd rev. ed.; Chicago: Chicago University Press, 1970).

2

Intertextuality, Revelation, Pentecostalism: The Roundabout of Meaning

> Competing interpretations of Revelation are not simply either right or wrong, but they constitute different ways of reading and constructing socio-historical and theo-ethical meaning. What is appropriate in such a rhetorical paradigm of biblical scholarship is not detached value-neutrality, but an explicit articulation of one's rhetorical strategies, interested perspectives, ethical criteria, theoretical frameworks, religious presuppositions, and sociopolitical locations for the critical discussion.[1]

1. Introduction

In this chapter, I attempt to offer an articulation of my theoretical framework (i.e. intertextuality). Intertextuality is a literary theory which suggests among other things that all (literary) texts are products of other texts (the *déjà lu*). This is obvious in the case of a monograph where multiple works are cited in the bibliography, yet intertextuality reaches far beyond direct quotations to include allusions and echoes which occur when one text reminds the reader of another text. Intertextuality does not stop with allusions or echoes but goes further into the life and community of the reader so that the 'interested perspectives, ethical criteria, theoretical frameworks, religious presuppositions, and sociopolitical locations' serve as (con)textual forces that converge with the literary texts.

At times, intertextuality is described as an intersection where two roads converge. Within the intersection it is impossible to differentiate between the roads. No longer on a single road, a driver is located at

[1] E. Schüssler Fiorenza, *Revelation: Vision of a Just World* (Edinburgh: T. & T. Clark, new edn, 1993), p. 3.

(or within) the intersection of the two. In the case of literary texts, the intersection would be the location of meaning. Though somewhat helpful, the analogy of the intersection is problematic because it over-simplifies the concept. While all analogies fail eventually, the image of a roundabout or traffic circle may better represent intertextuality. In a roundabout multiple roads are coming together and the right of way is a bit more fluid than at an intersection. Cars enter the circle and leave in accordance with certain rules; however, the driver may negotiate staying within the circle (if she or he misses the desired road). Signs and signals play a role in the negotiation of the roundabout as do other drivers. For me, as a North American studying in England, driving (or for that matter riding) through a roundabout was quite hectic at first. Although I eventually learned to manage, driving through a round-about still requires an interpretative process (no matter how unconscious) as to how to negotiate the meaning of the signs and signals as well as being aware of how others are currently interpreting those same signifiers. This chapter serves as a (textual) roundabout, where literary theory, studies on Revelation, Old Testament texts, and contextual theology all come together. My hope is to negotiate the roundabout bringing along some passengers/readers with me while not doing too much damage to the roads (or the passengers). The chapter begins with an investigation of the theory of intertextuality,[2] followed by an examination of the ways in which the method has been practiced in studies on Revelation. The chapter concludes by investigating ways in which intertextuality as a method correlates with contextual theologies thereby plotting the contextual vantage point from which an interpretation of the role of the Spirit may be offered.

2. Intertextuality: Its Origin and Its Future (in Biblical Studies)

When employing use of the term 'intertextuality', a certain amount of specification seems imperative due to the variety of definitions which have been assigned to the word.[3] In fact, J. Kristeva (who is credited

[2] Note the often cited remark by T. Eagleton that 'hostility to theory ... (usually) means an opposition to other people's theories and an oblivion of one's own' (T. Eagleton, *Literary Theory: An Introduction* [Minneapolis: University of Minneapolis Press, 1983], p. viii).

[3] For a discussion on the theory and practice of intertextuality see H.F. Plett, ed., *Intertextuality* (Research in Text Theory, 15; Berlin: de Gruyter, 1991); J. Clayton and

with coining the term)[4] chose to abandon its use because in her opinion so many others were using it incorrectly. She writes in her dissertation, 'since (intertextuality) has often been understood in the banal sense of "study of sources", we prefer the term *transposition* because it specifies that the passage from one signifying system to another demands a new articulation of the thetic'.[5] Within biblical studies a debate wages over the use of the term, the definition of which remains a point of discussion in its native discipline of literary studies as well.[6]

The majority of biblical scholars seem to be using 'intertextuality' as a general rubric for discussing the use of Scripture within Scripture.[7] In these cases, intertextuality can be described as a category for identifying allusions to pre-texts (i.e. texts written chronologically earlier than the focus [or generated] text from which literary influence or allusion can be identified). In practice, there appears to be little difference between many of the new intertextual readings and the traditional source or redaction analysis, which raises the question, 'Why use the term?' Some scholars who have critically reflected on the use of intertextuality would respond that its use is being propelled solely by its popularity. In other words, it is fashionable or trendy.[8] At a time when biblical scholars are increasingly diving into interdisciplinary explorations (especially with literary criticism), the appropriation of new vocabulary gives the appearance of a successful navigation of the interdisciplinary waters. J. van Ruiten's article, 'The Intertextual Relationship between

E. Rothstein, eds., *Influence and Intertextuality in Literary History* (Madison, WI: University of Wisconsin Press, 1991); M. Worton and J. Still, eds., *Intertextuality: Theories and Practices* (Manchester: Manchester University Press, 1990).

[4] J. Kristeva, 'Bakhtine, le mot, le dialogue et le roman', *Critique* 33 (1967), pp. 438-465; published in English as 'Word, Dialogue and Novel', in *Desire in Language: A Semiotic Approach to Literature and Art* trans. L.S. Roudiez (New York: Columbia University Press, 1980), pp. 64-91; also in T. Moi, ed., *The Kristeva Reader* (Oxford: Basil Blackwell, 1986), pp. 34-61. References are to the latter publication.

[5] Published in English as *Revolution in Poetic Language* trans. Margret Waller (New York: Columbia University Press, 1984), pp. 59-60.

[6] H.F. Plett, 'Intertextualities', in *Intertextuality,* ed. H.F. Plett (Berlin: de Gruyter, 1991), pp. 7-18.

[7] The use of the term is not restricted to the 'Use of the Old Testament in the New', but also includes analysis of the use of Scripture within the Old Testament, e.g., D.N. Fewell ed., *Reading between Texts: Intertextuality and the Hebrew Bible* (Louisville, KY: John Knox Press, 1992).

[8] E. van Wolde, 'Trendy Intertextuality', in *Intertextuality in Biblical Writing, ed.* S. Draisma (Festschrift for B. van Iersel; Kampen: Kok, 1989), pp. 43-49; T.R. Hatina, 'Intertextuality and Historical Criticism', *Bib Int* 7 (1999), pp. 28-43.

Isaiah 65:17-20 and Revelation 21:1-5b', is an example of this kind of misplaced appropriation.[9] Other than the use of the term 'intertextuality' in the title, van Ruiten does not refer to intertextuality in the text, its summary, or in the footnotes. Instead, van Ruiten's paper delves into the influence which the Isaiah text exerts on the text in Revelation. The highlighting of van Ruiten's misappropriation should not be understood as disparaging the piece as a whole. Indeed, the piece is a first-rate source-critical analysis. Nevertheless, some scholars would question the use of 'intertextuality' simply as new nomenclature, because it seems to nullify the theoretical force which the term is capable of generating.[10]

One such scholar, T.R. Hatina, argues that intertextuality and historical criticism are incompatible owing to the ideological and theoretical origins of intertextuality. Hatina delineates three characteristics of intertextuality which historical scholars fail to consider when employing the term: '(1) the ideological context wherein the term was coined; (2) the inherently related concept of text; and (3) the distinction between influence and intertextuality'.[11] These characteristics deserve careful consideration.

2.1. The Ideological Context of Intertextuality

In 1966, Kristeva, a twenty-five-year-old Bulgarian, arrived in Paris to pursue doctoral studies in literary theory.[12] Her background prepared her well for the intellectual climate she was entering. With a solid grounding in Marxist theory (as well as being fluent in Russian), Kristeva was able to make an immediate impact upon the world of literary theory by introducing (along with her compatriot T. Todorov) the work of Mikhail Bakhtin, the Soviet theorist from whose work

[9] J. van Ruiten, 'The Intertextual Relationship between Isaiah 65:17-20 and Revelation 21:1-5b', *Estudios Bíblicos* 51 (1993), pp. 473-510.

[10] For example, G. Aichele and G.A. Phillips, 'Introduction: Exegesis, Eisegesis, Intergesis', *Semeia* 69/70 (1995), pp. 7-18; T.R. Hatina, 'Intertextuality and Historical Criticism', 28-43; K. Nielsen, 'Intertextuality and Biblical Scholarship', *Scandinavian Journal of the Old Testament* 2 (1990), pp. 89-95; G. Snyman, 'Who is Speaking? Intertextuality and Textual Influence', *Neot* 30/2 (1996), pp. 427-449; B.D. Sommer, 'Exegesis, Allusion and Intertextuality in the Hebrew Bible: A Response to Lyle Eslinger', *Vetus Testamentum* 44:4 (1996), pp. 479-489.

[11] Hatina, 'Intertextuality and Historical Criticism', p. 29.

[12] The biographical information on Kristeva as well as the assessment of the cultural and intellectual environment in 1960's France closely follows T. Moi, 'Introduction', in T. Moi, ed., *The Kristeva Reader,* pp. 1-22.

Kristeva would develop her notion of intertextuality. Kristeva was soon to be associated with *Tel Quel,* a literary group known for its *avant garde* approach to literature. Led by P. Sollers, who would later become Kristeva's husband, the *Tel Quel* group included such names as Foucault, Derrida and Barthes. Not unlike structuralism, the focus of *Tel Quel* was 'on *language* as the starting-point for a new kind of thought on politics and the subject ... [T]he group based its work on a new understanding of history as *text;* and of writing (*écriture*) as *production,* not representation.'[13] In terms of traditional literary studies, these ideas are quite revolutionary. If writing is production rather than representation then the power to determine meaning shifts from the bourgeois establishment's assessment of authorial intent to the readers at large. This anti-establishment sentiment not only pervaded the work of these (poststructural) theorists, but also found a public voice.

In May 1968, a social uprising occurred in France, where students and workers revolted against the oppression of the ruling communist party.[14] The intellectual left abandoned French communism, claiming it to be a revisionist regime of the Soviet Union. The *Tel Quel* group opted instead for Maoism (a Chinese form of Marxism led by Mao Zedong). From the viewpoint of the French intellectual community, Mao's China appeared to be the answer (i.e. Marxism as it was meant to be). Kristeva (with her background in Eastern Europe) was not as optimistic as other members of *Tel Quel.* She traveled to China, hoping to see how Marxism operated in a different cultural background which did not have a monolithic religion; however, her discovery was unsettling, especially with regard to the situation of women. Not until Mao's death did the world learn of the torture and death which occurred under the authority of Chairman Mao.[15] Thus, Hatina argues that the ideological origin of intertextuality is one of cultural and literary revolution, a context which is completely contrary to the ideological assumptions of historical criticism.[16]

[13] Moi, 'Introduction', p. 4.

[14] Moi, 'Introduction', p. 4.

[15] Kristeva became disenchanted with collective political action and later claims in her essay, 'A New Type of Intellectual: the Dissident', that the politically active intellectual is hopelessly caught in the very logic of power he or she is seeking to undermine (idem, 'A New Type of Intellectual: the Dissident', in T. Moi, ed., *The Kristeva Reader,* pp. 292-300).

[16] Conversely, one could argue that historical criticism has been more than a little revolutionary.

Hatina's complaint that historical scholars have not sufficiently considered the ideological context of intertextuality is congruent with the earlier assessment of the editors of *Semeia* 69/70, who discuss the ideological context of intertextuality in their introductory essay.[17] They claim that certain conservative biblical scholars have illegitimately grafted the word 'intertextuality' into a conservative paradigm, attempting to nail down authorial intent and literary influence. The irony, the editors claim, is that 'intertextuality is not some neutral literary mechanism but is rather at root a means of ideological and cultural expression and of social transformation'. In order to support this thesis, the editors describe how Kristeva was politically involved in France during the 1960s. Aichele and Phillips, the editors, claim that intertextuality should not be used to serve conservative aims (i.e. authorial intent and literary history) because the authorial intent and literary history of intertextuality are not conservative. However, the careful reader sees that indictment lose its force in its own enactment.

Following a similar argument to that of Aichele and Phillips, Hatina insists that intertextuality is grounded in post-structuralism. He finds it ironic that historical critics who normally are very sensitive to context have chosen to ignore the ideological context which, according to Hatina, gives intertextuality 'its distinct meaning'.[18] This argument is problematic as well because post-structuralism calls into question the validity of a 'distinct meaning'. The basic notion of intertextuality is that words have meaning in relationship to other signs, yet those signifiers are not stable but are in constant flux. According to M. Worton and J. Still, 'every quotation distorts and redefines the "primary" utterance by relocating it within another linguistic and cultural context'.[19] In the final analysis, the ideological argument that conservative scholars should abandon the use of intertextuality as a rubric of study fails to convince.[20] However, if conservative scholars continue to use jargon which is contrary to their own political stance, they would be well served to articulate their theoretical framework. In addition to reveal-

[17] Aichele and Phillips, 'Introduction: Exegesis, Eisegesis, Intergesis', pp. 7-18.

[18] Hatina, 'Intertextuality and Historical Criticism', p. 43.

[19] M. Worton and J. Still, 'Introduction', in *Intertextuality: Theories and Practices,* ed. M. Worton and J. Still (Manchester: Manchester University Press, 1990), p. 11.

[20] Not all scholars who acknowledge the post-structural characteristics of intertextuality accede to the ideology of those who first used the term; cf. e.g. K. Nielsen, 'Intertextuality and Biblical Scholarship', pp. 89-95.

ing the political climate of intertextuality's origin, the examination of the ideological context raises the question of the poststructural concept of text (or textuality) which pervades the work of the originators of 'intertextuality'.

2.2. (Inter)textuality

R. Barthes (Kristeva's teacher) describes writing as 'that neutral, composite, oblique space where our subject slips away, the negative where all identity is lost, starting with the very identity of the body of writing'.[21] Barthes's rhetorical move points to the shift in emphasis within literary criticism from authorial intention to the reader's response. '[A] text', according to Barthes,

> is made of multiple writings, drawn from many cultures and entering into mutual relations of dialogue, parody, contestation, but there is one place where this multiplicity is focused and that place is the reader, not, as was hitherto said, the author. The reader is the space on which all the quotations that make up a writing are inscribed without any of them being lost; a text's unity lies not in its origin but in its destination.[22]

The epistemological stance inherent within Barthes's comment not only illustrates the tension between poststructuralism and historical criticism but also highlights a tension between poststructuralism and narrative approaches to the biblical texts. Barthes announces the death of the author[23] but he also calls into question the unity of the final form of the text, which is a major premise of the narrative approaches. In theory, intertextuality calls into question the notion of the autonomous text. In other words, all texts are products of other texts (i.e. textuality). As Hatina proposes, the concept of textuality is a vital characteristic of intertextuality and one that is rarely considered by histori-

[21] R. Barthes, *Image Music Text* trans. S. Heath (New York: Hill and Wang, 1977), p. 142.

[22] Barthes, *Image Music Text,* p. 148. Cf. the comments of Ricoeur, 'Writing renders texts autonomous with respect to the intention of the author. What the text signifies no longer coincides with what the author meant' (P. Ricoeur, *Hermeneutics and the Human Sciences* [Cambridge: University Press 1981], p. 139). Likewise Derrida writes that a text is 'no longer a finished corpus of writing. Some content enclosed in a book or its margins, but a differential network, a fabric of traces, referring to other differential traces' (J. Derrida, 'Living On'/'Border Lines', in H. Bloom et al., *Deconstruction and Criticism* [London: Routledge and Kegan Paul 1979], p. 84).

[23] Barthes proclaims, 'the birth of the reader must be at the death of the Author' (Barthes, *Image Music Text,* p. 148).

cal scholars who employ the term. A thorough definition of textuality exposes the incompatibility between intertextuality and traditional historical studies.

2.2.1. *A Fishian Concept of Text(uality)*

The literary theory of S. Fish has been chosen in order to express the significance of text as production, followed by a critique of Fish by J. Culler.[24] Although his name is not automatically associated with post-structuralism (unlike Derrida, Foucault, Lacan, Barthes or Kristeva), Fish's theory is a good choice. He is frequently used to represent the culmination of reader-response criticism as well as an introduction into postmodernism.[25] Like Wittgenstein, whose work is often described as early (Wittgenstein) or late (Wittgenstein), Fish experiences a similar categorization by his critics, having undergone a metamorphosis between 1970, when he published 'Literature in the Reader: Affective Stylistics',[26] and 1980, when he published, *Is There a Text in This Class?*[27] Furthermore, his popularity has not been diminished either by his lucid writing style (bearing no resemblance to the idiolect of Derrida and company) or his controversial (and often misrepresented) formulation of interpretative communities.

Fish[28] first wrote about the role of the reader in 1967 in his book *Surprised by Sin: The Reader in Paradise Lost.*[29] He argues that *Paradise*

[24] Culler offers a critique not only of Fish but all reader-oriented criticisms (J. Culler, *On Deconstruction: Theory and Criticism after Structuralism* [Ithaca, NY: Cornell University Press, 1982], pp. 64-83). For other critiques see E. Freund, *The Return of the Reader: Reader-Response Criticism* (New York: Methuen, 1987). The theological criticisms of Fish will be treated later.

[25] For a survey of the development of reader-response criticism see J.P. Tompkins, ed., *Reader-Response Criticism: From Formalism to Post-Structuralism* (Baltimore: Johns Hopkins University Press, 1980).

[26] S. Fish, 'Literature in the Reader: Affective Stylistics', *New Literary History* 2 (1970), pp. 123-62.

[27] The first representation of the late Fish may be located with the publication of S. Fish, 'Interpreting the *Variorum*', *Critical Inquiry* 2 (1976), pp. 465-485.

[28] Overviews of Fish's development abound. See E. Freund, *The Return of the Reader, passim;* F. Burnett, 'Postmodern Biblical Exegesis: The Eve of Historical Criticism', *Semeia* 51 (1990), pp. 51-80; S. Moore, 'Negative Hermeneutics, Insubstantial Texts: Stanley Fish and the Biblical Interpreter', *JAAR* 4 (1988), pp. 707-719; idem, *Literary Criticism and the Gospels: The Theoretical Challenge* (New Haven, CN: Yale University Press, 1989), pp. 108-130.

[29] S. Fish, *Surprised by Sin: The Reader in Paradise Lost* (Berkeley: University of California Press, 1967).

Lost guides the reader through the initial human experience as she is fooled by Satanic rhetoric only to recognize her need for grace and solidarity with Adam and Eve. In his next book-length contribution, *Self-Consuming Artifacts: The Experience of Seventeenth-Century Literature,*[30] Fish (still in his formalist mode) analyzes the way in which seventeenth-century authors mislead the reader into premature conclusions which are subsequently invalidated, diminishing the reader's confidence.

Fish the anti-formalist did not really appear until 1975, when he published 'Interpreting the *Variorum*', where he initially develops his understanding of interpretative communities. In 1980, he published a collection of essays (most of which had been previously published) under the title, *Is There a Text in This Class? The Authority of Interpretative Communities.* The collection chronicles his development from 'Literature in the Reader: Affective Stylistics' (an essay published in 1970) to a group of four new essays (including the title essay). Each previously published essay begins with an introductory note describing the circumstances in which it was originally written and frequently offering a corrective as well.

Fish prefaces this volume with the following explanation of its title,

> The answer this book gives to its title question is "there is and there isn't". There isn't a text in this or any other class if one means by text what E.D. Hirsch and others mean by it, "an entity which always remains the same from one moment to the next", ...but there is a text in this and every class if one means by text the structure of meanings that is obvious and inescapable from the perspective of whatever interpretative assumptions happen to be in force.[31]

This basic principle is the heart of Fishian literary theory. It underpins the argument of the entire book and indeed Fish's subsequent work as well.[32] He claims that this fundamental concept is simple, but the implications are far-reaching and often misunderstood, which is

[30] S. Fish, *Self-Consuming Artifacts: The Experience of Seventeenth-Century Literature* (Berkeley: University of California Press, 1972).

[31] S. Fish, *Is There a Text in This Class? The Authority of Interpretative Communities* (Cambridge, MS: Harvard University Press, 1980), p. vii. The full reference for the quotation is E.D. Hirsch, *Validity in Interpretation* (New Haven: Yale University Press, 1967), p. 69.

[32] Including S. Fish, *Doing What Comes Naturally: Change, Rhetoric, and the Practice of Theory in Literary and Legal Studies* (Oxford: Oxford University Press, 1989); idem, *There is No Such Thing as Free Speech: And It's a Good Thing Too* (Oxford: Oxford University Press, 1994).

why he took ten years to comprehend this point and takes four hundred pages to elaborate it.

In 'Literature in the Reader', Fish claims to be an anti-formalist, embracing the Affective Fallacy of W.K. Wimsatt and M.C. Beardsley, by promoting a style of reading which can best be explained as 'reading moment-by-moment'. The operative question of the critic changes from 'What does this poem mean?' to 'What does this word, phrase, or sentence do?' J. Tompkins explains that affective stylistics regards literature 'not as a fixed object of attention but as a sequence of events that unfold within the reader's mind'.[33] According to Fish, literature is a 'kinetic art'.[34] However, the text maintains a primary role (and a significant amount of potential energy) because it provokes the rules of competence immanent in the author and the erudite reader.

This closet formalism is abandoned in 'Interpreting the *Variorum*', where the text disappears. Fish completely forsakes the idea of agency in authorial intention as well as the notion that the text contains 'formal features'. According to Fish, interpretation creates everything (intention and formal features). For Fish, even the 'facts' of grammar are products of interpretation. 'The history of linguistics', writes Fish,

> is the story of competing paradigms, each of which offers a different account of the constituents of language. Verbs, nouns, cleft sentences, transformations, deep and surface structures... – now you see them, now you don't, depending on the descriptive apparatus you employ. The critic who confidently rests his (or her) analyses on the bedrock of syntactic descriptions is resting on an interpretation; the facts he (or she) points to *are* there, but only as a consequence of the interpretative (human-made) model that has called them into being.[35]

There are no more eternally accepted universal foundations. At first this might appear as if Fish is promoting a general relativism, but that could not be farther from the truth. According to Fish, what one perceives is always given shape by interpretative acts.

Faced with the paradoxical question of interpretational stability on the one hand and interpretational instability on the other, Fish sharpens his conception of interpretative communities.

[33] J.P. Tompkins, *Reader-Response Criticism*, pp. xvi-xvii.
[34] Fish, *Is There a Text in This Class?*, p. 43.
[35] Fish, *Is There a Text in This Class?*, p. 167.

> Interpretative communities are made up of those who share interpretative strategies not for reading (in the conventional sense) but for writing texts, for constituting their properties and assigning their intentions. In other words, these strategies exist prior to the act of reading and therefore determine the shape of what is read rather than, as is usually assumed, the other way around ... The notion of interpretative communities thus stands between an impossible ideal and the fear which leads them to maintain it ... It is the fragile but real consolidation of interpretative communities that allows us to talk to one another, but with no hope or fear of ever being able to stop.[36]

He is referring to the impossible ideal of a solid text (the Hirschian text) and the fear of never being able to communicate (a formalist fear). The ideal of a solid text and the fear of etiolating communication are not confined to the world of literary studies but penetrate to the heart of biblical studies as well. According to S. Moore, Fish 'has managed to take ... the theme of language as world construction, which pervaded philosophy and linguistics for generations (Nietzsche, Pierce, Wittgenstein, Heidegger, Foucault, Derrida), and to lay it squarely on the doorstep of an unsuspecting and indignant critical institution.'[37] A. Thiselton, one of Fish's chief opponents on theological grounds, critiques the Fishian concept of interpretative communities on these two points (i.e. the need for a solid text and the fear of not being able to be critiqued from the outside). However, before examining the theological critique of Thiselton the critique of J. Culler is offered, thereby meeting Fish initially on his own ground (literary theory) before examining the theological implications of his literary theory.

2.2.2. *J. Culler, A Literary Critique of Fish*

In his book on deconstruction, Culler examines reader-response criticism and finds it wanting.[38] He distinguishes between feminist criticism and male reader-response criticism, though both incur the same criticism. E. Freund declares that Culler has written the obituary for reader-response criticism. Indeed, the forcefulness with which Culler vitiates reader-response criticism is astounding. Culler raises three fundamental questions concerning reader-response criticism: (1) Who is in control, the text or the reader? (2) What is *in* the text? and (3) Why do

[36] Fish, *Is There a Text in This Class?*, pp. 171-172.
[37] Moore, *Literary Criticism and the Gospels*, p. 170.
[38] Culler, *On Deconstruction*, p. 66.

stories of reading always have such happy endings? Although he critiques other theorists besides Fish, the focus of this discussion is limited to Culler's comments on Fish, including the comments that relate Fish to other theorists.

Culler's question of control penetrates to the heart of the difficulty within reader-response criticism. The contenders in the power game include the reader and the text. Do readers decisively act or do they automatically respond to the text? This critique is directed primarily at the early Fish, and loses a bit of its force insomuch as Fish has already critiqued himself at this point. Nevertheless, I will follow Culler's argument.

Culler points to Fish's claims (in *Surprised by Sin* and *Self Consuming Artifacts*)[39] that he portrayed the actual experience of readers. Fish has regressed from that point, declaring, 'I was not revealing what readers had always done but trying to persuade them to a set of community assumptions so that when they read they would do what I did.'[40] Culler complains that Fish's reader never learns anything and is always disturbed by the second half of the sentence. Culler expects any 'real reader, especially one striving to be informed, to notice that premature guesses often prove wrong and to anticipate this possibility as he reads.' Fish's explanations of the reader's experience, according to Culler, do not equal Fish reading but Fish imagining a Fishian reader.[41] Thus, Culler identifies two aporias, (1) the gap between a reported experience and a presumed experience, and (2) even more to the point, what counts as 'experience'?

According to Culler, 'Fish lives in contradiction without shame' with an undeniably divided 'experience of expecting resolved senses to come unresolved, yet also confidently resolving a sense as though it could not be unresolved.'[42] The impasse of the divided nature of experience (Culler's 'suspension of disbelief') constitutes not only Culler's main complaint concerning the location of control, but also his complaint concerning the contents of a text. Culler notes that Fish offers the notion of interpretative communities as a corrective for the divided and deferred nature of the reader's experience; however, Culler

[39] See notes 29 and 30.

[40] Fish, *Is There a Text in This Class?*, p. 15.

[41] Culler, *On Deconstruction*, p. 66. Culler correctly identifies the Fishian reader with the anti-hero of Barthes; cf. R. Barthes, *The Pleasure of the Text* (trans. R. Miller; New York: Hill & Wang, 1975).

[42] Culler, *On Deconstruction*, p. 66.

debases this concept. He declares that Fishian interpretative communities take 'the differences and problems *within* reading and project them into the differences *between* interpretative communities, assuming the unity and identity of each reader's and each community's procedures and experiences'.[43] Demeaning the idea of interpretative communities, Culler declares that the divided nature of reading requires that experience be construed into a narrative. This narrative (or story of reading) tells of the manipulation of a reader by a text. According to Culler, '[t]he re-emergence of the text's control, in stories that sought to recount just the opposite (here Culler is referring to 'Literature in the Reader'), is a powerful illustration of the constraints discursive structures impose on theories that claim to master or describe them.'[44] Therefore, Culler proposes that the flux between a reader's decisive action and automatic responses is not a mistake but an essential structural feature of the situation.

Culler's argument is persuasive. He ends with the example of a joke. A joke is only a joke if someone laughs, and therefore the reader/hearer is in control just as the reader-response critics would prefer. However, one does not (always) will to laugh. A laugh is often spontaneous. Thus, one may say, 'the joke made me laugh.' Hence, Culler seems to seal the coffin on the question of control. Although not peaceably, control is shared ultimately by both the text and the reader. Culler's assessment is helpful but it also raises other questions.

The divided and deferred nature of communication to which Culler refers assumes that 'interpretational risk only incurs when conditions of communication are characterized by distance and etiolation', but J. Derrida repudiates this metaphysics of presence which is assumed by claiming that all communication is characterized by distance. In his essay, 'Signature, Event, Context', Derrida meditates his way through J.L. Austin's book, *How To Do Things with Words,* and concludes that all communication is mediated.[45] In this case, 'reading' is

[43] Culler, *On Deconstruction,* p. 68.

[44] Culler, *On Deconstruction,* p. 72.

[45] J. Derrida, 'Signature Event Context', *Glyph* 1 (1977), pp. 172-197. Derrida's unique style makes negotiating his work quite difficult. The corpus of secondary literature on Derrida can be very helpful. See Culler, *On Deconstruction, passim*; Fish, *Doing What Comes Naturally,* pp. 37-67. For engagement with Derrida in biblical studies see (among others) A.C. Thiselton, *New Horizons in Hermeneutics: The Theory and Practice of Transforming Biblical Reading* (London: Harper Collins, 1992), pp. 80-141; S. Moore, *Literary Criticism and the Gospels,* pp. 131-170; idem, *Mark and Luke in Post-*

understood as a creation of meaning; and therefore, 'reading' is merely a trope for 'writing'. Derrida refers to the ancient Greeks as misconstruing the conception of writing. The Greek adage proposes that '[m]en in a state of communicating their thoughts by means of sounds, felt the necessity of imaging new signs capable of perpetuating those thoughts and of making them *known* to persons who are *absent*'[46] (Derrida's emphasis). But this assumes presence! In other words, the adage is based on the philosophical notion that privileges presence over absence; however, Derrida deconstructs this binary opposition.

In agreement with the axiom of Barthes ('the death of the author'), Derrida pushes the theory a step further. He claims that it does not matter if the author is dead or alive, present (in physical form) or absent. The presence of the author does not help because all communications are mediated.[47] Even for the author, authorial intent is not known without mediation – she must consult herself with categories of interrogation that limit in advance the image she can have of herself. Even if present the author would not be an unmediated entity either to herself or to her audience.[48]

J.L. Austin had tried to explain the difference between a direct speech act where the intention of the speaker (or author) is evident and a performative speech act where the intention of the speaker is once removed. Austin refuses to use a fictional text to describe direct speech-acts, because it creates a fictional world as opposed to a serious (non-fictional) text which relates to empirical fact. Austin utilizes the metaphor of a stage utterance to represent an utterance that is removed

structuralist Perspectives: Jesus Begins to Write (New Haven: Yale University Press, 1989), *passim*. Derrida is working with J.L. Austin, *How to Do Things with Words* (Cambridge: Harvard University Press, 1975).

[46] J. Derrida, 'Signature Event Context', p. 176.

[47] Note the similar sentiments of C.S. Lewis commenting on his novel *Till We Have Faces*: 'an author doesn't necessarily understand the meaning of his own story better than anyone else' (W.H. Lewis, ed., *Letters of C.S. Lewis* [New York: Harcourt, Brace and World, 1966], p. 273).

[48] An acknowledgement that the self is also a text to be interpreted is the basis of psychoanalysis which has become the primary discipline of J. Kristeva. For the theoretical argument of the self as text see W.B. Michaels, 'The Interpreter's Self: Pierce on the Cartesian "Subject"', *Georgia Review* 31 (1977), pp. 383-402; A. Jefferson, 'Autobiography as Intertext: Barthes, Sarraute, Robbe-Grillet', in *Intertextuality: Theories and Practices,* ed. M. Worton and J. Still, pp. 108-129; T. Rajan, 'Intertextuality and the Subject of Reading/Writing', in *Influence and Intertextuality in Literary History,* ed. J. Clayton and E. Rothstein, pp. 61-74.

(i.e. the performer does not contain the intention of the words but rather the playwright). However, Derrida suggests that persons are always already removed (even in the case of face-to-face communication). Therefore, all utterances are stage utterances. All communication is mediated. (This is an abbreviated domestication of the Derridan concept of iterability).

Although an author is always removed, communication does occur, and Derrida insists that it be accounted for, even if there had only been a single occurrence of communication. How does communication occur? Derrida begins by suggesting that occurrence is not concretely definable from the outside because there is no 'totally saturated context'. Occurrence is the agreement between two. Successful performable acts 'occur by means of shared assumptions which enable speakers and hearers to make the same kind of sense of the words they exchange.'[49] Even contexts are constructs. Local constraints are all one has. As Fish puts it, the texts (and the readers) that exist are products of interpretative communities. 'The only "proof" of membership is fellowship, the nod of recognition from someone in the same community.'[50] Thus, the joke is not an example of the normative divided and deferred character of reading, but rather, the nod of recognition within an interpretative community. Fish writes that a 'coincidence of concerns is serendipitous rather than probable because one party is speaking or writing to a heterogeneous audience and hoping that the right-minded listener or reader is tuning in.'[51] Furthermore, the '[s]hape of belief (either about another or about one's self) is responsible for the shape of the interpretation.'[52] Therefore, Culler's first question, 'Who is in control, the text or the reader?' may be answered with an ambiguous yes, but this does not suggest that the text or the reader can be analyzed without the mediation of an interpretative community.

Moving on to Culler's second question, 'What is *in* the text?' Fishian literary theory and the critique of it by Culler is quite the magical show, with text disappearing and reappearing, 'now you see it now you don't', and it is not only the text that disappears but theories of reading as well. Fish declares:

[49] Fish, *Doing What Comes Naturally,* p. 52.
[50] Fish, *Is There a Text in This Class?,* p. 173.
[51] Fish, *Doing What Comes Naturally,* p. 38.
[52] Fish, *Doing What Comes Naturally,* p. 43.

> At a stroke, the dilemma that gave rise to the debate between the champions of the text and the champions of the reader (of whom [Fish] had certainly been one) is dissolved because the competing entities are no longer perceived as independent. To put it another way, the claims of objectivity can no longer be debated because the authorizing agency, the center of interpretative authority, is at once both and neither.[53]

According to Culler, the consequence of Fishian literary theory is a radical monism. Culler claims that Fish's 'radical monism' is a 'logical result of analysis that shows each entity to be a conventional construct; but the distinction between subject and object is more resilient than Fish thinks and will not be eliminated "at a stroke".'[54] Buying into Culler's description of Fish, Stephen Moore writes, 'Fish may cause the text to disappear but it reappears as soon as one attempts to talk about interpretation.'[55] According to Culler, theories of reading blur the distinctions between fact and interpretation, text and reader, and thus, Culler concludes, theories of reading lead the critic (Fish in this example) into monism.

When quoting Fish from 'Interpreting the *Variorum*', Culler stops at the end of the rhetorical question, 'What is that act an interpretation *of?*' which highlights as a logical impasse Fish's confessed inability to answer the question. Culler continues by insisting that stories of reading will not allow this question to go unanswered. However, pausing for a moment to take a closer look at Fish's answer to his own question, one can see that Fish claims that the question is unanswerable.

> This then is my thesis that the form of the reader's experience, formal units, and the structure of intention are one, that they come into view simultaneously, and that therefore the questions of priority and independence do not arise. What does arise is another question: what produces *them?* That is, if intention, form, and the shape of the reader's experience are simply different ways of referring to (different perspectives on) the same interpretative act, what is that act an interpretation *of?* I cannot answer that question, but neither, I would claim, can anybody else.[56]

According to Culler, Fishian theory is a radical monism which subverts traditional criticism's subject-object distinction. Ignoring the unanswerability of the question, Culler moves forward by suggesting

[53] Fish, *Is There a Text in This Class?,* p. 14.

[54] Culler, *On Deconstruction,* p. 74.

[55] Moore, *Literary Criticism and the Gospels,* p. 118.

[56] Fish, *Is There a Text in This Class?,* p. 165.

that readers function on the level of imagination, citing R. Rorty as an analogue for a possible way forward.[57] Rorty writes,

> it is not as if we had some deep insight into the nature of reality which told us everything save atoms and the void was "by convention" (or "spiritual" or "made up"). Democritus's insight was that a story about the smallest bits of things forms a background for stories about changes among things made of these bits. The acceptance of this genre of world-story (fleshed out successively by Lucretius, Newton, and Bohr) may be definatory of the West, but it is not a choice which could obtain, or which requires, epistemological or metaphysical guarantees.[58]

Culler concludes that the distinction between an external text and a reader is a necessary background for arguments about interpretation and accounts of interpretation. He cites E.D. Hirsch that reading and interpreting must maintain a certain level of dualism where the text and the reader are easily differentiated. In theory, Fish may cause the text to dissolve but in practice reading requires a subject-object distinction. Although Culler uses Hirsch to discuss the need for dualism, he does not agree with Hirsch's claims that the 'meaning' of any given text is fixed based on the intention of author and that only the 'significance' of the text can change.[59] Echoing Rorty's final statement that there are no epistemological or metaphysical guarantees, Culler writes that readers 'employ such distinctions all the time because our stories require them, but they are variable and ungrounded concepts.'[60] At this point, Culler has emasculated the theory of texts as represented in 'Interpreting the *Variorum*'; however, he fails to appreciate (as he cites the reprint of the essay in *Is There a Text in This Class?*) that Fish has already addressed the dualistic nature of reading. The Fishian theory (as represented in *Is There a Text in This Class?*) continues 'to account within the new model, for everything that had been recognized under the old model as being constitutive of the literary institution: texts,

[57] Rorty is answering the question which T. Kuhn has raised concerning the interpretative paradigms in science: Are there properties *in* nature that scientists discover, or do their conceptual frameworks *produce* such entities as subatomic particles, light waves, etc.? (T. Kuhn, *The Structure of Scientific Revolutions* [Chicago: University of Chicago Press, 1970]).

[58] R. Rorty, *Philosophy and the Mirror of Nature* (Princeton: Princeton University Press, 1980), pp. 344-45.

[59] E.D. Hirsch, *Aims of Interpretation* (Chicago: University of Chicago Press, 1976), *passim*.

[60] Culler, *On Deconstruction*, p. 77.

authors, periods, genres, canons, standards, agreements, disputes, values, changes, and so on.'[61] However, Fish's claim that the new model continues to account for the same things as the old model does not mean that everything remains the same. Life is different without epistemological and metaphysical guarantees. The Fishian text is 'the structure of meaning that is obvious and inescapable from the perspective of whatever interpretative assumptions happen to be in force.'[62]

The real thrust of Fish's comment that no one can know '[w]hat acts of interpretation are interpretation of?' is that raw data are not accessible without some form of interpretation. The crux of the problem surrounds the confusion over the meaning of the word 'text'. What disappears in the essay 'Interpreting the *Variorum*' is the (Hirschian) text. Text as defined by Fish always exists. Fish argues that 'there always is a text (just as there always is an ordinary world) but that what is in it can change, and therefore at no level is it independent of prior interpretations.'[63]

Fish's claim that 'interpretation is the only game in town'[64] repudiates a radical monism! Culler fails to appreciate that the text which disappears is the formal independent entity (a Hirschian text) and not the structure of meaning (a Fishian text) which never disappears though it may change. Therefore, the (Hirschian) text does not reappear. Culler's maxim concerning the resiliency of the subject-object distinction must be reconceived as constructs of an interpretative community.

In summary, the magic show is a mild disappointment. Although Fish causes the (Hirschian) text to disappear, Culler fails to make it reappear. The occurrence of communication is not based on a solid text or the capriciousness of the reader but rather on the interpretative strategy which was already in place. The confusion between the various definitions of 'text' is dramatically revealed in the title essay of Fish's volume *Is There a Text in This Class?* In this essay, a student at Johns Hopkins University approached her lecturer and asked 'Is there a text in this class?' The lecturer, a colleague of Fish, responded positively, naming the *Norton Anthology of Literature*. However, the student had previously taken a course with Fish and her question was not con-

[61] Fish, *Is There a Text in This Class?,* p. 17.
[62] Fish, *Is There a Text in This Class?,* p. vii.
[63] Fish, *Is There a Text in This Class?,* p. 272.
[64] Fish, *Is There a Text in This Class?,* p. 355.

cerned with the required textbook for the class. The student retorted, 'No, no, I mean in this class do we believe in poems and things, or is it just us?' She wanted to know the theoretical stance of the lecturer, concerning the existence of a solid text. Fish explains that in order to hear what the student intended, his colleague had to move into a position where the comment could be understood, at which time his colleague thought, 'Ah! there's one of Fish's victims.' If his colleague had not been able to understand, the student would have had to

> make a new start, although she would not have had to start from scratch (indeed starting from scratch is never a possibility); but she would have to back up to some point at which there was a shared agreement as to what was reasonable to say so that a new and wider basis for agreement could be fashioned.[65]

Thus the answer to Culler's second question, 'What is *in* the text?' cannot simply be answered in abstraction but requires a contextual situation.

Culler's third question, 'Why do stories of reading always have such happy endings?' may now be considered briefly. His complaint is the perpetual optimistic tone, which stories of reading always seem to maintain. This sentiment has been voiced recently in biblical criticism with a fascination of reading 'against the grain'. Readings 'against the grain' are popular in biblical studies because they subvert the status quo ideology of the establishment. However, if grain (i.e. *the* meaning) does not exist separate from interpretation then reading against the grain turns out to be a reading against someone's interpretation. In other words, although positive readings may be perpetuating an acceptance of the establishment, negative readings cannot claim the 'critical' higher ground because they are simply driven by an anti-establishment position.[66]

A more direct answer to Culler's question concerning the positive nature of the stories of reading would be, 'context'. Context provides a certain stability and context is always already provided. Fish proposes that

> A sentence is never not in a context. We are never not in a situation. A statue is never not read in the light of some purpose. A set of interpretative

[65] Fish, *Is There a Text in This Class?*, p. 315.

[66] For more on this concept of confessionalism vs. criticism see Chapter 3 n. 12.

> assumptions is always in force. A sentence that seems to need no interpretation is already the product of one.[67]

'It follows then that while no sentence is ambiguous in the sense that it has (as a constitutive property) more than one meaning, every sentence is ambiguous in the (undistinguishing) sense that the single meaning it will always have can change'.[68]

Culler's criticisms of Fish are helpful in pointing out key elements in the theory, and yet in the end Fish seems able to answer these charges.[69] Thus, the Fishian concept of text(uality) lies latent within the concept of intertextuality, at least as it is used in this study. All (con)texts, whether they are literary, religious or social, remain constructs of an interpretative community. While it may be impossible for me to delineate completely the composition of my own interpretative community, certain characteristics can be articulated. For example, my interpretative assumptions bear the markings of a convergence with professional biblical studies (particularly the version found in Sheffield)[70] as well as a merging with poststructural literary theory. Yet, my interpretative assumptions (as I see them) are formed primarily in relation to my Pentecostal faith, the lens through which I perceive all reality. The correlation between the ethos and spirituality of Pentecostalism with the concept of a Fishian interpretative community raises further questions. In addition to literary criticism, Fish has also received criticism on theological grounds.

[67] Fish, *Is There a Text in This Class?,* p. 284.

[68] Fish, *Is There a Text in This Class?,* p. 283. This Fishian concept echoes the Platonic notion of ambiguous sentences. According to Plato, the 'ideal' sentence is ambiguous, but the 'actual' sentence (which is always in context) is not ambiguous.

[69] In addition to the criticism of Culler, Fish (and Culler) receive an interesting critique from J. Tompkins. Tompkins highlights that both Fish and Culler wish to secure a high moral status for their literary theories. By giving up the claim to objectivity and a uniquely correct (and thereby powerful) interpretation of a given text, Fish admits that his interpretation is only one among many. While this nod towards egalitarian interpretation seems politically humble, the theory which Fish proposes prevents him, according to Tompkins, from securing such a position. For if the interpretative community of which Fish is a part is responsible for the interpretation that is reached, then Fish was not free to offer one interpretation among many as he claims.

[70] Note the comment of S. Fowl that it 'is no secret that what counts as meaning in Sheffield most certainly does not count as meaning in Cambridge' (idem, *The Bible in Three Dimensions* [Sheffield: Sheffield Academic Press, 1988], p. 69).

2.2.3. *Theological Implications of Fishian Literary Theory*

According to S. Moore, 'in the new Fishian dispensation, the rationalist mandate of modern criticism (serving truth and objective knowledge) gives way to a postmodern mandate (serving the critic and his or her community)'. Assessments not unlike this one have led many to criticize postmodern concepts of texts as promoting subjectivism and relativism. At this point the comments of A. Thiselton become most relevant.[71] Thiselton seems to have two primary concerns with Fishian literary theory.[72] First, he argues that Fishian literary theory supports a communal solipsism (i.e. the community is all that can be known). In other words, the interpretative community controls what can be known and furthermore the only things that can be known are *within* the community. Thus, if Fish is correct then a text can never reform a group *from the outside.*

According to Thiselton, Fish has faltered with his 'all or nothing' mentality concerning a choice between 'the sharply-bounded crystalline purity of formalist concepts and the unstable concepts of contextual pragmatism'.[73] Thiselton suggests that there is a middle ground on which one can stand which acknowledges 'the working distinction between how the knowing subject or agent *conditions* raw data and what this subject or agent *constructs* independently of raw data' (Thiselton's italics).[74] Relying on Wittgenstein's theory of language games, Thiselton argues that 'concepts may function with a measure of operational stability but with "blurred edges".' In my opinion, Thiselton's position is more slippery than he admits. As W.J. Lyons has argued, the fact that 'raw data' exist is not questioned by the Fishian theory

[71] Thiselton, *New Horizons in Hermeneutics,* pp. 502-550. Others have critically engaged Fish on theological grounds though to a lesser degree including D.A. Carson, *The Gagging of God* (Grand Rapids: Eerdmans, 1996), pp. 57-137; W.W. Klein, C.L. Blomberg and R.L. Hubbard, *Introduction to Biblical Interpretation* (Dallas: Word Books, 1993), pp. 438-40; G. Osborne, *The Hermeneutical Spiral* (Downers Grove: InterVarsity Press, 1991), pp. 377-380; K. Vanhoozer, *Is There a Meaning in This Text? The Bible, the Reader and the Morality of Literary Knowledge* (Grand Rapids, MI: Zondervan, 1998), *passim;* N.T. Wright, *The New Testament and the People of God* (Minneapolis: Fortress, 1992), pp. 18-144.

[72] For a more thorough engagement of Thiselton and his critique of Fish (an argument which is followed closely here) see W.J. Lyons, *Canon and Exegesis: Canonical Praxis and the Sodom Narrative* (Sheffield: Sheffield Academic Press, 2002), *passim.*

[73] Thiselton, *New Horizons in Hermeneutics,* p. 541. See S. Fish, 'Introduction: Going Down the Anti-Formalist Road', in *Doing What Comes Naturally,* pp. 1-33.

[74] Thiselton, *New Horizons in Hermeneutics,* p. 541.

but rather that one cannot move from such data to the human subject without interpretation.[75] Furthermore, Thiselton fails to distinguish successfully his concept of conditioning raw data from Fish's notion of interpretation. In either case there is no unmediated access to the data.[76]

[75] Lyons, *Canon and Exegesis, passim.*

[76] See J.K.A. Smith, *The Fall of Interpretation: Philosophical Foundations for a Creational Hermeneutic* (Downers Grove: InterVarsity Press, 2000). Smith looks closely at the overriding assumption in modern hermeneutics that interpretation is an unfortunate, lamentable obstacle to immediacy. Smith highlights a couple of evangelical theologians who argue for a present immediacy that forgoes the necessity of interpretation, namely R. Koivisto, *One Lord, One Faith: A Theology for Cross-Denominational Renewal* (Wheaton, IL: Bridgepoint/Victor, 1993) and R. Lints, *The Fabric of Theology: A Prolegomenon to Evangelical Theology* (Grand Rapids: Eerdmans, 1993). As noted by Smith, the impact of W. Dilthey and later M. Heidegger has focused such attention on the 'situationality and locality' of human existence that subsequent (sophisticated) engagements in philosophical hermeneutics have been unable to argue for a present immediacy model. See W. Dilthey, *The Essence of Philosophy* (trans. S.A. Emery; New York: AMS, 1969) and M. Heidegger, *Being and Time* (trans. J. Macquarrie and E. Robinson; New York: Harper & Row, 1962). Nevertheless, significant contributors to the hermeneutical debate have maintained a *hope* that immediacy may one day be regained. Referring to the latter model as 'eschatological immediacy', Smith places in this group H.-G. Gadamer, *Truth and Method* (trans. A. Lingis; Pittsburg: Duquesne Press, 1969), J. Habermas, 'On Hermeneutics' Claim to Universality', in *The Hermeneutics Reader*, ed. K. Mueller-Vollmer (New York: Continuum, 1985), 294-319, and W. Pannenberg, *Metaphysics and the Idea of God* (trans. P. Clayton; Grand Rapids: Eerdmans, 1990). Acknowledging the oddity of pairing Gadamer and Habermas, Smith argues convincingly that despite their differences concerning the role of context and tradition, Gadamer and Habermas, as well as Pannenberg, hold the concept that at a future point interpretation will be overcome and immediacy will reign. Contrary to both positions (i.e., present immediacy and eschatological immediacy), Smith describes what he calls the *violent mediation* model of M. Heidegger and his greatest disciple, J. Derrida. Smith will agree with Heidegger and Derrida that mediation is an essential part of being human; however, on the basis of a reading of Augustine, Smith will argue (contrary to Heidegger and Derrida) that mediation *necessarily* produces violence. Beginning with the (Christian) assumption that creation is good, Smith argues that mediation and the necessity of interpretation are also good because they are distinctives of being a creature. Thus, interpretation is part of the creative process and need not be avoided either now or in the eschaton. Cf. J.K.A. Smith, 'How to Avoid Not Speaking: Attestations', in *Knowing Other-wise: Philosophy on the Threshold of Spirituality,* ed. J.H. Olthuis, Perspectives in Continental Philosophy (Bronx: Fordham University Press, 1997), pp. 217-34; idem, 'Originary Violence: The Fallenness of Interpretation in Derrida', *Concept* 19 (1996), pp. 27-41; idem, 'The Art of Christian Atheism: Faith and Philosophy in Early Heidegger', *Faith and Philosophy* 14:1 (1997), pp. 71-81.

According to Thiselton, the Fishian theory allows the reader (or the interpretative community) to make a text mean anything and thereby preventing someone outside of a community from presenting the group with the gospel. If this were the case then I too would reject Fishian literary theory; however, I am not convinced by Thiselton's reading of Fish. What is denied is not that a group can be reformed from the outside but rather the grounds from which such a claim can be made. Therefore, the text may remain a dialogue partner for a group despite the fact that the text is a product of interpretative assumptions. R. Rorty argues that the threat of relativism is only an illusion.

> Except for the occasional cooperative freshman, one cannot find anybody who says that two incompatible opinions on an important topic are equally good. The philosophers who get *called* relativists are those who say that the ground for choosing between two opinions is less algorithmic than had been thought. ... So the real issue is not between those who think one view is as good as another and people who do not. It is between those who think our culture, or purposes, or intuitions, cannot be supported except 'conversationally', and people who still hope for other sorts of support.[77]

There are two sides to this debate which may be described as an anti-foundational hope and an anti-foundational fear. Fish shatters the hope of anti-foundationalists of ever being able to shake their convictions and relieves the suspicious formalists of being able to substantiate their fears. 'Anti-foundationalists can never have', according to Fish,

> the consequences for which some of its proponents hope, the consequences of freeing us from the hold of unwarranted absolutes so that we may more flexibly pursue the goals of human flourishing of liberal conversation. The reasoning behind this hope is that since we now know that our convictions about truth and factuality have not been imposed on us by the world ... but are derived from practices of ideologically motivated communities, we can set them aside in favor of convictions that we choose freely. But this is simply to imagine the moment of unconstrained choice from the other direction, as a goal rather than an abyss ... Those who express [anti-foundationalist fear] are concerned lest we kick ourselves loose from constraints; those who profess [anti-foundationalist hope] look forward to finally being able to do so.[78]

[77] R. Rorty, 'Texts and Lumps', *New Literary History* 17 (1985), p. 12.
[78] Fish, *Doing What Comes Naturally,* p. 323.

Confidence remains in a person's interpretations even though the interpretations are conditioned by the community. Consequences abound for all because the right loses its fear and the left loses its hope. The fundamentalists lose their claim to objectivity and the liberals lose their claim to liberalism. It is an old argument that a scholar cannot approach a text without presuppositions; however, the implications of such a statement have rarely been plumbed quite this far. Presuppositions affect interpretation in ultimate ways.

> The mind is not a static structure, but an assemblage of related beliefs any one of which can exert pressure on any other in a motion that can lead to a self-transformation ... [R]ather than being an object of which one might ask, 'how does it change', the mind (and, by extension, the community) is an engine of change, an on going project whose operations are at once constrained and the means by which those same constraints are altered. The outside is always an *interpreted* outside. The distinction between the outside and the inside is not empirical and absolute, but rather, an interpretative distinction between realms that are interpreted rather than discrete.[79]

Contrary to Thiselton's assumption that interpretative communities cannot speak with one another, 'It is the fragile but real consolidation of interpretative communities that allows us to talk to one another, but with no hope or fear of ever being able to stop.'[80] The relationship between contextualization and catholicity is examined further in the final section of this chapter.

It is possible to couch the theological implications of Fishian literary theory in more philosophical terms. The entire matter is an issue of epistemology. Those with non-foundational fear can roughly be placed within a modernistic worldview relying primarily (but not entirely) on an epistemology of reason, longing for foundations based on propositional truth(s). Those with non-foundational hope can roughly be categorized as having a postmodern worldview and relying primarily (but not entirely) on an epistemology of experience (i.e. locally conditioned data). What is missing from this discussion is what both Wesley and Kierkegaard refer to as an epistemology of faith.[81] At one level,

[79] Fish, *Doing What Comes Naturally*, p. 146.

[80] Fish, *Is There a Text in This Class?*, p. 172.

[81] See R.D. Matthews, 'Religion and Reason Joined: A Study in the Theology of John Wesley', Ph.D. thesis (Harvard University, 1986), pp. 184-246. See also S. Kierkegaard, *Concluding Unscientific Postscript to the "Philosophical Fragments"* (trans. D.F. Swenson; ed. W. Lowrie; Princeton: Princeton University Press, 1941), p. 106.

faith is essential to all epistemologies yet Wesley will, on the one hand, maintain a special category called 'saving faith'. Kierkegaard, on the other hand, reserves faith for the highest level of knowing. His 'leap of faith' allows a person to transcend both reason and experience and have a relationship with God.

In conclusion, it becomes quite clear that the argument of Hatina is certainly correct with regards to the inherently related concept of text within the theory of intertextuality. The theoretical concept of text differs greatly between the historical (biblical) scholars who are employing intertextuality and the poststructural scholars who employ the term in literary theory. Our discussion of textuality has been lengthy, but it is necessary to define what constitutes a text since the larger argument maintains that meaning resides in the relationship of different texts. In the next section attention is turned to Hatina's final point of consideration. What is the relationship between intertextuality and literary influence?

2.3. Intertextuality and the Influence of Influence

While the question of what constitutes a text is essential to understanding intertextuality theoretically, the practice of intertextuality must answer the question of its relationship to literary influence.[82] Attempts to explain intertextuality in terms of the influence of chronologically earlier texts have been criticized strongly as a failure to appreciate the textuality of texts and the situationality of readers.[83] Hence,

[82] The relationship between intertextuality and influence has been the focus of several studies: e.g. T.K. Beal, 'Ideology and Intertextuality: Surplus of Meaning and Controlling the Means of Production', in *Reading Between Texts: Intertextuality and the Hebrew Bible,* ed. D.N. Fewell (Louisville: Westminster, 1992), pp. 27-40; J. Clayton and E. Rothstein, 'Figures in Corpus: Theories of Influence and Intertextuality', in *Influence and Intertextuality in Literary History,* ed. J. Clayton and E. Rothstein, pp. 3-36; Aichele and Phillips, 'Introduction: Exegesis, Eisegesis, Intergesis', pp. 7-18; G. Snyman, 'Who is Speaking? Intertextuality and Textual Influence', pp. 427-449; A.D. Weiner, 'Sidney/Spencer/Shakespeare: Influence/Intertextuality/Intention', in *Influence and Intertextuality in Literary History,* ed. J. Clayton and E. Rothstein, pp. 245-270.

[83] In terms of biblical interpretation, this is H. Knight's principal flaw. While he clearly recognizes the contextualization of all interpretation, he seems oblivious to the fact that privileging the biblical account over the horizon of the readers is purely a semantic move. I do not disagree with the premise that divine revelation should be guarded from 'cultural accommodation, ideological captivity and reductionism' (cf. H. Knight, *A Future for Truth: Evangelical Theology in a Postmodern World* [Nashville: Abingdon Press, 1997], p. 165). Nevertheless, Yong is correct when he writes, 'It is

intertextuality is sometimes defined in such ways to make it appear as an enlargement of influence. Thus, as J. Culler defines the concept, 'intertextuality is not the investigation of sources and influences as traditionally conceived; it casts its net wider to include anonymous discursive practices, codes whose origins are lost, that make possible the signifying practices of later texts.'[84]

The difficulty arises because intertextuality is described theoretically as the infinite discursive space where all texts interact with one another. However, in practice it is difficult (if not impossible) to make such a discursive space the object of attention. In Culler's words:

> intertextuality is a difficult concept to use because of the vast and undefined discursive space it designates, but when one narrows it so as to make it more usable one either falls into source study of the traditional and positivistic kind (which is what the concept was designed to transcend) or else ends by naming particular texts as pre-texts on grounds of interpretative convenience.[85]

Thus, to work with the concept of intertextuality one must focus the attention of the analysis in ways that undermine the very concept that is being employed.

In an ironic twist, the attempt to define the edge where intertextuality and influence can be differentiated has not produced 'blurred edges' (*à la* Wittgenstein) but rather a blurred center (*à la* Derrida). By trying to bring the edges of intertextuality into focus the center has

unrealistic and self-deceiving to think oneself and one's community able to preserve the priority of biblical revelation since it is precisely such mechanisms which allow the ideological captivity Knight fears' (A. Yong, *Discerning the Spirit(s): A Pentecostal-Charismatic Contribution to Christian Theology of Religions* [Sheffield: Sheffield Academic Press, 2000], p. 318).

[84] J. Culler, *The Pursuit of Signs: Semiotics, Literature, Deconstruction* (London: Routledge & Kegan Paul, 1981), p. 103. For similar assessments see J. Clayton and E. Rothstein, 'Figures in Corpus: Theories of Influence and Intertextuality', p. 3; J. Frow, *Marxism and Literary Theory* (Oxford: Blackwell, 1986), p. 156. For Vorster, intertextuality differs from *Redaktionsgeschichte* in three significant ways, 'First of all it is clear that the phenomenon of text has been redefined. It has become more a network of references to other texts (intertexts). Secondly it appears that more attention is to be given to "text" as a process of production and not to the sources or their influences. And thirdly it is apparent that the role of the reader is not to be neglected in this approach to the phenomenon of text' (W. Vorster, 'Intertextuality and Redaktionsgeschichte', in *Intertextuality in Biblical Writings*, ed. S. Draisma [Festschrift B. van Iersel; Kampen: Kok, 1989], p. 21.

[85] J. Culler, *The Pursuit of Signs*, p. 109.

fallen out of focus, causing a denial of a key element (the supposition that all signs contain traces of other signs). In other words, differentiating intertextuality from the concept of literary influence is not as easy as some theorists imagine. Certainly, traces of influence are irreducibly a part of intertextuality despite the rigor with which it is denied. Thus, bringing the notions of intertextuality and influence together is not failing to appropriate properly intertextuality but on the contrary this method appreciates the nature of intertextuality and the inability of any sign to delimit the trace of another sign which may infiltrate it. The resiliency of influence is never more evident than when Kristeva explicitly acknowledges the influence which the work of M. Bakhtin has had on her own literary theory.

Although intertextuality and influence cannot be kept from tainting one another one should not conclude that an attempt to differentiate the two is futile. The approaches may use similar vocabulary but (as Snyman suggests) intertextuality and literary influence have different connotations concerning the following concepts:

1. *information:* sources are regarded as extrinsic phenomena, independent of human perception, whereas intertextuality's assumption of textual links rests on the ability of the reader to create such links.
2. *form and criticism:* textual influence distinguishes between the act of influence and any discussion about it in a typical object-subject relationship, while intertextuality sees the reader and the text both as texts refracting one another.
3. *ideology:* source criticism and textual influence do not take into account the ideology of the observer, because science, art and morality belong to distinct forms of logic. Intertextuality maintains that all views are ideological, reflecting biases of a particular time.
4. *structure:* source criticism and textual influence focus on ordering and structuring, smoothing over inconsistencies and contradictions. Intertextuality uses these contradictions and inconsistencies as the result of human communication where meaning is always deferred.
5. *understanding:* source criticism and influence work with parallels between human patterns in order to explain and order systems. Intertextuality emphasizes the uniqueness of each situation and the particular nature of the circumstances.[86]

Each of these points deserves brief attention. In terms of information and ideology, the role of the reader is certainly highlighted within

[86] G. Snyman, 'Who is Speaking? Intertextuality and Textual Influence', p. 446.

intertextuality in ways that are inimical to traditional source-critical studies where the situationality of the reader is to have little (or no) bearing on the analysis. On the one hand, intertextuality blurs the subject-object distinction in a dialogical relationship which the linear causality of source criticism does not address. On the other hand, the dialogicity of intertextuality offers little help in the pursuit of historical questions such as origin. With regards to structure, source criticism and intertextuality are not that far apart. Both approaches focus on contradictions and inconsistencies and both conclude that these lacunae are signs of multiplicity within the text. However, they differ in that source criticism assumes that the appearance of aporias in the text is an anomaly while intertextuality assumes that the difficulties are a part of all texts. Contrary to the assessment of G. Synman, intertextuality does not support the view that meaning is always deferred but rather that meaning has the *potential* of being deferred. In relation to the final point on understanding, the uniqueness of each situation produces a meaning which may change but is not *necessarily* deferred.

2.4. Summary

In this section the relationship between intertextuality and source criticism has been explored in three areas. First, examination of the ideological origin of intertextuality highlights a particular poststructural characteristic of the concept but the arguments that conservative aims should not be coupled with intertextuality owing to ideological differences ultimately fail to convince. Secondly, it has been argued that the inherent concept of texts in the theory of intertextuality is radically different from the historical-critical conception of text. The inference is not that historical critics should necessarily stop employing the term but rather that readers should understand that not all intertextual analysis is of the poststructural kind. Thirdly, the influence of influence also proves to be enigmatic. Nevertheless, intertextuality in practice may not simply be equated with source criticism, owing to different presuppositions as well as different goals. Attention is now turned to attempts to practice an intertextual analysis on Revelation.

3. Intertextuality in Revelation Studies

Within the subdiscipline of Revelation studies, intertextuality is most often appropriated as new nomenclature for the traditional rubric, 'Use of the Old Testament in the New Testament'. In addition to the Old Testament, other literary sources have also been identified as pre-texts for Revelation, including the synoptic Gospels[87] as well as non-canonical Jewish writings.[88] Nevertheless, the use of the Old Testament in Revelation has received the lion's share of attention,[89] despite the fact that Revelation never quotes the Old Testament explicitly. How-

[87] L.A. Vos, *The Synoptic Traditions in the Apocalypse* (Kampen: Kok, 1965); R.J. Bauckham, 'Synoptic Parousia Parables and the Apocalypse', *NTS* 23 (1977), pp. 162-76; cf. M.E. Boring, 'The Apocalypse as Christian Prophecy', in *Society of Biblical Literature Seminar Papers,* ed. G. MacRae (Missoula, MT: Scholars Press), pp. 43-62; J.M. Court, *Myth and History in the Book of Revelation* (London: SPCK, 1979).

[88] P.-M. Bogaert, 'Les apocalypses contemporaines de Baruch, d'Esdras et de Jean', in *L'Apocalypse johannique et l'apocalyptique dans le Nouveau Testament,* ed. J. Lambrecht (Leuven: Leuven University Press, 1980), pp. 47-68; G.K. Beale, 'The Problem of the Man from the Sea in IV Ezra 13 and its Relation to the Messianic Concept in John's Apocalypse', *NovT* 25 (1983), pp. 182-188; L.W. Hurtado, 'Revelation 4-5 in the Light of Jewish Apocalyptic Analogies', *JSNT* 25 (1985), pp. 105-124; R.J. Bauckham, 'The Book of Revelation as a Christian War Scroll', *Neot* 22 (1988), pp. 17-40; E. Lupieri, 'The Seventh Night: Visions of History in the Revelation of John and the Contemporary Apocalyptic', *Henoch* 14 (1992), pp. 113-32.

[89] The most significant recent works include: G.K. Beale, *The Use of Daniel in Jewish Apocalyptic Literature and the Revelation of St John* (Lanham, MD: University Press of America, 1984); J.M. Vogelgesang, 'The Interpretation of Ezekiel in the Book of Revelation', Ph.D. thesis (Harvard University, 1985); J. Paulien, *Decoding Revelation's Trumpets: Literary Allusions and Interpretation of Revelation 8:7-12* Andrews University Seminary Doctoral Dissertation Series, 21 (Berrien Springs, MI: Andrews University Press, 1987); J.-P. Ruiz, *Ezekiel in the Apocalypse: The Transformation of Prophetic Language in Revelation 16,17-19,10* (Frankfurt am Main: Peter Lang, 1989); R.J. Bauckham, *The Climax of Prophecy: Studies in the Book of Revelation* (Edinburgh: T. & T. Clark, 1993); J. Fekkes, *Isaiah and Prophetic traditions in the Book of Revelation: Visionary Antecedents and their Development* (Sheffield: Sheffield Academic Press, 1994); S. Moyise, *The Old Testament in the Book of Revelation* (Sheffield: Sheffield Academic Press, 1995); G.K. Beale, *John's Use of the Old Testament in Revelation* (Sheffield: Sheffield Academic Press, 1998); cf. also A. Schlatter, *Das Alte Testament in der johanneischen Apokalypse* (Gütersloh: Bertelsmann, 1912); A. Vanhoye, 'L'utilisation du livre d'Ezéchiel dans l'Apocalypse', *Bib* 43 (1962), pp. 436-476; A. Lancellotti, 'L'Antico Testamento nell' Apocallise', *Rivista Biblica* 14 (1966), pp. 369-384; L.P. Trudinger, 'Some Observations Concerning the Text of the Old Testament in the Book of Revelation', *JTS* 17 (1966), pp. 82-88; F. Jenkins, *The Old Testament in the Book of Revelation* (Marion, IN: Cogdill Foundation, 1972); A. Gangemi, 'L'utilazzione del Deutero-Isaia nell' Apocalisse di Giovanni', *Euntes Docete* 27 (1974), pp. 109-144; B. Marconcini, 'L'utilaazaoine del T.M. nelle citazioni isaiane dell' Apocalisse', *Rivista Biblica* 24 (1976), pp. 113-136; M.D. Goulder, 'The Apocalypse as an Annual Cycle of Prophecies', *NTS* 27 (1981), pp. 342-367. See also the discussion of recent literature in F.J. Murphy, 'The Book of Revelation', *CR:BS* 2 (1994), pp. 181-205.

ever, the lack of direct quotations has failed to deter scholars from focusing attention on allusions to the Old Testament, owing in large part to the overwhelming extent to which the language of the Old Testament permeates the book. Indeed, by most accounts there are more allusions to the Old Testament in Revelation than in any other New Testament book.[90] Although it can be said that 'intertextuality is now a common word in Revelation studies',[91] the majority of the work appropriating the term has maintained a more traditional nature.[92] Key exceptions to this trend have been the works of J.-P. Ruiz and S. Moyise. While their scholarship may not be fully equated with poststructuralism, the attention given to the situationality of the contemporary reader places their work closer to the theory of intertextuality as it is defined in literary studies.[93] The following two sections critically engage the works of Ruiz and Moyise, respectively. However, since G.K. Beale has already offered a substantial critical survey of both Ruiz and Moyise, the assessments that follow will engage his questions and critiques as well.[94]

[90] The exact number of allusions is difficult to determine because the criteria used to identify allusions vary from one scholar to the next. Beale demonstrates the ambiguity of numbering the allusions by citing the contradictory assessments of different Greek texts and commentators: UBS 3rd edition lists 394 allusions; Nestle-Aland 26th edition lists 635 allusions; British and Foreign Bible Society Greek text lists 493; E. Hühn, *Die alttestamentlichen Citate und Reminiscenzen im Neuen Testament* (Tübingen: J.C.B. Mohr, 1900), pp. 269-271 lists 455; cf. G.K. Beale, *John's Use of the Old Testament in Revelation,* p. 60.

[91] Murphy, 'The Book of Revelation', p. 205.

[92] D. Aune, 'Intertextuality and the Genre of the Apocalypse', in *Society of Biblical Literature Seminar Papers* 30, ed. E.H. Lovering, Jr. (Atlanta: Scholars Press, 1991), pp. 142-160; J. van Ruiten, 'The Intertextual Relationship between Isaiah 65:17-20 and Revelation 21:1-5b', pp. 473-510; cf. the comment by R.J. Bauckham that Revelation 'is a book to be read in constant intertextual relationship with the Old Testament' (idem, *The Climax of Prophecy,* p. xi).

[93] Ruiz, *Ezekiel in the Apocalypse;* Moyise, *The Old Testament in the Book of Revelation.* See also W.S. Vorster, '"Genre" and the Revelation of John: A Study in Text, Context and Intertext', *Neot* 22 (1988), pp. 103-123; S. Freyne, 'Reading Hebrews and Revelation Intertextually', in *Intertextuality in Biblical Writings,* ed. S. Draisma, pp. 83-93.

[94] Beale, in a critical survey of works on the use of the Old Testament in Revelation, grouped Ruiz and Moyise together under the heading, 'Hermeneutical Studies', while the following come under the rubric 'Exegetical Studies': Beale, *The Use of Daniel;* Vogelgesang, 'The Interpretation of Ezekiel'; Paulien, *Decoding Revelation's Trumpets;* Bauckham, *The Climax of Prophecy;* Fekkes, *Isaiah and Prophetic Traditions in the Book of Revelation* (Beale, *John's Use of the Old Testament in Revelation,* pp. 13-59).

3.1. J.-P. Ruiz

Ruiz's work focuses on the allusions to Ezekiel in Rev. 16:17–19:10. Critically building on previous work on the use of Ezekiel in Revelation, Ruiz's primary contribution (especially in relation to this study) centers around his conclusion that readers of the Apocalypse should engage in 'sapiential reflection' on John's hermeneutical use of the Old Testament. Using John's hermeneutics as a model the readers should interpret John's text in a similar manner.[95] The implications of such a practice escalate when Ruiz describes John's reading as a re-appropriation of the Old Testament tradition which produces genuinely new meanings, 'which are not simply repetitions or combinations of the old ones'.[96] Ruiz understands reading as a production of meaning which is unlimited, 'a continuous fertility of the metaphoric terrain'. Therefore, the production of meaning will continue as long as a dialogue continues between the text and its interpreters.[97] Ruiz argues that John's words 'gather meaning over time', and thus interpretative communities may produce endless meanings of Revelation.[98] In his assessment of Ruiz, G.K. Beale correctly identifies his method as 'a form of reader-response criticism'.[99]

Ruiz defends his hermeneutical position on four grounds. First, he identifies the church's liturgical setting as the intended context in which the book should be read and interpreted.[100] Other commentators have reached a similar conclusion partially based on their reading of the first beatitude in Rev. 1:3 ('Blessed is the one who reads and those who hear the words of the prophecy, and keep what is written in them, for the time is near'). However, Ruiz offers a new focus on the role of hearers/readers in *interpreting* the prophecy and not merely reading and hearing.[101] Offering Rev. 19:1-10 as an example of the liturgical setting, Ruiz argues that the readers are 'active participants in

[95] Ruiz, *Ezekiel in the Apocalypse,* p. 224. Contra this position see R. Longenecker, 'Can We Reproduce the Exegesis of the New Testament?', *TynBul* 21 (1970), pp. 3-38.

[96] Ruiz, *Ezekiel in the Apocalypse,* p. 228.

[97] Ruiz, *Ezekiel in the Apocalypse,* p. 222.

[98] Ruiz, *Ezekiel in the Apocalypse,* p. 223.

[99] The preceding description of Ruiz's work has basically summarized Beale's overview. See Beale, *John's Use of the Old Testament in Revelation,* pp. 29-31.

[100] Ruiz, *Ezekiel in the Apocalypse,* pp. 184-189.

[101] See a similar independent argument in R. Waddell, 'Hearing What the Spirit Says to the Churches: A Profile of a Pentecostal Reader of the Apocalypse', a paper presented to the 28th annual meeting of the SPS, March 1998.

the interpretation of the book'.[102] Likewise, Ruiz understands the admonition not to worship an angel as directed to the readers and not solely to John. Conceding the doxological nature of Rev. 19:1-10, Beale rightly affirms Ruiz's idea that the readers are invited along with John to worship God alone; however, the further assumption that the readers are also invited (or even encouraged) to interpret the text, according to Beale, is questionable.[103]

Secondly, Ruiz investigates the significance of certain imperatives found in the text and argues that they too have hermeneutical implications. The imperatives he cites include the hearing formula, 'who ever has an ear, *let him hear*' (cf. the letters and 13:9) and the command to have 'wisdom' and 'understanding' (Rev. 13:18; 17:9).[104] In response to Ruiz's appeal to the imperatives, Beale acknowledges that they may include an exhortation to interpret, but the primary thrust is *ethical* and not intellectual. Beale attempts to support his critique in two ways: (1) by investigating the Old Testament background to Rev. 13:18 and 17:9, which he sees as Daniel 11–12; and (2) by comparing John's use of the word 'wisdom' with an Old Testament definition of 'wisdom'.

The context of Daniel 11–12 is a prophecy about a tribulation where an evil king will persecute the saints. The instruction to have wisdom is understood by Beale as a directive to discern keenly true saints from hypocrites. Thus when John instructs his readers to have wisdom, Beale suggests that he is exhorting them to be aware of the end-time deception prophesied in Daniel. As he writes,

> The readers don't need any sophisticated or penetrating interpretative ability to interpret the hidden meaning of Daniel, but they do need to perceive that what had been understood and expected in previous generations from the prophecy of Daniel 11–12 was beginning to be fulfilled.[105]

Beale is apparently wanting to distinguish between *interpreting* the meaning of the text and *discerning* the ethical implication of the text. According to Beale the manner in which 'wisdom' is used in Revelation is analogous to its connotation in Old Testament wisdom literature (e.g. in Proverbs): 'applying to life situations the truth which is

[102] Ruiz, *Ezekiel in the Apocalypse,* p. 523.
[103] Beale, *John's Use of the Old Testament in Revelation,* p. 32.
[104] Ruiz, *Ezekiel in the Apocalypse,* pp. 190-214.
[105] Beale, *John's Use of the Old Testament in Revelation,* p. 33.

already known in the mind'.[106] However, the sublime life described in Proverbs does not correlate easily with the tumult of Revelation. Indeed, the wisdom of Job (or Ecclesiastes) would serve as a better parallel for Revelation, in which case traditional wisdom is turned on its head, subverted by an epistemology of suffering. In Job, wisdom is not applying what you know but rather re-interpreting life from a new perspective. The tension of theodicy is not resolved in Job. In the end, God shows up and that is sufficient for Job. It could be said that Job had an apocalypse. He came to the end of himself when God was unveiled before him.[107]

Although Beale concedes that a certain level of interpretation is necessary for the readers to understand, he maintains that the interpretative element is secondary to the ethical admonition. The emphasis Beale places on the moral dimension of the exhortations is especially helpful, though Ruiz had not failed to highlight the moral implications of the imperatives.[108] Furthermore, Beale's critique may be problematic owing to the strict dichotomy which he maintains between volition and cognition. Separating the heart from the mind may represent the modern reader but not necessarily the ancient reader (and certainly not the Pentecostal reader). Indeed, the nature of an apocalypse is to rely not on what one knows but rather on what is revealed in the heart as much as in the head. Beale argues that the 'hermeneutical imperatives' would be better understood as 'moral imperatives' or *merely* 'paraenesis'.[109] However, in a tradition like Pentecostalism where the sermons are more dialogical than monological, even paraenesis contains a not insignificant amount of interpretation.

The third aspect of Revelation which Ruiz understands as an invitation to interpret is John's use of μυστήριον. Conversely, Beale sees the references to mystery as relating to John individually and not the readers. He argues further that John does not interpret the mystery himself, but rather the mystery is explained to him by a heavenly mediator. Beale understands the mystery in an objective sense, viz. the revelation of God's unfolding plan, while Ruiz includes the subjective idea of the

[106] Beale, *John's Use of the Old Testament in Revelation,* p. 34; idem, 'The Danielic Background for Revelation 13:18 and 17:9', *TynBul* 31 (1980), pp. 163-170.

[107] Cf. R.D. Moore, 'The Integrity of Job', *CBQ* 45:1(1983), pp. 17-31.

[108] Ruiz notes that the hearing formulas encourage the readers 'to come thereby to an understanding of their situation and of what the risen Christ expects from them' (J.-P. Ruiz, *Ezekiel in the Apocalypse,* p. 196).

[109] Beale, *John's Use of the Old Testament in Revelation,* p. 35.

process of interpretation where the revelation must be 'received, discerned, and appropriated'.[110] In agreement with Beale, a Pentecostal reader would acknowledge that John does not resolve the mystery by himself but rather with the help of a heavenly mediator. However, contrary to Beale, this does not rule out the truth of Ruiz's assumption. The mystery is an invitation to interpret but only with the agency of the Spirit, who speaks the words of Christ to the churches.

Ruiz's final observation concerning the necessity of interpretation surrounds John's idiosyncratic Greek. According to Ruiz, John employs such difficult Greek 'to confound an ordinary reading of the text'.[111] In response to the alternative grammar and syntax, the readers focus additional attention on that passage causing them 'to understand the new meaning which the text offers'.[112] In addition to causing the reader to focus more intently on certain phrases, Beale suggests that the odd Greek is caused by a Semitic influence.[113] Although Beale agrees with Ruiz that the solecisms cause the reader to reflect on the passage, Beale insists that the reflection is on John's intended meaning and not on the creation of meaning by the reader. Beale will concede that John creates new meanings of Old Testament texts but he qualifies the new meanings as 'organically developed' in a 'redemptive historical sense'.

Throughout his critique, Beale has repeatedly questioned the assumption made by Ruiz that the text has endless meanings. Beale's standard rebuttal is that such an assumption lacks exegetical support. In other words, the text cannot have multiple meanings because it does not explicitly make that claim. According to Beale, if the text contained endless multiple meanings then 'a solid rationale would be provided for readers to follow John's purported creative method of rereading Scripture.'[114] The absence of such a rationale has led Beale to conclude that Ruiz's assumption is a 'theological statement without exegetical support, which corresponds better to ecclesiological traditions in which revelation is viewed as an ongoing process throughout the history of the church'.[115] On the one hand, I am in considerable agreement with Beale. The concept of polyvalency in literary texts

[110] Ruiz, *Ezekiel in the Apocalypse,* p. 214.

[111] Ruiz, *Ezekiel in the Apocalypse,* p. 220.

[112] Ruiz, *Ezekiel in the Apocalypse,* p. 220.

[113] Cf. Beale, *John's Use of the Old Testament in Revelation,* pp. 318-355.

[114] Beale, *John's Use of the Old Testament in Revelation,* p. 40.

[115] Beale, *John's Use of the Old Testament in Revelation,* p. 40.

derives more from a theological position than an exegetical discovery. On the other hand, Beale seems subject to his own criticism. His idea of new 'organically developed' meanings is not exegetically supported but rather rests on his theological assumption that the Old Testament should be read through the lens of Christ's redemptive work. Although I share the conviction that Christians should read the Old Testament differently because of Christ, I also share the conviction that revelation is an ongoing process. My point is that to some extent every reading is supported by theological grounds and no reading is supported solely on exegetical grounds. Beale seems to be making an argument along similar lines when he writes, 'whatever conclusion one reaches, it is not based only on raw exegetical considerations but on the theological presupposition of the individual interpreter!'[116]

3.2. S. Moyise

S. Moyise has developed the fullest appropriation of intertextuality in Revelation studies.[117] Challenging earlier historical studies which have argued that the message of the seven letters is understood best in the light of a historical reconstruction of the original context,[118] Moyise proposes that allusions to the Old Testament within the seven letters serve as the best interpretative grid with which to understand this biblical text. In addition to chapters on the use of Daniel and Ezekiel, he also offers an examination of the Dead Sea Scrolls as a possible intertext for Revelation. While many scholars have recognized the centrality of the Old Testament in Revelation, most of the work done on

[116] G.K. Beale, 'Did Jesus and His Followers Preach the Right Doctrine from the Wrong Texts?', An Examination of the Presuppositions of Jesus' and the Apostles' Exegetical Method', in *The Right Doctrine from the Wrong Texts? Essays on the Use of the Old Testament in the New,* ed. G.K. Beale (Grand Rapids: Baker Books, 1994), p. 397.

[117] S. Moyise, 'Intertextuality and the Book of Revelation', *ExpTim* 104 (1993), pp. 295-298; idem, 'Does the New Testament Quote the Old Testament Out of Context?', *Anvil* 11 (1994), pp. 133-143; idem, *The Old Testament in the Book of Revelation* (Sheffield: Sheffield Academic Press, 1995); idem, 'The Old Testament in the New: A Reply to Greg Beale', *IBS* 21 (1999), pp. 54-58; idem, 'Intertextuality and the Study of the Old Testament in the New Testament', in *The Old Testament in the New Testament: Essays in Honour of J.L. North,* ed. S. Moyise (Sheffeild: Sheffield Academic Press, 2000), pp. 25-32.

[118] C.J. Hemer, *The Letters to the Seven Churches of Asia in their Local Setting* (Sheffield: Sheffield Academic Press, 1986); W.M. Ramsay, *The Letters to the Seven Churches of Asia and their Place in the Plan of the Apocalypse* (London: Hodder & Stoughton, 1904).

this topic has remained in the historical arena. The historical approach can be valuable in helping to eliminate dubious parallels and by adding a higher level of conviction to the clearer allusions.[119] However, Moyise suggests that this is only a partial solution. In an attempt to be certain that the original author intended an allusion, scholars may overlook more subtle but nevertheless important references in favor of those that can be more or less proven. Using the analogy of a symphony, he suggests that a music critic is not expected 'to limit his or her comments to the loudest instruments in the orchestra!'[120]

Moyise addresses the significance of the original context of an allusion, positioning his work between two alternatives. On the one hand, he cites G.K. Beale as a representative of a position that maintains that the Old Testament is determinative for the meaning in the New Testament.[121] Beale's thesis is that key sections of Revelation (namely 1, 4-5, 13, 17) are simply a midrash on Daniel 7. On the other hand, Moyise cites Schüssler Fiorenza as a representative of a position that holds that the Old Testament merely offers the vocabulary for John and therefore the original Old Testament meaning does not come into play.[122] In either case the reader is being led to a fixed interpretative resolution.[123]

Moyise offers an alternative, suggesting that the reader is to struggle with an intersection of textual surfaces where the question is no longer a matter of respect (or the lack thereof) for literary context. He asks,

[119] Cf. S. Sandmel, 'Parallelomania', *JBL* 81 (1962), pp. 1-13.

[120] Moyise, *The Old Testament in the Book of Revelation,* p. 18.

[121] Moyise, *The Old Testament in the Book of Revelation,* p. 22. Beale challenges this classification as misrepresenting his view. According to Beale, the Old Testament serves as both servant and guide in the formation of the thought in the Apocalypse.

[122] Schüssler Fiorenza, *The Book of Revelation: Justice and Judgment,* p. 135. 'John does not interpret the Old Testament but uses its words, images, phrases, and patterns as a language arsenal in order to make his own theological statement or express his own prophetic vision'.

[123] These two positions correspond to two forms of imitation (namely *reproductive* and *eclectic*) described in T.M. Greene, *The Light of Troy: Imitation and Discovery in Renaissance Poetry* (New Haven: Yale University Press, 1982), pp. 16-53. Beale seems to adhere to an understanding of reproductive imitation, described by Greene as a view that sees the pretext as being 'beyond alteration and beyond criticism'. According to Beale, John is simply informing his contemporaries that the prophecies of Daniel are becoming for them a reality. Schüssler Fiorenza's understanding of the use of the Old Testament in Revelation can be categorized under eclectic imitation, which sees a variety of vocabulary from a variety of pretexts as means to evoke powerful images without necessarily involving intentional interpretation of the pretexts.

'how does the Old Testament context interact with the New Testament context?'[124] This question is somewhat different from the traditional argument over whether the New Testament authors respected the context of the Old Testament texts they employed. Respect for context (or the lack thereof) becomes a moot point in this kind of analysis because intertextuality assumes that 'every quotation distorts and redefines the 'primary' utterance by relocating it within another linguistic and cultural context'.[125]

Following the example of R.B. Hays,[126] Moyise builds a method based on the literary work of J. Hollander[127] and T.M. Greene.[128] Hollander and Greene have developed a concept of literary echo. In this metaphor, a text serves as a sound chamber where other echoes (texts) may be heard. While some echoes may be clear many are often faint and are only distinguishable by the careful/informed hearer. 'Thus one aspect of a criticism attuned to echoes is to point out the "cave of resonant significance" so that others are enabled to "listen in".'[129] Once an allusion or echo has been identified the work of the scholar has only begun for the task remains to explain the manner in which the two contexts affect one another.[130] In other words, the scholar must read in two directions. Not only does the old effect the new but the new affects the way in which one reads the old.

Although Moyise uses the term intertextuality approvingly, he does not employ it uncritically. Indeed, he has offered a most helpful classification which provides parameters on defining the discursive ways in which the term may be used.[131] Moyise rightly notes that 'intertextuality' has become an umbrella term covering 'traditional source criti-

[124] Moyise, *The Old Testament in the Book of Revelation,* p. 19.

[125] M. Worton and J. Still, 'Introduction', p. 11.

[126] R.B. Hays, *Echoes of Scripture in the Letters of Paul* (New Haven: Yale University Press, 1989).

[127] J. Hollander, *The Figure of Echo: A Mode of Allusion in Milton and After* (Berkeley: University of California Press, 1981).

[128] T.M. Greene, *The Light of Troy: Imitation and Discovery in Renaissance Poetry* (New Haven: Yale University Press, 1982).

[129] Moyise, *The Old Testament in the Book of Revelation,* p. 110.

[130] R.B. Hays writes, 'The twofold task of a criticism attuned to such echoes, then, is (a) to call attention to them so that others might be enabled to hear; and (b) to give an account of the distortions and new figurations that they generate' (R.B. Hays, *Echoes of Scripture in the Letters of Paul,* p. 19).

[131] S. Moyise, 'Intertextuality and the Study of the Old Testament in the New Testament', *passim.*

cism, Jewish midrash, typology and what Fishbane calls "inner biblical exegesis".'[132] The popularity of the term is indicative of both its evocative power and a new emphasis that a text cannot be studied in isolation. Furthermore, intertextuality philosophically supports the notion that 'the way that a text has been interpreted down the ages is not irrelevant ... even if it cannot be shown that a particular interpretation was present in the mind of the author.'[133] The discursive use of the term, as has been noted above, makes its use confusing, causing some to suggest the term be abandoned.[134] As opposed to abandoning the term, Moyise offers sub-categories to indicate the individual scholar's focus, namely (1) *Intertextual Echo* (2) *Dialogical Intertextuality* and (3) *Postmodern Intertextuality.*

3.2.1. *Intertextual Echo*

In studies on the use of the Old Testament in the New, references have often been divided into three groupings: (1) quotations, (2) allusions, and (3) echoes. 'Quotation', the highest classification, is reserved for clear breaks in the author's style to introduce words from another text which are often accompanied by an introductory formula like καθὼς γέγραπται or Μωΰσῆς λέγει. Secondly, allusions are less precise than quotations and often receive additional scrutiny in terms of authenticity. R.B. Hays has offered seven tests: availability, volume, recurrence, thematic coherence, historical plausibility, history of interpretation and satisfaction. While these guidelines are useful they by no

[132] Moyise, 'Intertextuality and the Study of the Old Testament in the New Testament', p. 15. Likewise Miscall, "Intertextuality' is a covering term for all the possible relations that can be established between texts' (P.D. Miscall, 'Isaiah: New Heavens, New Earth, New Book', in *Reading between Texts: Intertextuality and the Hebrew Bible,* ed. D.N. Fewell [Louisville, KY: Westminster/JohnKnox Press, 1992], p. 44). Cf. G. Buchanan, *Introduction to Intertextuality* (Lewiston, NY: Edwin Mellen Press, 1994).

[133] Moyise, 'Intertextuality and the Study of the Old Testament in the New Testament', p. 16. Cf. U. Luz, *Matthew in History: Interpretation, Influence, and Effects* (Minneapolis: Fortress, 1994); E.B. Powery, 'Ulrich Luz's *Matthew in History:* A Contribution to Pentecostal Hermeneutics?' *JPT* 14 (1999), pp. 3-17; U. Luz, 'A Response to Emerson B. Powery', *JPT* 14 (1999), pp. 19-26. Dubbed *Wirkungsgeschichte,* this method of appreciating the multiple readings a text has had is not unrelated to the contextualization of postmodern culture.

[134] S.E. Porter, 'The Use of the Old Testament in the New Testament: A Brief Comment on Method and Terminology', in *Early Christian Interpretation of the Scriptures of Israel: Investigations and Proposals,* ed. C.A. Evans and J.A. Sanders (Sheffield: Sheffield Academic Press, 1997), pp. 79-96.

means serve as 'objective' criteria.[135] Last (but not least), echoes represent the faintest of references which may even be the result of the unconscious mind, which is so thoroughly soaked with a text that references are almost unavoidable.[136] At one point Moyise compares this phenomenon with the interpretation of glossolalia in (English-speaking) Pentecostal churches which is often delivered in the phraseology of the King James Bible.[137] Although some may question the authenticity of an interpretation in the King's English, suggesting the message is not from God but solely drawn from the mind of the speaker, this is certainly not a necessary conclusion; nor would it be necessary to conclude that John failed to have an authentic vision but merely wove a text together from his own mind.[138] The importance of the echo should not be measured either by its volume or its originality[139] but rather by its power to evoke a desired image. R.B. Hays writes, 'Echoes linger in the air and lure the reader... back into the symbolic world of Scripture. Paul's allusions gesture toward precursors whose words are already heavy with tacit implication.'[140] Intertextual

[135] R.B. Hays, *Echoes of Scripture in the Letters of Paul,* pp. 32-33. Hays acknowledges the limited value of the criteria stating: 'Despite all the careful hedges that we plant around texts, meaning has a way of leaping over, like sparks'. For other attempts to objectify the process of discerning allusions or echoes see G.K. Beale, *The Use of Daniel,* p. 43; J. Paulien, 'Elusive Allusions: The Problematic Use of the Old Testament in Revelation', *BR* 33 (1988), pp. 40-48.

[136] Caird describes John's use of the Old Testament in Revelation saying: 'He constantly echoes the Old Testament writings (without ever actually quoting them), partly because this was the language which came most naturally to him, partly because of the powerful emotive effect of familiar associations, and partly no doubt because his vision had actually taken its form, though not its content, from the permanent furniture of his well stocked mind' (G.B. Caird, *A Commentary on the Revelation of St. John the Divine,* 74).

[137] Moyise, *The Old Testament in the Book of Revelation,* p. 40. Cf. a similar comment by C. Rowland, *Revelation,* p. 6.

[138] In favor of the idea that despite John's use of the Old Testament, he truly experienced a vision see: Bauckham, *The Climax of Prophecy, passim;* D.E. Aune, *Prophecy in Early Christianity and the Ancient Mediterranean World* (Grand Rapids: Eerdmans, 1983), *passim.*

[139] T.S. Eliot writes of the poet that, 'not only the best, but the most individual parts of his work may be those in which the dead poets, his ancestors, assert their immortality most vigorously' (T.S. Eliot, *Selected Essays* [3rd edn; London: Faber, 1951], p. 14). Also cited in Moyise, *The Old Testament in the Book of Revelation,* p. 108.

[140] Hays, *Echoes of Scripture in the Letters of Paul,* p. 155.

echo is the sub-category that the majority of biblical scholarship would fall under at this point.

3.2.2. *Dialogical Intertextuality*

Dialogical intertextuality seeks to take the next step beyond intertextual echo by investigating the effects not only of the pre-text on the latter text but vice versa. In this case, the 'task of intertextuality is to explore how the source text continues to speak through the new work and how the new work forces new meanings from the source text.'[141] Likewise, Worton and Still say, 'Every literary imitation is a supplement which seeks to complete and supplant the original and which functions at times for later readers as the pre-text of the "original".'[142]

Moyise finds dialogical intertextuality especially helpful with texts in which conflicting images are placed in close juxtaposition, creating a tension that is often unresolved. The image of the lion and the lamb in Rev. 5:5-6 is illustrative of this kind of tension. The 'Lion of the tribe of Judah, the Root of David', an allusion to Gen. 49:9 and Isa. 11:1, 10, has been understood by most (if not all) scholars as a symbol in Jewish literature for the victory of the Messiah over the enemies of God[143] vis-à-vis the image of the lamb, which is seen in the Old Testament primarily in reference to the sacrifice of the lamb[144] and as a metaphor for the Servant of God (Isa. 53:10). Placed in such proximity, the reader is faced with the challenge of resolving the tension, a task that for many has become easier with the influential comments of G.B. Caird.

> Wherever the Old Testament says "Lion", read "Lamb". Wherever the Old Testament speaks of the victory of the Messiah or the overthrow of the enemies of God, we are to remember that the gospel recognizes no other way of achieving these ends than the way of the Cross.[145]

[141] Moyise, *The Old Testament in the Book of Revelation,* p. 111.

[142] Worton and Still, 'Introduction', p. 7. See also H. Bloom: 'In Milton's grand metaleptic reversal, the account of Creation in Genesis has become a Midrash upon Milton' (H. Bloom, *The Breaking of the Vessels* [Chicago & London: University of Chicago Press, 1982], p. 84).

[143] Cf. *Targ. Neof.* and *Targ. Ps.-J.* of Gen. 49:9-12; *Tanh.* Gen 12:12; *Gen. R.* 97; 1QSb 5:21-29.

[144] Cf. Exod. 12:1-20; 29:38-46; Lev. 4:1-5, 13.

[145] Caird, *A Commentary on the Revelation of St. John the Divine,* 75. Many have cited Caird with approval including: M.E. Boring, *Revelation* (Louisville, KY: Westminster/John Knox Press, 1989), p. 110; J.P.M. Sweet, *Revelation* (London: SCM Press,

Following Caird, many interpreters have resolved the tension by allowing the image of a self-sacrificing lamb to devour any notion of a powerful lion. However, for others such a resolution is unconvincing, a view best represented in the commentary of J.M. Ford.[146] Citing the pseudepigraphal *Testament of Joseph* in support, Ford proposes that the image of the lamb begs for comparison with the power of the lion rather than contrast because the apocalyptic lamb is a symbol of strength which will destroy evil in the last days.[147] She strengthens her position by noting the subsequent references to the 'lamb', which describe kings hiding from the wrath of the lamb (Rev. 6:16) as well as the lamb engaging in a victorious war (Rev. 17:10, 17). While Ford's view has gained few supporters, her position accentuates difficulties in uncritically accepting Caird's position.

The solution to this conundrum, according to Moyise, is that John did not intend for his readers simply to replace one image with another, because the images require mutual interpretation.[148] This notion of a dialogical relationship between texts in the different testaments is supported somewhat by Beale who writes, 'the New Testament interprets the Old and the Old interprets the New.'[149] However, Beale maintains that the juxtaposition of contrasting images is simply an aspect of John's Semitic style and does not result in ambiguity. He seems especially concerned with Moyise's comment that by 'utilizing past texts, the author has produced a fresh composition which invites the

1990), p. 125; G.K. Beale, *The Book of Revelation* (Grand Rapids: Eerdmans, 1999), p. 353. Beale includes an additional notion that eschatologically the Lamb may indeed have a more 'literal' defeat of the enemy so that the Lamb may be a lion after all? Cf. Bauckham, *The Climax of Prophecy,* p. 183. Bauckham acknowledges that the vision of the Lamb does not negate the hopes embodied in the messianic titles, and yet he too cites Caird, stating that a new symbol has been forged of conquest by sacrificial death.

[146] J.M. Ford, *Revelation* (Garden City, NY: Doubleday, 1975), pp. 87-95. See also the comments on John 1:29 by R. Brown, 'Thus we suggest that John the Baptist hailed Jesus as the lamb of Jewish apocalyptic expectation who was to be raised up by God to destroy evil in the world, a picture not too far from that of Rev xvii 14' (R. Brown, *The Gospel according to John* [2 vols.; Garden City, NY: Doubleday, 1966], p. 60).

[147] The passage in *T. Jos.* 19:8 actually links the images of a 'lion' and a 'lamb'. Indeed, C.K. Barrett disputes *T. Jos.* 19:8 as a possible background for John 1:29 since it 'recalls the conquering lamb of Revelation' (C.K. Barrett, *The Gospel According to St John* [London: SPCK, 1978], p. 147).

[148] Moyise, *The Old Testament in the Book of Revelation,* pp. 127-132.

[149] Beale, *John's Use of the Old Testament in Revelation,* p. 127.

reader to participate and *create meaning*'.[150] Beale, citing E.D. Hirsch for support, proposes that Moyise is guilty of a 'hermeneutical flaw', confusing 'meaning' with 'significance'.[151] Within this distinction, 'meaning' is to be reserved for the intention of the original author and 'significance' relates to a variety of implications throughout the history of interpretation and beyond. In order to illustrate his point, Beale offers the following analogy of an apple:

> We can compare an author's original, unchanging meaning to an apple in its original context of an apple tree. When someone removes the apple and puts it into another setting (say, in a basket of various fruits in a dining room for decorative purposes), the apple does not lose its original identity as an apple, the fruit of a particular kind of tree, but the apple must now be understood not in and of itself but *in relation to the new context* in which it has been placed. This new contextual relationship is called 'significance'. The context does not annihilate the original identity of the apple, but now the apple must be understood in its relation to its new setting.[152]

The latent theory in this statement suggests that the 'significance' of the allusions to the Old Testament may change by virtue of a new contextualization but that 'meaning' is stable and does not change. While the analogy of the apple is not unreasonable, Moyise rightly questions whether this does justice to the text of Revelation. In the case of the lion/lamb allusion, the messianic expectancy which energized generations of Jews is radically re-interpreted as 'self-sacrifice'. Although Beale explains this development as John 'offering new understandings of Old Testament texts and fulfillments of them which

[150] Moyise, *The Old Testament in the Book of Revelation,* p. 142. Also cited in Beale, *John's Use of the Old Testament in Revelation,* p. 49 (Beale's emphasis).

[151] E.D. Hirsch, *Aims of Interpretation,* p. 14. Cf. I. Paul, 'The Value of Paul Ricoeur's Hermeneutic of Metaphor in Interpreting the Symbolism of Revelation Chapters 12 and 13', unpublished Ph.D. thesis (Nottingham: Nottingham Trent University, 1998), pp. 151-154. Paul discusses the issues surrounding authorial intention and proposes a middle ground between what he calls 'strong affirmation' (*à la* Hirsch) and 'negation', which he assigns to radical forms of reader-response criticism. Paul claims to occupy a middle position, which he identifies as 'weak affirmation'. He defines weak affirmation as a consistent demonstration of 'the value of assuming that it is reasonable to talk of the intention of the author, and perhaps have some considerable understanding of it, without having to appeal to it – beyond the text – in order to justify a particular interpretative strategy'.

[152] Beale, *John's Use of the Old Testament in Revelation,* pp. 51-52. See Moyise's response in S. Moyise, 'The Old Testament in the New: A Reply to Greg Beale', *IBS* 21 (1999), pp. 54-58.

may have been surprising to an Old Testament audience',[153] I agree with Moyise that it seems 'quite arbitrary to call this a change of "significance" but not a change of "meaning".'[154]

Moyise has responded with his own analogy of a fruit salad, refusing Beale the possibility of having his apple and eating it too. Dialogical intertextuality focuses on the fact that texts are in relationships but these relationships exert more force on the texts (or fruit) than Beale wants to admit. A better analogy is that pieces of apples, bananas, and pears are all mixed into a single bowl. The proverbial apple has been peeled, diced and 'severed from its core'. Although the fruit salad is a step in the right direction, it does not go far enough. As Moyise writes,

> the real problem with this type of analogy is its corporeality. Texts do not have hard surfaces that protect them from change of context. They are more like the ripples on a pond, which spread out, intersect with other ripples and form new patterns. Or even less corporeal, texts are like sound waves which "interfere" with one another, producing a series of harmonics and distortions.[155]

In theory, dialogical intertextuality as a sub-category represents a central characteristic of the larger umbrella of 'intertextuality', the notion that all texts (in the broadest sense of the term) are interrelated. Thus interpretative communities construct their identity in comparison to and in contrast with other communities. In terms of practice, dialogical intertextuality must be selective. It is impossible to frame all of reality (i.e. Derrida's *le texte général*) as an object for observation.[156]

[153] Beale, *John's Use of the Old Testament in Revelation,* p. 128.

[154] Moyise, 'Intertextuality and the Study of the Old Testament in the New Testament', p. 32. If such strict restraints were placed on the use of 'meaning' then it might be said that, owing to the situationality of humans, everyone only deals with 'significance', placing 'meaning' solely within the realm of Platonic forms; but that is hardly helpful.

[155] Moyise, 'Intertextuality and the Study of the Old Testament in the New Testament', p. 32.

[156] While the expanse of the general text may necessarily require a limitation on the number of intertexts which can be identified in any given analysis, the possibilities of interpretation remain open. 'They remain open not because the reader can make the sentence mean anything whatever but because other specifications of context or interpretations of the "general text" are always possible' (J. Culler, *On Deconstruction,* p. 131).

The selection process is a task of the reader; and this leads us into a discussion of postmodern intertextuality.

3.2.3. *Postmodern Intertextuality*

Like feminist and liberation interpretations, postmodern intertextuality serves to highlight the contextual significance of the interpreter within the reading process. Furthermore, postmodern intertextuality accentuates that 'no text is an autonomous and self-sufficient entity'.[157] The presence of other texts within a primary text leads to the potentiality of multiple meanings (i.e. polyvalency). However, the existence of multiple interpretations within biblical studies is indisputable as a simple perusal of secondary sources would quickly prove. So what is the value of emphasizing the inherently flawed nature of interpretations? Moyise gives three answers to this question.

First, postmodern intertextuality does not deny the possibility of meaning but it does insist that meaning is not ideologically neutral. To support this Moyise cites several interpretations of Revelation which question the level of violent language and the comparatively meager language of love and forgiveness. Although Christians can argue that the violence is shaped by a principle of self-sacrifice, this sympathetic reading is certainly not the only possible interpretation.[158] Second, by juxtaposing a selected intertext with a focus text a new light is cast in ways that reveal previously unseen characteristics. Third, postmodern intertextuality is true to some degree because, according to Moyise, 'it is clearly impossible for any one individual to perfectly grasp the meaning of a text.'[159] The significance of this statement depends on whether human finitude is accepted as a simple truism or seen as a critical element within interpretation. If the latter is true then attention to the circumstances of the reader will play a vital hermeneutical role, deserving careful study. Commonly, those who deny the significance of human finitude are in positions of power and have the privilege of presenting their interpretations as (the) truth, often giving the less

[157] I.R. Kitzberger, 'Introduction', in *The Personal Voice in Biblical Interpretation,* ed. I.R. Kitzberger (London: Routledge, 1999), p. 6.

[158] Cf. H. Bloom, *The Revelation of St John the Divine* (Modern Critical Interpretations, NY: Chelsea House, 1988), pp. 4-5; S.D. Moore, 'Revolting Revelations', in *The Personal Voice in Biblical Interpretation,* ed. I.R. Kitzberger (London: Routledge, 1999), pp. 183-200.

[159] S. Moyise, 'Intertextuality and the Study of the Old Testament in the New Testament', p. 40.

powerful (women, racial minorities and the poor) the short end of the stick, at times across their backs.

3.3. Excursus on G.K. Beale: The Right Doctrine from the Wrong Texts?

The crux of the issue is respect (or lack of it) for the context of the Old Testament passages employed by New Testament writers.[160] Beale is convinced that the authors of the New Testament wrote with complete respect for the context of the passages they cite or to which they (consciously) allude. Furthermore, he suggests that the exegetical methods found within the New Testament should be mimicked by Christians today, albeit with a humble lack of certainty regarding the success of contemporary interpretations.

Beale is disputing a widely-held opinion that Jesus and the New Testament writers utilized the atomistic exegetical methods of their Jewish contemporaries, methods which few scholars would consider legitimate today.[161] Indeed, R.N. Longenecker argues that despite the apostles' ahistorical methods they were nevertheless ensured valid interpretations owing to their unique revelatory status. Beale concedes that if Longenecker is correct then modern readers may certainly not use the exegetical methods of the apostles. However, he contends that the methods of the New Testament writers were contextually sensitive and for that matter so were many of their contemporaries.[162] His theory begins with two observations. First, it should not be assumed that the non-contextual exegesis commonly associated with early Pharisaic and Qumran interpretations predates AD 70 because most of the examples of such readings are after AD 70.[163] Second, contextual sensitivity is not

[160] G.K. Beale, 'Did Jesus and His Followers Preach the Right Doctrine from the Wrong Texts?, An Examination of the Presuppositions of Jesus' and the Apostles' Exegetical Method', *Them* 14 (1989), pp. 89-96.

[161] E.g. R.N. Longenecker, 'Who Is the Prophet Talking About? Some Reflections on the New Testament's Use of the Old', *Them* 13 (1987), pp. 4-8; M.D. Hooker, 'Beyond the Things That Are Written? St. Paul's Use of Scripture', *NTS* 27 (1981-82), pp. 295-309; B. Lindars, 'The Place of the Old Testament in the Formation of New Testament Theology', *NTS* 23 (1977), pp. 59-66.

[162] Contrary to Beale's position C. Rowland argues that John's use of the Old Testament 'is an indication of "visionary language" rather than a deliberate attempt to write a commentary on these texts ... this is not exegesis in any conventional sense' (C. Rowland, *Revelation,* p. 6).

[163] For support Beale cites D.I. Brewer, *Techniques and Assumptions in Jewish Exegesis before 70 C.E.* (Tübingen: Mohr, 1992).

uncharacteristic in Qumran or in Jewish apocalyptic.[164] Moreover, Beale asserts that his position is defensible even if these observations are proven to be faulty. The existence of non-contextual exegesis among the contemporaries of Jesus and the apostles does not necessarily prove they all shared the identical hermeneutical method, especially given the obvious separation in terms of the Messianic fulfillment.

He argues that allusions to the Old Testament within the New Testament which appear to be contradicting their original sense are not the result of a lack of contextual respect but simply indicative of the new presuppositional stance of the writers formed by their understanding of Jesus as the fulfillment of Old Testament prophecy. '*Granted the legitimacy of these presuppositions,* John's interpretation of the Old Testament shows respect for Old Testament contexts.'[165] According to Beale, the apostles were simply employing a form of canonical typology which can only mistakenly be equated with non-contextual allegorical readings.[166] In cases where non-contextual uses of the Old Testament are undeniable Beale assumes the allusion to be a product of the author's mind, which is so thoroughly saturated with particular passages that the Old Testament verbiage is used without much forethought. Thus, the reader should assume that the allusion is unintentional.[167] He cites the following as an example:

[164] Cf. Beale, *The Use of Daniel, passim.*

[165] Beale, *John's Use of the Old Testament in Revelation,* p. 45. Moyise finds this discussion inadequate. He acknowledges that 'John shows an "awareness" of the Old Testament contexts but his Christian presuppositions nevertheless allow him to change, modify and even (on occasions) invert them' (Moyise, 'Intertextuality and the Study of the Old Testament in the New Testament', p. 33 n. 58). It is not that I disagree with Beale's assumption that Christ as the center of history is the key to interpreting portions of the Old Testament but rather that historical, contextually sensitive exegesis of the modernistic kind is not the sole arbiter of truth for the biblical authors or for (Christian) readers today.

[166] Beale does not defend this assumption in detail but he does cite the following in support: L. Goppelt, *Typos* (Grand Rapids: Eerdmans, 1982); A.T. Hanson, *Studies on Paul's Technique and Theology* (Grand Rapids: Eerdmans, 1974), p. 186; Foulkes, *Acts of God* (London: Tyndale, 1958), p. 35; O. Cullmann, *Salvation in History* (London: SCM, 1967), pp. 132-33.

[167] In a post-Freudian culture, it is precarious to argue that a person only reveals insights about the self intentionally. In other words, authors may communicate something about themselves which they did not intend. U. Eco, *Interpretation and Overinterpretation* (Cambridge: Cambridge University Press, 1992), gives some personal examples of where readers have pointed out allusions in his own writings that he had not been aware of at the time of writing, which he nevertheless agrees in retrospect are

> the phrase "I turned *to see the voice which was speaking*" (Rev. 1:12a) is probably drawn from Dan. 7:11 (LXX), but there it refers to the "boastful words" of the beast. This may have been drawn in unconsciously because of the clear influence of Daniel 7 in Rev. 1.7-14.[168]

I find this paradoxical. On the one hand, I am asked to believe that John is careful never to disregard the context of the Old Testament passages he employs, and on the other hand, I am asked to believe that the same John, whose mind is saturated with the Old Testament, will inadvertently identify Christ with the words used by Daniel to identify the beast! It seems to me far better to acknowledge that John may not be as bound by contextual obligation as Beale wishes.

To the question, 'Did Jesus and his followers preach the right doctrine from the wrong texts?', Beale responds with an emphatic 'No'. Indeed, he asserts that imitating the exegetical method of the apostles is normative as long as one holds the same presuppositions and acknowledges a lower degree of epistemological certainty. The fact that typology has been misused as a method in church history 'illegitimately focusing on minutiae as typological foreshadowing', does not negate the legitimate use of this hermeneutical method. In other words, abuse does not negate proper use.

In conclusion, I have a few concerns with Beale's hermeneutics. Although I highly value Beale's detailed analysis of John's use of the Old Testament in the Apocalypse, in the final analysis, as a Pentecostal I find it inadequate. He leaves insufficient room for John to be recording an actual vision as opposed to solely exegeting scripture. When I read the text I assume John is interpreting and relaying an experience in the Spirit, albeit not devoid of Old Testament allusions.[169] The Apocalypse ought not to be reduced solely to a contextually sensitive exegesis.[170] Beale represents John as an informed Christian

allusions. Perhaps this is what Hays means when he writes, 'connotations bleed over' (R.B. Hays, *Echoes of Scripture,* p. 142).

[168] Beale, *John's Use of the Old Testament in Revelation,* p. 74.

[169] Likewise see M.R. Mulholland, *Revelation: Holy Living in an Unholy World* (Grand Rapids: Zondervan, 1990), pp. 17. He insists that in order to 'develop a more holistic understanding of Revelation, the reality and nature of visionary experience must be taken seriously as a primary factor in interpretation'.

[170] Cf. J.E. Stanley, 'Elements of a Postmodern Holiness Hermeneutic Illustrated by the way of the Book of Revelation', *WTJ* 28 (1993), pp. 23-43. Stanley proposes that a holiness hermeneutic is (1) confessional and communal, (2) comprehensive in

reader who wishes to explicate the meaning of Scripture for his contemporaries, a representation that is strikingly similar to how I would characterize Beale. In fact, it seems to me that in an attempt to describe John and his activities Beale has produced at best a caricature of himself and at worst a first-century Hal Lindsay (the ecclesiastical 'chicken little') telling his contemporaries that the prophecies of Daniel are surely taking place in their day. One only needs to see the signs! In response, Beale could say that my reading of the Apocalypse presents John as a caricature of a Pentecostal reader, seeing visions and existentially hearing the word of God. Of course, John never claims to be exegeting Scripture but he does claim to be seeing a vision in the Spirit.

Second, Beale seems to be arguing that readers should only take their cues on how to interpret a text solely from what a text explicitly instructs.[171] However, this is untenable from Beale's position because the text never indicates that it contains a singular meaning or that the meaning should be identified with the intention of the author. Beale could respond that these assumptions are simply basic to understanding and communication. However, it would be even more difficult to argue cogently that the text instructs a reader to perform an historical (atomistic) exegesis, and yet the lack of such instruction has not prevented volumes from being written in this manner including works by Beale himself. It seems far more faithful to the concept of a liturgical worshiping community to take its cues from the manner in which its early leaders handled biblical texts. In other words, I am persuaded by Ruiz's argument that the appropriate context in which the text is to be read, *interpreted* and followed is the worshiping community. The fact that different interpretations exist between communities (or even within them) is not a reason for remorse but rather exultation and it certainly does not imply that one interpretation is as good as another.

Third, while I am not opposed to 'imitating the apostles', I question the possibility of identifying the 'epistemological certainty' of the biblical writers. Did John think that he was writing Scripture as he recorded the Apocalypse? If so, why has the scriptural status of the

method, (3) values intertextuality, and (4) is open to the Spirit.

[171] Beale, *John's Use of the Old Testament in Revelation,* p. 40. Beale seems to me to be ambivalent on this point, arguing on the one hand that John is in a unique position as a prophet and therefore his method of interpretation should not be expected to be repeatable, and on the other hand, arguing that readers should employ the exegetical methods of the apostles.

Apocalypse been questioned by a not insignificant number of people? What is the relationship between the revelatory stance of the early church and the revelatory stance of the church today? What is the role of the Spirit in this revelatory process? Beale is unequivocal about the privileged position of the apostles and I suspect he would differentiate between the *inspiration* of apostolic writings and the *illumination* of Christian readings, in a manner analogous no doubt to the 'meaning' vs. 'significance' debate.

With the profusion of reader-response theories, the tendency to reserve 'inspiration' to the role of the Spirit in the writing process seems to be an attempt to safeguard the meaning from individualistic interpretations. Thus 'illumination' (i.e. the role of the Spirit in reading) is used to describe a process that contains a higher level of subjectivity. In premodern times this distinction did not occur. J. Wesley speaks of the inspiration of both writing and reading: 'The Spirit of God not only once *inspired* those who wrote it, but continually *inspires*, supernaturally assists, those that read it with earnest prayer.'[172] Contemporary theologians have also made the point that the activity of the Spirit in relation to reading should also be identified as 'inspiration'.[173] As C.H. Pinnock laments, textbooks on hermeneutics fail to discuss the role of the Spirit in interpretation.[174] Pinnock suggests the silence ensues because those who acknowledge a contemporary breathing of the Spirit often avoid the discussion to prevent opening the door to subjectivism while those who advocate subjectivism often allow only for a human contribution. Another possible reason for this silence derives from the preoccupation within Western culture with rationalism, 'which fosters

[172] J. Wesley, *Explanatory Notes upon the New Testament* (1755, repr. London: Epworth 1950), p. 794. One Wesleyan theologian takes the issue further in his systematic text, titling his section on biblical inspiration, 'It is the Person that is Inspired'. He writes that 'the inspiration of the Holy Spirit is not directed toward the papyrus, the pen, or the ink, but toward the persons inspired' (A.F. Gray, *Christian Theology* vol. 1 [Anderson, IN: Warner Press, 1944], p. 80).

[173] E.g. C.H. Pinnock, 'The Work of the Holy Spirit in Hermeneutics', *JPT* 2 (1995), pp. 3-23. Furthermore, the biblical text does not differentiate between inspiration and illumination (cf. 2 Tim. 3.16 and Eph. 1.17).

[174] Pinnock offers the following examples: G. Fee, *Gospel and Spirit: Issues in New Testament Hermeneutics* (Peabody, MA: Hendrickson, 1991); R.A. Muller, *The Study of Theology: From Biblical Interpretation to Contemporary Formulation* (Grand Rapids: Zondervan, 1991); G.R. Osborne, *The Hermeneutical Spiral: A Comprehensive Introduction to Biblical Interpretation* (Downers Grove, IL: InterVarsity Press, 1991); A.C. Thiselton, *New Horizons in Hermeneutics* (Grand Rapids: Zondervan, 1992).

a neglect of the Spirit'.[175] The flip-side of the coin is that mysticism is being devalued. 'Therefore, the only thing we leave the Spirit to do in interpretation is to rubber-stamp what our scholarly exegesis concludes.'[176] What would a hermeneutic look like where the Spirit is taken seriously as the agent of all revelatory communication including (inspired) reading as well as (inspired) writing?[177]

First, a Spirit-led interpretation must involve a broad epistemology that includes reason and yet transcends rationalism.[178] Both fundamentalist and liberal biblical scholars alike treat the text as a code that simply needs to be broken rather than as a casebook that includes multiple, diverse testimonies. Propositions, while not unimportant, are not the sole avenue for communicating truth. Thus a pneumatic hermeneutic will need to allow ample room for narrative both within the text and within the community, as well as room for songs and prophecy.

Second, discerning the movement of the Spirit is not always an easy task, for the Spirit moves where it wills. Thus, the interpretation can never stop with explanation but must always include an integration of ethical behavior, emphasizing truth in deed as well as in thought and word.[179] Analogous to the Hebrew שׁמע, the admonition in the hearing

[175] C.H. Pinnock, 'The Work of the Holy Spirit in Hermeneutics', *JPT* 2 (1995), p. 8.

[176] Pinnock, 'The Work of the Holy Spirit in Hermeneutics', p. 8.

[177] A brief discussion of some possible elements of a Spirit-inspired hermeneutic are provided here. The following chapter is dedicated to the topic of a Pentecostal hermeneutic.

[178] All that I am suggesting is that no single method is sufficient to exhaust the meaning of Scripture. Note well Moltmann's observation, 'History is undoubtedly the paradigm of modern European times, but it is not the final paradigm for humanity' (J. Moltmann, *The Way of Jesus Christ: Christology in Messianic Dimensions* (trans. M. Kohl; Minneapolis: Fortress, 1990], p. 215). Cf. the comments of the liberationist J. Míguez Bonino: 'one hopes that Pentecostal scholarship will not recapitulate the fruitless debate between modernists and fundamentalists but will challenge both and facilitate the development of a multilevel hermeneutic' (J. Míguez Bonino, 'Changing Paradigms: A Response', in M.W. Dempster *et al., The Globalization of Pentecostalism: A Religion Made to Travel* [Oxford: Regnum, 1999], p. 118).

[179] Discussing the issue of ethical reading, Fowl and Jones write, 'the aim of Scriptural interpretation is to shape our common life in the situations in which we find ourselves according to the characters, convictions, and practices related in Scripture' (S.E. Fowl and L.G. Jones, *Reading in Communion: Scripture & Ethics in the Christian Life* [Grand Rapids: Eerdmans, 1991], p. 20). See also R. Wall, *Revelation NIBC* (Peabody, MA: Hendrickson, 1991), p. 37. Wall writes, 'The ultimate aim of Biblical interpreta-

formula implies heeding as well as hearing. Although Beale highlights the significance of the ethical dimension of the Apocalypse he demarcates too drastically the difference between propositional cognitive elements of truth and existential volitional realization of truth.

Third, the role of the Spirit is to lead the believers into all truth (John 16:13), which includes Scripture but not exclusively. As S. Land writes, the Spirit 'speaks scripturally but also has more to say than Scripture'.[180] Yet Scripture is not simply one of many testimonies. Rather, it holds a unique position over and against the community but not over and against the Spirit. In other words, the goal of a Spirit-inspired interpretation is to maintain the dialogical relationship between *'a law so righteous'* (the inscripturated revelation) and the *'God - so-near'* (charismatic revelation).[181] Or, more radically stated,

> The canon – that which keeps our weaving straight – I would propose, is the Holy Spirit, not a collection of writings. The Spirit of Christ is the norm or standard of the faith, and that Spirit stands in authority over *both Scripture and prophecy*. It is not Scripture that is the ultimate norm, but Christ. As such, prophecy is not subject to the standard of written Scripture but rather the *kanon* of the Spirit as it operates in the discernment of the community.[182]

Fourth, implicit within the previous points is the notion of an existential experience with the Spirit. At this point, Schleiermacher becomes a helpful dialogue partner owing to his emphasis on the experience of the Spirit. However, experience is only part of a pneumatic epistemology which must be complemented with faith and reason in the context of a tradition.[183] 'First of all you must understand this, that

tion is to acquire knowledge that determines and shapes the identity of God's people in history'.

[180] S.J. Land, *Pentecostal Spirituality: A Passion for the Kingdom* (Sheffield: Sheffield Academic Press, 1993), p. 100.

[181] R.D. Moore, 'Canon and Charisma in the Book of Deuteronomy', *JPT* 1 (1993), p. 92.

[182] J.K.A. Smith, 'The Closing of the Book: Pentecostals, Evangelicals, and the Sacred Writings', *JPT* 11 (1997), p. 68.

[183] The relationship between the community decision making and Scripture has been often addressed in relation to the so-called Jerusalem council in Acts 15. Cf. L.T. Johnson, *Religious Experience in Earliest Christianity: A Missing Dimension in New Testament Studies* (Minneapolis: Fortress Press, 1998), *passim;* J.C. Thomas, 'Reading the Bible from within Our Traditions: A Pentecostal Hermeneutic', in *Between Two Horizons: Spanning New Testament Studies & Systematic Theology*, ed. M. Turner and J.B.

no prophecy of Scripture is a matter of one's own interpretation' (2 Pet. 1:21). Thus, the community (or some may say tradition) serves as a safeguard against idiosyncratic interpretations. Nevertheless, the leading of the Spirit does not necessarily ensure a following of the Spirit which may result in misreadings or negative effects (i.e. the *Wirkungsgeschichte* of any given text may produce both positive and negative effects).

Fifth, closely related to the notion of communal safeguards, a Spirit-led interpretation will be ecumenical. Acknowledging the situationality of readers within a community does not suggest isolationism or, worse, sectarianism. The Spirit is working universally to draw all of creation back to God. The Spirit is eschatological; the Spirit is mission-focused; and the Spirit is catholic. The reality of human contextualization does not mute ecumenical dialogue but rather insists that true catholicity exists only with diversity and not uniformity.

3.4. Summary

As the above survey of the use of intertextuality in Revelation studies progressed, the thoughts of Ruiz and Moyise have been critically engaged and I have attempted to answer the challenges put forward by Beale. Hermeneutically, I am very close to Ruiz and especially Moyise. The emphasis placed by Ruiz on the liturgy rings true with my belief that reading the biblical texts is one of the primary functions of a community of faith. The initial beatitude, 'Blessed is the one who reads and those who hear', suggests the involvement of the whole community participating in worship. The public reading of a text may allow for only a single reader while all others are hearing, and yet the reader joins with the hearers/believers as all participate in an act of worship. Thus a worship service is the place where reading is kept faithful and communal *(pro nobis)*. The difficulty in appreciating this view lies in the apotheosis of the individual which permeates fundamentalism and biblical criticism. Within these paradigms, the texts are understood as self-evident artifacts that the individual believer or scholar simply needs to dissect, reducing the role of the Spirit and the community to minor items. If Ruiz's hypothesis is accepted that read-

Green (Grand Rapids: Eerdmans, 2000), pp. 108-122; J.B. Shelton, 'Epistemology and Authority in the Acts of the Apostles: An Analysis and Test Case of Acts 15:1-29', a paper presented to the 28th annual meeting of the SPS, March 1998.

ing the Apocalypse is intended to reside in the liturgy, then the community may no longer be incidental.[184]

A creative hermeneutic such as that of Ruiz or Moyise need not be seen as inimical to communication but rather as a characteristic of human finitude. 'Such an "interpretation of interpretation" *re*-values embodiment and ultimately ends in an ethical respect for difference as the gift of a creating God who loves difference and who loves differently.'[185] The challenge is to be ecumenical while maintaining distinctives. To lose the distinctives would be defeating the purpose of having differences, but to remain sectarian would defeat the purpose as well.

4. Intertextuality and Contextualization: A Theology for Diversity

Scholars have advocated the utilization of intertextuality for a variety of reasons. D. Aune sees it as an alternative to narrative approaches, which he feels have failed to appreciate the value of source criticism owing to a presupposed unity of the text, a notion which is central to narrative criticism (at least within biblical studies). Aune writes that source criticism

> has benefited from the relatively recent development of a new emphasis in literary criticism, *intertextuality,* a way of reading a text that sees it as a nexus of other texts and cultural systems, whether in the horizon of the author or of the reader.[186]

In what might be considered a completely opposite rationalization, Moyise views intertextuality as an alternative to source and redaction criticism, which he sees as being overly preoccupied with authorial intention.

> However, this emphasis on the author's 'intention' has been largely abandoned in New Testament study and replaced by a focus on the text itself or on the role of the reader. This has been for both practical (we have no ac-

[184] Cf. S. Hauerwas, *Unleashing the Scriptures: Freeing the Bible from Captivity to America* (Nashville: Abingdon, 1993), pp. 19-28. He writes, 'no text can substitute for the people of God'.

[185] J.K.A. Smith, *The Fall of Interpretation,* p. 23.

[186] Aune, *Revelation 1–5,* p. cvi. Aune insists it is not his intention to defend the source-critical method, believing that 'It needs no defense'. See also Aune, 'Intertextuality and the Genre of the Apocalypse', pp. 142-160.

> cess to the author's 'intention') and theoretical reasons (meaning is not a 'given' but has to be 'created' by the reader).[187]

While Moyise may have overstated the extent to which the author's intention has been abandoned, a gross exaggeration according to Beale,[188] attention in biblical studies to reading theory has at the very least increased in recent years. However, drawn into the spotlight of critical observation the reader would be wise to heed the caveat of the so-called Marcan apocalypse, 'ὁ ἀναγινώσκων νοείτω'. One of the most significant contributions reader-response theories have offered the greater guild of biblical studies is an awareness that not all persons read alike.

A phenomenon within theological studies which parallels reader-response criticism is a movement dubbed 'contextualization'.[189] An odd term to be sure, contextualization highlights a recognition among theologians that the socio-cultural context of a group plays a vital role in the formation of its theology.[190] Characteristics of contextualization that are important for this study include: (1) contextualization is not a rejection of Christianity on the whole but rather a critique of the captivity of Christianity within the dominant European cultural form; (2) contextualization is at heart a renewal movement that wishes to prioritize participation;[191] and (3) contextualization devalues long-range universals in favor of short-range situation-oriented norms. In order to value local contexts many contextual theologians avoid attempts at 'formulating comprehensive theological systems, developing instead a multiplicity of local theologies'.[192] Shifting the paradigm exclusively to parochial norms begs the question of the 'catholic' dimension of Christianity. As D. Irvin puts it, 'Have contextual theologies aban-

187 Moyise, *The Old Testament in the Book of Revelation,* p. 142.

188 Beale, *John's Use of the Old Testament in Revelation,* p. 50.

189 For a definition of contextualization see, among others, J. Ukpong, 'What is Contextualization?', *NZM* 43 (1987), pp. 161-168.

190 Not unlike reader-response theories, contextualization has received mixed reviews in theological circles with some scholars preferring to maintain a contextually neutral theology.

191 In particular, liberation theology especially emphasizes orthopraxis. Cf. G. Gonzalez, *A Theology of Liberation: History, Politics and Salvation* (Maryknoll, NY: Orbis, 1973), p. 10.

192 D.T. Irvin, 'Contextualization and Catholicity: Looking Anew for the Unity of the Faith', *Stud Theo* 48 (1994), p. 84.

doned the notion of the essential unity of Christian churches beyond the local context, their catholicity?'[193]

Before offering his own answer to this question, Irvin begins by citing a few other attempts. These attempts appeal to the incarnation of the Word as a divine form of contextualization, serving as a model for contextual theologies.[194] Based on this notion, the unity in Christ is an essential guide for the diversity of contextual theologies. L. Russell argues:

> Such diversity is an authentic basis for unity, for it allows us to discover the many ways our Lord can be known ... (and) affords us with a much richer expression of our one faith in Christ, and leads us to expect Christ's presence in many unexpected contexts.[195]

In other words, Christ is seen as the central text which can be relocated into new contexts. However, this is somewhat problematic for it grants a universal status to a particular historical situation, namely the apostolic era, thereby undercutting the very notion of contextual theologies. The difficulty with a context-free or transcendent central text is that it stands above its contexts, passing over them rather than through them.[196] Thus the conundrum remains, if contextual theologies remain unable to employ a common transcontextual center, then is the only alternative in theology 'a new tribalism'? Irvin answers this question with an emphatic No!

> Contextualization is not in fact an invitation to new tribalism in theological discourse. The commonalties and cross-fertilizations are too prominent, and the dialogical gains too rich for us to investigate them as monadic or isolated phenomenon. Yet the question remains ... what encompasses a viable Christian ecumenical vision that does not require adherence to abstracted dogmatic formulations of Scripture or Tradition, nor assign privileged status to a particular theological articulation?[197]

Irvin proposes intertextuality as a possible solution for moving beyond the local while remaining contextual. Once texts and contexts

[193] Irvin, 'Contextualization and Catholicity', p. 84.

[194] E.g. S. Coe, 'In Search of Renewal in Theological Education', *Theo Ed* 9 (1973), pp. 233-243; L. Russell, 'Exploring the Context of our Faith', in *Changing Contexts of Our Faith,* ed. L. Russell (Philadelphia: Fortress, 1985), pp. 21-35.

[195] Russell, 'Exploring the Context of our Faith', p. 29.

[196] Irvin, 'Contextualization and Catholicity', p. 85.

[197] Irvin, 'Contextualization and Catholicity', pp. 87-88.

are both conceived as textual weavings, boundaries may be crossed without collapsing into a universal truth. Relying on M. Bakhtin's notion of dialogicity, Kristeva describes a literary word as an '*intersection of textual surfaces* rather than a point (a fixed meaning), as a dialogue among several writings: that of the writer, the addressee (or the character), and the contemporary or earlier cultural context'.[198] According to Irvin, intertextuality 'takes seriously the manner in which theologies are situated historically, the manner in which they form the limits for each other, and the manner in which they are analogous and oppositional at the same time'.[199]

What are the theological implications of utilizing intertextuality as a means of facilitating ecumenical discussion? First, intertextuality provides the necessary theory to speak meaningfully of contextual readings. In Irvin's words, 'Intertextuality is decentering without being destructive to context.'[200] According to H. Cox, Pentecostalism serves as an example of the convergences of various texts and contexts which interlace to form new fabrics of faith which are nevertheless woven together by common strands.[201] While Cox's view of Pentecostalism has received some criticism for not fully distinguishing between indigenous spiritualities and Pentecostalism,[202] a few Pentecostal scholars have followed Cox's observations and carried them further albeit not without critical reflection.[203] Second, memory plays a preeminent role, recalling the stories of the community. Memory is formed intertextu-

[198] Kristeva, *Desire and Language*, p. 65.

[199] Irvin, 'Contextualization and Catholicity', pp. 89-90.

[200] Irvin, 'Contextualization and Catholicity', p. 90.

[201] H. Cox, *Fire from Heaven: The Rise of Pentecostal Spirituality and the Reshaping of Religion in the Twenty-first Century* (Reading, MA: Addison-Wesley, 1995). Cox's thesis is that Pentecostalism will continue to do well in a variety of places around the world because it incorporates elements of *primal spirituality,* including ecstatic speech, mystical piety and millennial fervor. An example of intertextual relationships is the similarities (and differences) between glossolalia and the kind of 'scat singing' Louis Armstrong made famous. 'Both are forms of verbal expression that transcend the normal limitations of language, though they are used for quite different purposes in these contexts' (H. Cox, *Fire from Heaven,* p. 148).

[202] J.R. Williams, 'Harvey Cox and Pentecostalism: A Review of *Fire form Heaven*', *APS* 1 (1998), pp. 23-26; G. McGee, 'Review of *Fire from Heaven: The Rise of Pentecostal Spirituality and the Reshaping of Religion in the Twenty-first Century* (Reading, MA: Addison-Wesley, 1995), by H. Cox', *Missiology* 24 (1996), p. 421.

[203] A. Yong's work on a pneumatological approach to a Christian Theology of Religions is by far the most thorough engagement with the questions posed by Cox (A. Yong, *Discerning the Spirit(s), passim*).

ally by a variety of authoritative texts. Typically, scripture and tradition have served as the common historical memories that form the identity of a Christian community;[204] however, in recent years cultural identity and interreligious dialogue have also played a significant role in communal memory. 'So it is with collective memory that one is linked to others in community creating something that can meaningfully be called a collective identity.'[205] Third, catholicity need not entail uniformity of creed nor commitment. Contextual theologies should allow room for alternative interpretations of reality. Of course Christian contextual theologies when trying to converse with other religions will inevitably run into the Christological impasse.[206]

5. Conclusion

In this chapter, two primary avenues have been investigated, namely literary theory and biblical studies, or more directly intertextuality and its application in studies on Revelation. Although Pentecostalism has been referred to in passing, it remains the last major avenue that needs to be investigated at length. In keeping with the theory of intertextuality as presented above, the context of the interpreter (in this case Pentecostalism) serves as another text which intersects with the text of Revelation and the Old Testament texts within Revelation. Viewing Pentecostalism as a text which (in)forms interpretations of Scripture is not unique to this study. Note the comment of M.W. Dempster concerning Pentecostal hermeneutics. He writes,

> The agenda of Pentecostal hermeneutics is changing on three basic fronts: the conception of what constitutes a text, the issue of the pre-understanding of the interpreter, and the relationship between a text and an interpreter that produces meaning. Hermeneutics still has as its object the interpreta-

[204] More radically stated, '[A] classical position distinguishes between Scripture and tradition, requiring that tradition be subject to Scripture as its norm. However, I would argue that this is a naive distinction: Scripture itself is the product of a tradition or better, a plurality of traditions (while other traditions were excluded). If Scripture itself is part of the tradition, then it must also be "normed" by a criterion outside of tradition, namely, the Spirit of the living Christ as he resides and abides within the community of the faithful' (J.K.A. Smith, 'The Closing of the Book', *JPT* 11 [1997], pp. 68-69, n. 68).

[205] Irvin, 'Contextualization and Catholicity', p. 93.

[206] Overcoming the obstacles that prevent dialogue between Christianity and other religions is the goal of Yong's *Discerning the Spirit(s)*.

> tion of texts. However, the notion of what constitutes a text has broadened considerably. For example, one can conceive of the meaningful action of a faith community as a social text which is subject to hermeneutical investigation.[207]

Later he writes, 'Meaningful actions are now included in the intertextual relationships of hermeneutical activity.'[208] The next chapter is an attempt to offer an articulation of the theological context from which my interpretation of the role of the Spirit in the Apocalypse is offered.[209]

[207] M.W. Dempster, 'Paradigm Shifts and Hermeneutics: Confronting Issues Old and New', p. 129.

[208] Dempster, 'Paradigm Shifts and Hermeneutics', p. 129.

[209] Following a similar method, but from a different vantage point, N.P. Frantz offers intertextuality as a means for Anabaptist women to engage in the larger theological discussion on Scripture without losing their distinctive pietist/feminist perspective. See her article, 'The (Inter)Textuality of Our Lives: An Anabaptist Feminist Hermeneutic', *CGR* 14 (1996), pp. 131-144.

3

Hearing What the Spirit Says to the Churches: Profile of a Pentecostal Reader of the Apocalypse

1. In(tro)duction to Pentecostalism: A Text to be Interpreted

This chapter seeks to venture in a postmodern direction by unequivocally acknowledging my own socio-religious context, namely Pentecostalism.[1] There are distinctives within the worldview of Pentecostalism which have predisposed the manner in which I interpret the biblical texts.[2] Thus in this chapter, I sketch the contours of Pentecostalism and suggest a possible hermeneutic which is faithful to the ethos of the movement. Following the delineation of a Pentecostal hermeneutic, I examine the work on the role of the Spirit in the Apocalypse by a few Pentecostal scholars to see to what extent their theological persuasion has affected their work. The chapter ends with a turn toward the Apocalypse to see what additional insights the book might contain toward further development of the hermeneutic.

The previous chapters contained two latent methodological slogans which provide the impetus for the following characterization of the ethos of Pentecostalism. The first can be referred to as the 'contextualization of interpretation'. I.T. Beckwith acknowledges that the supposedly impartial exegeses of biblical texts, often showcasing 'the ingenuity of interpreters', have consistently been swayed by the scholar's circumstances, either political or ecclesiastical, and by the methodology

[1] For a prospectus on the future of Pentecostal scholarship see the Society for Pentecostal Studies presidential address of J.C. Thomas, 'Pentecostal Theology in the Twenty-First Century', *Pneuma* 20 (1998), pp. 3-19; repr. in idem, *The Spirit of the New Testament* (Blandford: Deo Publishing, 2005), pp. 4-22.

[2] S.A. Ellington has explored the relationship between a distinctive Pentecostal worldview and the Pentecostal appropriation of scripture (S.A. Ellington, 'Pentecostalism and the Authority of Scripture', *JPT* 9 [1996], pp. 16-38).

and hermeneutic applied to the text.[3] Like the interpreters before me, I too have been influenced by my circumstances along with my presuppositions concerning the text of the Apocalypse. As a member of a Pentecostal community of faith, I acknowledge that I am influenced by a particular Gestalt or pretext which predisposes my interpretation of the biblical texts. Any reading that is explicitly *pro nobis* must concede that the context of the community (in)forms the interpretation.[4] In a similar vein, E. Schüssler Fiorenza accentuates the 'plurality of meaning' (the second methodological slogan) when she observes that the imaginative language of Revelation need not be exegetically reduced to a one-to-one meaning but rather be allowed to evoke 'imaginative participation'.[5]

[3] I.T. Beckwith, *The Apocalypse of John* (Grand Rapids: Baker Book House, 1967, repr. of 1919 edition), p. 319. Surprisingly, as early as 1919, Beckwith foreshadows the emphasis within biblical studies that has recently been placed on the reception of the text. Noting the tacit subjectivism in his observation, Beckwith advises close attention to the historical situation of the original author and his or her audience as well as attention to the literary influences of the text, in the case of the Apocalypse primarily Jewish apocalypses and the Old Testament. I understand this advice to be Beckwith's attempt to set boundaries for the proper influences on the scholar in order to produce an accurate interpretation.

[4] For an excellent example of a Pentecostal *pro nobis* reading see F. Cimpean, 'From Margins to Center: Pentecostal and Orthodox Readings of Romans 8 in Romania', *JPT* (forthcoming). Cimpean argues that the theological crux of Romans is life in the Spirit as recorded in ch. 8, the center of the book. The Western interpretation which focuses on justification by faith is practically mute in the Eastern context of Romanian Pentecostalism and the Eastern Orthodox church. See also S.E. Fowl, ed., *The Theological Interpretation of Scripture: Classic and Contemporary Readings* (Cambridge: Blackwell, 1997), a reader of theological interpretations of scripture; idem, 'The New Testament, Theology and Ethics', in *Hearing the New Testament,* ed. J.B. Green (Grand Rapids: Eerdmans, 1995), pp. 394-410; S.E. Fowl and L.G. Jones, *Reading in Communion: Scripture and Ethics in Christian Life* (Grand Rapids: Eerdmans, 1991); S. Fish, *Is There a Text in This Class? The Authority of Interpretative Communities* (Cambridge, MA: Harvard University Press, 1980), pp. 303-371.

To refer to a Pentecostal reading as being *pro nobis* does not engender solipsism because the reading is formed by what God is presently saying through the scriptures. The participation between God and the community which is taking place when scriptures are interpreted is analogous to the synergistic involvement of God and the individual in salvation. S. Land writes that salvation requires an 'affective transformation', because, '[s]oteriology is not simply the exposition of redemption accomplished and applied, though it is grounded in what God has done for us. But the 'for us' is grounded in the 'in himself' (the *pro nobis* in the *a se*)' (S.J. Land, 'A Passion for the Kingdom: Revisioning Pentecostal Spirituality', *JPT* 1 [1992], p. 201).

[5] E. Schüssler Fiorenza, *The Book of Revelation*, p. 22. Note the way in which Fio-

'Contextualization' and 'plurality' serve as a pair of shibboleths for a paradigm shift which has been hotly debated in the guild of biblical studies, a shift away from the diachronic historical critical method toward more synchronic narrative methods. Historically, professional biblical scholars examined texts in terms of source criticism and subsequently redaction criticism, focusing on the *Sitz im Leben* of the author and/or the original audience. These historical methods seek to provide an *objective* ground where a critical distance between the scholar and the text can be maintained so that the exegesis is not tainted with the experience of the interpreter. Attempting to discover the historical and literary sources which produced the text, these traditional forms of criticism give little attention to the final form of the text.[6]

In a belated response to New Criticism, a movement within literary studies that concentrated solely on the final form of the text, biblical studies has produced volumes of scholarship concentrating on the narrative integrity of the biblical texts.[7] Although the dominance of the historical-critical approach within biblical scholarship has waned, narrative approaches, which are increasingly claiming a larger portion of the academic pie, continue to maintain a prominent place for the pursuit of objective meaning, albeit *within* the text, as opposed to historical criticism whose attention is primarily *behind* the text.[8] The emphasis

renza's words resonate with Pentecostal theology. 'In the Spirit [Pentecostals] participate in the marriage supper but also live in the 'not yet' of a lost world... the Spirit acts... via the Word, enabling the believer to travel backward and forward in salvation history and to *imaginatively participate* in the events that have been and are yet to be' (S.J. Land, *Pentecostal Spirituality*, p. 98 [italics mine]).

6 An early example of an attempt to rescue a text from the unsatisfactory conclusions of historical criticism is D.J.A. Clines, *I, He, We, and They* (Sheffield: Sheffield Academic Press, 1976). Clines offers a 'rhetorical' reading of Isaiah 53, maintaining the passage's integrity as a poem and avoiding the historical temptation to crack the code.

7 Very little work has been done on Revelation from a narrative-critical viewpoint with the exception of the very good work by David L. Barr, 'The Apocalypse as a Symbolic Transformation of the World: A Literary Analysis', *Int* 38 (1984), pp. 39-50; idem, 'The Apocalypse of John as Oral Enactment', *Int* 40 (1986), pp. 243-256; idem, *New Testament Story: An Introduction* (Belmont: Wadsworth, 1987). Also see R.J. Bauckham's work, which is not necessarily narrative-critical but does give due regard to the final form of the text. For the most part, narrative criticism in biblical studies seems oblivious to New Criticism's demise in its native discipline. Cf. S.D. Moore, *Literary Criticism and the Gospels* (New Haven: Yale University Press, 1989), pp. 108-130.

8 For an explanation of narrative criticism in biblical studies see N.R. Peterson,

on the text within narrative criticism has given way (at least in some parts of the academy) to an emphasis on the reader and his or her context (i.e. reader response and poststructural criticism).[9] These newer approaches, while not abandoning attention to the final form of the text, attach importance to what the reader brings to the text as a vital component in the interpretation of meaning.[10]

Despite the rise of synchronic methods and in the face of the popularity and acceptance of contextual readings (e.g. gender and racial interpretations), the debate continues concerning the extent to which biblical scholars should explicitly integrate their theological convictions[11] when they engage in biblical studies. Be that as it may, Pente-

Literary Criticism for New Testament Critics (Philadelphia: Fortress, 1978); M.A. Powell, *What is Narrative Criticism?* (Minneapolis: Fortress, 1990); G.R. Osborne, *The Hermeneutical Spiral: A Comprehensive Introduction to Biblical Interpretation* (Downers Grove: Inter Varsity Press, 1991), pp. 153-173. W.R. Tate offers an excellent introduction to biblical hermeneutics by dividing scholarship into three sections (the world *behind* the text, the world *within* the text, and the world *in front* of the text) (W.R. Tate, *Biblical Interpretation: An Integrated Approach* [Peabody, Mass.: Hendrickson, 1991]). The origin of modern narrative theory is traced back to T. Todorov, who coined the term 'narratology' in 1969: *Grammaire du Décaméron* (The Hague: Mouton, 1969). See also G. Genette, *Narrative Discourse* (Ithaca: Cornell University Press, 1980); idem, *Narrative Discourse Revisited* (Ithaca: Cornell University Press, 1988).

[9] Reader response criticism is so discursive that it may have been placed alongside narrative criticism; however, the juxtaposition of 'reader response' with 'poststructuralism' reflects the method's deconstructive accent. See S.D. Moore, *Literary Criticism and the Gospels;* idem, *Poststructuralism and the New Testament: Derrida and Foucault at the Foot of the Cross* (Minneapolis: Fortress, 1994); J.P. Tompkins, ed., *Reader-Response Criticism: From Formalism to Post-Structuralism* (Baltimore: Johns Hopkins University Press, 1980).

[10] Examples of these contextual readings would include feminist readings, African American readings, psychoanalytical readings, liberation readings and many other voices from the margins which have taught that the view from the fringe is not always identical with the traditional interpretation of sacred texts.

[11] See R.D. Moore's testimonial introduction, where he deconstructs the binary opposites so prevalent in the academy of criticism and confession. Scholarship has long favored criticism regulating confession to the church but Moore shows how these opposites are not as exclusive as previously thought. Cf. R.D. Moore, 'Deuteronomy and the Fire of God: A Critical Charismatic Interpretation', *JPT* 7 (1995), p. 20; idem, 'Canon and Charisma in the Book of Deuteronomy', *JPT* 1 (1993), p. 92. In the latter article, Moore brings together another binary opposite (written revelation and spoken revelation). Contrary to J. Derrida, Moore does not privilege writing nor does he privilege speech but rather holds the two in a continual tension, maintaining a harmony between *'a law so righteous'* (the inscripturated revelation) and the *'God -so-near'* (charismatic revelation). I will comment more on this later. Al-

costals (especially those of the rank and file) read the Bible theologically as divinely inspired scripture which can and will speak directly to their present situations and will affect every aspect of their lives.[12] Thus, a Pentecostal reading would be both synchronic, focusing on the final form of the text, and theological, allowing the ethos and experience of the tradition to inform the interpretation theologically. Perhaps owing to the strong ecclesiastical commitments of most Pentecostal biblical scholars, theological implications have always been an implicit part of their hermeneutical *telos*, yet I am proposing that an explicit theological hermeneutic,[13] applied throughout the interpretive process and not restricted to *a posteriori* reflection, is essential in order to produce a Pentecostal reading of a text.

By proposing that a Pentecostal reading must be theological, I am not disparaging historical methods or non-theological interpretations, for they continue to offer vital insights into the biblical texts which serve to enlighten the academy.[14] Indeed it is possible for a Pentecostal

though he advocates a synchronic method, Moore questions the infatuation with the *'final form'* using the words of Moses as a warning, 'Take heed to yourselves, since you saw no form on the day that Yahweh spoke to you at Horeb out of the midst of the fire' (Deut. 4:15, the translation from the Hebrew is Moore's). In God there is no form, only the consuming fire. Moore concludes with a deconstruction of deconstructionism, calling into question the idolatry of 'smashing idols (cf. Jehu in 2 Kgs. 10)'. For Moore, God is the ultimate deconstructionist.

[12] Pentecostals do not have a monopoly on reading the Bible theologically. Indeed, Christians, particularly those not involved in professional biblical studies, have always read theologically. Therefore, the claim that a Pentecostal reading must be theological is not exclusive, although a Pentecostal reading will look somewhat different from other theological readings owing to the differences in the respective socio-religious contexts.

[13] F. Watson, *Text Church and World, passim.* Watson builds on the work of B.S. Childs, *Introduction to the Old Testament as Scripture* (London: SCM Press, 1979); idem, *The New Testament as Canon: An Introduction* (London: SCM Press, 1984); H.W. Frei, *The Eclipse of Biblical Narrative: A Study in Eighteenth and Nineteenth Century Hermeneutics* (New Haven: Yale University Press, 1974). See R. Morgan with J. Barton, *Biblical Interpretation* (Oxford: Oxford University Press, 1988); and A.C. Thiselton's critical appreciation of Morgan's work in A.C. Thiselton, 'On Models and Methods: A Conversation with Robert Morgan', in *The Bible in Three Dimensions,* pp. 337-356.

[14] Hollenweger has argued that Pentecostals should embrace the findings of historical criticism in their congregations and not limit these historical insights to their seminaries (W.J. Hollenweger, 'Intellectual Honesty and Healing the Wounds of Division' [keynote address presented to the 28th Annual Meeting of the Society for Pentecostal Studies, 1999]). The value of historical criticism for a Pentecostal or any Christian congregation is debatable. See the dissident comment by S.E. Fowl, 'Until

scholar to address a topic of interest for Pentecostals without employing an explicitly Pentecostal method.[15] However, I wish to differentiate between the examination of a topic which interests Pentecostals and the explicitly Pentecostal examination of a topic. In this study, it is my intention to follow the latter method as I investigate the role of the Spirit in Revelation. The following section is a description of the origins and theological ethos of Pentecostalism which will serve as a contextual intertext[16] for both the development of a Pentecostal herme-

the historical-critical method becomes critical of its own theoretical foundations and develops a hermeneutical theory adequate to the nature of the text which it is interpreting it will remain restricted... to the guild and the academy, where the question of truth can endlessly be deferred' (S.E. Fowl, ed., *The Theological Interpretation of Scripture,* p. 26).

[15] See J.C. Thomas, *Footwashing in John 13 and the Johannine Community* (Sheffield: Sheffield Academic Press, 1991). While not explicitly engaging in a Pentecostal method, Thomas did participate in process of formation within a worshiping and praying Pentecostal community that innately affected his research and interpretations, thereby leaving traces in the monograph of his Pentecostal theology and praxis. See also J.C. Thomas, 'Reading the Bible from within Our Traditions: A Pentecostal Hermeneutic', in *Between Two Horizons,* ed. J.B. Green and M. Turner (Grand Rapids: Eerdmans, 2000), pp. 108-122. Thomas ends with an autobiographical conclusion in which he delineates the formation and impact provided from his faith community.

[16] The notion of a Pentecostal ethos serving as an intertext has previously been discussed in the Fall 1993 issue of *Pneuma.* These articles encompass the conviction *à la* Gadamer (and Ricoeur) that the shared experience of a community may be envisioned as a text which in turn intersects with a literary text forming the crossroads (or roundabout) of meaning. Utilizing the popular hermeneutical metaphor of a 'fusion of horizons', these scholars envision the relationship between a text and an interpreter: R.D. Israel, D.E. Albrecht and R.G. McNally, 'Pentecostals and Hermeneutics: Texts, Rituals and Community', *Pneuma* 15:2 (1993), pp. 137-161; T.B. Cargal, 'Beyond the Fundamentalist-Modernist Controversy: Pentecostals and Hermeneutics in a Postmodern Age', *Pneuma* 15:2 (1993), pp. 163-187; J-D. Plüss, 'Azusa and Other Myths: The Long and Winding Road from Experience to Stated Belief and Back Again', *Pneuma* 15:2 (1993), pp. 189-201; J. Byrd, 'Paul Ricoeur's Hermeneutical Theory and Pentecostal Proclamation', *Pneuma* 15:2 (1993), pp. 203-214. See also the editorial, M.W. Dempster, 'Paradigm Shifts and Hermeneutics: Confronting Issues Old and New', *Pneuma* 15:2 (1993), pp. 129-135. The preceding issue of *Pneuma* contained four responses which to varying degrees serve as retorts to the articles previously cited. R.P. Menzies offered the most antagonistic retort: 'Jumping Off the Postmodern Bandwagon', *Pneuma* 16:1 (1994), pp. 115-120.

The acknowledgment of the relationship between the context of the reader and the literary text is not unique to theological studies but rather was derived from parallels in the discipline of literary theory. For a sampling, see A. Jefferson, 'Autobiography

neutic and the application of that hermeneutic to the text of Revelation. Beyond the conventional perfunctory justification, the preceding description of my interpretational context contains personal viewpoints.

2. The Origins and Theological Ethos of Pentecostalism

Since the birth of the movement at the beginning of the twentieth century, Pentecostalism has affected almost every facet of Christianity.[17] Despite its vast size and perhaps owing to the movement's demographics, the impact of Pentecostalism on biblical scholarship has been minimal in comparison to the movement's growth. The majority of Pentecostals are located on the margins of society, but nevertheless constitute twenty-one percent of organized global Christianity. According to a 1988 survey, seventy-one percent of the Pentecostals in the world are non-white. The same survey classifies Pentecostals as being 'more urban than rural, more female than male, more children (under eighteen) than adults, more third world than western world, more living in poverty than affluence, more family-related than individualist'.[18] The gender, racial, and socio-economic characteristics of the movement have been immanent since its inception.

The origins of Pentecostalism can be traced back to a revival held at the Bethel Bible School in Topeka, Kansas in January 1901, when a teenage girl by the name of Agnes Ozman became the first person in modern times to be 'baptized in the Spirit and speak in other tongues'. The Bethel Bible School was under the direction of Charles F. Parham

as Intertext: Barthes, Sarraute, Robbe-Grillet', in *Intertextuality: Theories and Practices,* ed. M. Worton and J. Still (Manchester: Manchester University Press, 1990), pp. 108-129.

[17] To access the history and development of Pentecostalism, a good place to begin is V. Synan, ed., *The Holiness-Pentecostal Movement in the United States* (Grand Rapids: Eerdmans, 1971); R.M. Anderson, *Vision of the Disinherited: The Making of American Pentecostalism* (Peabody: Hendrickson, 1972); W.J. Hollenweger, *The Pentecostals* (Peabody: Hendrickson, 1972); D.W. Dayton, *Theological Roots of Pentecostalism* (Metuchen: Scarecrow, 1987); S.J. Land, *Pentecostal Spirituality;* H. Cox, *Fire From Heaven: The Rise of Pentecostal Spirituality and the Reshaping of Religion in the Twenty-first Century* (Reading: MA: Addison-Wesley, 1995); D.W. Faupel, *The Everlasting Gospel: The Significance of Eschatology in the Development of Pentecostal Thought* (Sheffield: Sheffield Academic Press, 1996). For bibliographical resources see G. Wacker, 'Bibliography and Historiography of Pentecostalism (U.S.)', *DPCM,* pp. 65-76.

[18] D.B. Barrett, 'Statistics, Global', *DPCM,* p. 811.

who had been teaching that the chief distinctive which had been present at Pentecost as recorded in Acts 2 but was absent in the church of his day was glossolalia, popularly referred to as 'speaking in tongues'. The effect of the 1901 revival was not felt on a world wide scale until William J. Seymour, a one-eyed black holiness preacher who had been influenced by Parham's teaching, moved to Los Angeles, California. It was in Los Angeles that Seymour led a revival at the Azusa Street Mission which lasted for three years (1906-1909). Those who attended Azusa Street and the hundreds of other Pentecostal revivals that had sprung up around the world experienced a resurgence of the gifts of the Spirit as recorded in 1 Corinthians 12, which had only been practiced in the ecclesiastical margins, at least in the West, through the centuries.

In addition to the new emphasis on spiritual gifts, Pentecostalism was also experiencing a new-found equality that was cutting across traditional lines of race, gender and socio-economic class.[19] Seymour attributed the diversity of the earliest participants to divine providence, offering an opportunity to experience the refreshing of the Spirit to those who were otherwise marginal in society. Seymour rejoices over the benefit of his eclectic congregation in his newspaper, *The Apostolic Faith:*

> If it had started in a fine church, poor colored people and Spanish people would not have got it, but praise God it started here. God Almighty says He will pour out His Spirit on all flesh... It is noticeable how free all nationalities feel. If a Mexican or German cannot speak in English, he gets up and speaks in his own tongue and feels quite at home for the Spirit interprets through the face and people say amen. No instrument that God can use is rejected on account of color or dress or lack of education. This is why God has so built up the work.[20]

Unfortunately, the unity of the early Pentecostal movement suffered from theological divisions centering on the nature of the Trinity and the essence of sanctification. The movement was further fragmented

[19] Some observers outside the tradition have wrongly deduced that Pentecostalism primarily consisted of an escapist theology that appealed to the lower economic status: R.M. Anderson, *Vision of the Disinherited: The Making of American Pentecostalism* (Peabody: Hendrickson, 1972); L. Pope, *Mill Hands and Preachers: A Study of Gastonia* (New Haven: Yale University Press, 1965).

[20] W.J. Seymour, *The Apostolic Faith* 1:1 (1906), p. 1. Previously cited in S.J. Land, *Pentecostal Spirituality*, p. 17.

by racial divisions and a marginalization of women which infiltrated the movement as it evolved into separate denominations and was compromised by affiliations with non-Pentecostal organizations. This initial phase of Pentecostalism, dubbed 'classical Pentecostalism', is represented primarily in the U.S.A. by the Assemblies of God, Springfield, Missouri; the Church of God, Cleveland, Tennessee; the Church of God in Christ, Memphis, Tennessee; and the International Church of the Foursquare Gospel, Los Angeles, California.

Beginning in the late 1950's the spiritual renewal which marks Pentecostalism experienced a resurgence, this time in the mainline churches.[21] Unlike the classical Pentecostals, who for the most part left their parent Holiness denominations, those involved in the 'Charismatic Renewal' (as this phase is commonly labeled) remained within their churches of origin. This second phase gained national attention in the U.S.A. in 1959, when Dennis Bennett, the rector of St. Mark's Episcopal Church in Van Nuys, California, announced to his congregation that he had been baptized in the Holy Spirit and had spoken in tongues. Glossolalia, albeit a defining characteristic of the renewal, was only one of many charisms included in the worship of the Charismatics. The location of the Charismatic renewal was not limited to Protestant denominations but included scores of Catholics[22] as well as some in the Eastern Orthodox tradition.[23] Although the Charismatics were not primarily from lower socioeconomic classes, the adherents did

[21] P.D. Hocken, 'Charismatic Movement', *DPCM,* pp. 130-160; cf. the following: A. Bittlinger, ed., *The Church Is Charismatic* (Geneva: Renewal and Congregational Life, World Council of Churches, 1981); R. Quebedeaux, *The Charismatics II* (San Francisco: Harper & Row, 1983).

[22] F.A. Sullivan, 'Catholic Charismatic Renewal', *DPCM,* pp. 110-126; cf. the following: N.A. Abbott, ed., *The Documents of Vatican II* (New York: Guild Press, 1966); K. Ranaghan and D. Ranaghan, *Catholic Pentecostals* (Paramus: Paulist Press, 1969); idem, *As the Spirit Leads Us* (Paramus: Paulist Press, 1971); E.D. O'Connor, *The Pentecostal Movement in the Catholic Church* (Notre Dame: Ave Maria Press, 1971); E.D. O'Connor ed., *Perspectives on Charismatic Renewal* (Notre Dame: University of Notre Dame Press, 1974); R. Martin, *The Spirit and the Church: A Personal and Documentary Record of the Charismatic Renewal and the Ways it is Bursting to Life in the Catholic Church* (New York: Paulist Press, 1976); K. McDonnell, *Charismatic Renewal in the Churches* (New York: Seabury Press, 1976); K. McDonnell ed., *Presence, Power, and Praise: documents on the Charismatic Movement* (Collegeville: Liturgical Press, 1980).

[23] E.A. Stephanou, *The Charismatic Renewal in the Orthodox Church: 100 questions most frequently asked about the Orthodox Charismatic Renewal* (Fort Wayne: Logos Ministry for Orthodox Renewal, 1976).

share a desire with the classical Pentecostals to return to a more authentic New Testament experience.[24]

The differences between classical Pentecostalism and the Charismatic renewal have been delineated on two fronts, namely ecclesiology and eschatology. As mentioned above, the ecclesiology of the former movement was sectarian and therefore formed new denominations while the ecclesiology of the latter movement did not venture to establish any new organization, preferring to remain in the churches of origin. In matters of eschatology the classical Pentecostals have a distinctively greater emphasis on apocalypticism than those in the Charismatic renewal. Indeed, permeating every stratum of Pentecostal theology is an apocalyptic expectation that the parousia is imminent. The derivation of this apocalyptic accent is best equated with the Wesleyan Holiness revivals of the nineteenth century. Pentecostalism was not created *ex nihilo* but rather was the product of several convergent streams within the religious landscape, creating a current whose impact has yet to be ultimately determined. In addition to the Wesleyan Holiness doctrine of the pre-millennial coming of Jesus, Pentecostals have also maintained the Wesleyan distinctives of healing and sanctification, to which Pentecostals added their own understanding of the baptism in the Holy Spirit. This final characteristic has been the most conspicuous benchmark for the collective Pentecostal-Charismatic movement.

[24] This brief sketch of the origin of Pentecostalism will suffice for this study. However, the movement has experienced additional rejuvenations. Called the 'Third Wave', as distinct from the 'first wave' (classical Pentecostalism) and the 'second wave' (the Charismatic renewal), the third phase of the movement, whose participants are primarily evangelical Christians, shares the emphases on healing, exorcisms, and prophetic speech with the first two waves, but wishes to distinguish itself in several areas. Third-wavers insist that the baptism in the Holy Spirit occurs at conversion, as opposed to the Wesleyan view of subsequence. Furthermore, they avoid such self designations as 'charismatic' and 'Spirit-filled' in order to accommodate those in their congregations who do not participate in the charismatic style of worship; cf. C.P. Wagner, 'Third Wave', *DPCM,* pp. 843-844; idem, 'The Third Wave', *Christian Life* (September 1984), p. 90. The most recent rejuvenation of Pentecostal motifs in the church has been associated with the so-called 'Toronto Blessing'. For a critical appraisal cf. the following: F.D. Macchia, 'Guest Editorial: 'The Toronto Blessing': No Laughing Matter', *JPT* 8 (1996), pp. 3-6; M.M. Poloma, 'The Spirit Movement in North America at the Millennium: From Azusa Street to Toronto, Pensacola and Beyond', *JPT* 12 (1998), pp. 83-107; L. Pietersen, ed., *The Mark of the Spirit? A Charismatic Critique of the Toronto Blessing* (Carlisle: Paternoster, 1998).

The heart of Pentecostal theology is centered on five principal motifs which have comprised the major tenets of the so-called 'full gospel' (i.e. justification by faith in Christ, sanctification by faith as a second definite work of grace, baptism in the Holy Spirit evidenced by speaking in tongues, healing of the body provided in the atonement, and the pre-millennial return of Christ).[25] The emphasis these fundamentals have received throughout church history may be traced from Luther (justification) through Wesley (sanctification) to Cullis (healing) and the prophecy preachers of the nineteenth century (pre-millennial second coming), culminating in the Azusa Street revival (baptism in the Spirit). The full gospel developed a distinctively Christological accent within Pentecostalism as its early adherents testified that Jesus Christ was their Savior, Sanctifier, Spirit Baptizer, Healer, and Coming King.

Often attempts to pigeon-hole the Pentecostal movement by locating it within the broader stream of Christianity err in a reductionistic fashion, either by delimiting the movement as being 'essentially fundamentalist Christianity with a doctrine of Spirit baptism and gifts added on ... [or] as an experience which fits equally well in any spirituality or theological system – perhaps adding some needed zest of interest'.[26] Avoiding this reductionistic characterization, S.J. Land has offered a litany of paradoxical continuities and discontinuities between Pentecostalism and other streams of Christianity. Land writes:

> [Pentecostalism] is more Armenian than Calvinist in its approach to issues of human agency and perseverance. It is more Calvinist than Lutheran in its appreciation of the so-called 'third use of the Law' to guide Christian growth and conduct. It is more Eastern than Western in its understanding of spirituality as perfection and participation in the divine life (*theosis*) ... [it] is more Catholic than Protestant in emphasizing sanctification-transformation more than forensic justification, but more Protestant than Catholic in the conviction that the Word is the authority over the church and tradition for matters of faith, practice, government and discipline. In its origins Pentecostalism was more Anabaptist than the magisterial Reformation in its concern for peace and a covenanted believers' church where discipleship

[25] The extent to which the fivefold gospel has affected Pentecostalism can hardly be overstated, as is clearly demonstrated by S.J. Land, *Pentecostal Spirituality,* D.W. Faupel, *The Everlasting Gospel,* and D.W. Dayton, *Theological Roots of Pentecostalism*. Dayton represents a subtle difference in his work by focusing on a fourfold rather than a fivefold center by excluding any significant discussion on sanctification, though Dayton acknowledges the existence of the fivefold model.

[26] Land, *Pentecostal Spirituality,* p. 29.

> and discipline are essential features of congregational life. Pentecostalism has a more Holiness-evangelical hermeneutic than the fundamentalist-evangelical tradition in terms of its actual use of Scripture and understanding of the role of reason.[27]

As Land has argued, the ethos of Pentecostalism, albeit distinctive, intersects with every branch of Christianity. Thus, although a Pentecostal reading will be sectarian (i.e. *pro nobis*), there will certainly be times when the interpretation will resonate with an ecumenical ring. Indeed it is my hope that others will be able not only to differentiate themselves from my interpretations but also to find places of self-recognition.[28] For I suspect that Pentecostals have a distinctive contribution to offer to the academic disciplines of biblical studies and hermeneutics.

3. Toward a Pentecostal Theological Hermeneutic

Discussions concerning hermeneutics have preoccupied Pentecostal scholars for almost two decades. A large portion of the attention given to 'Pentecostal hermeneutics' has been primarily theoretical, arguing on the one hand the validity of a Pentecostal distinctive in biblical interpretation, and on the other hand arguing to what extent post-modern literary theory should be employed by a Pentecostal interpreter.[29] The present contribution to the discussion is by no means

[27] Land, *Pentecostal Spirituality*, pp. 29-30.

[28] I have gleaned these sentiments from Land, *Pentecostal Spirituality*, p. 7. See the Society for Pentecostal Studies presidential address of C. Bridges Johns, 'The Adolescence of Pentecostalism: In Search of a Legitimate Sectarian Identity', *Pneuma* 17 (1995), pp. 3-17; P.D. Hanson, 'Scripture, Community and Spirit: Biblical Theology's Contribution to a Contextualized Christian Theology', *JPT* 6 (1995), pp. 3-12; D.T. Irvin, '"Drawing All Together in One Bond of Love": The Ecumenical Vision of William J. Seymour and the Azusa Street Revival', *JPT* 6 (1995), pp. 25-53. Cf. W. Brueggemann, 'II Kings 18-19: The Legitimacy of a Sectarian Hermeneutic', *HBT* 8 (1985), pp. 1-42.

[29] For a bibliography see J.C. Thomas, 'Women, Pentecostals and the Bible: An Experiment in Pentecostal Hermeneutics', *JPT* 5 (1994), pp. 41-56, n. 4; see also K.J. Archer, 'Pentecostal Hermeneutics: Retrospect and Prospect', *JPT* 8 (1996), pp. 63-81. Cf. F.L. Arrington, 'Hermeneutics', *DPCM*, pp. 376-389; R. Stronstad, 'The Dynamics of a Pentecostal Pneumatology: Essays in Hermeneutics and Theology' (unpublished monograph); J.W. Wycoff, 'The Relationship of the Holy Spirit to Biblical Hermeneutics', Ph.D. thesis (Baylor University, 1990); M.S. Clark, 'An Investigation into the Nature of a Viable Pentecostal Hermeneutic', D.Th. thesis (Uni-

new. The acknowledgement that Bible reading should be interwoven with theological convictions and insights was endemic to all premodern biblical interpretation (e.g. Tertullian, whose Montanist persuasion resonates quite nicely with Pentecostals).[30] Tertullian shunned the idea of anyone attempting to interpret the biblical texts by means of philosophy, for 'what indeed has Athens to do with Jerusalem? What concord is there between the Academy and the Church? What between heretics and Christians?'[31] According to Tertullian, coalescing philosophy and revelation would result in unfaithfulness to the latter. I do not suspect that the average Pentecostal sitting on a church pew makes a conscious effort to read his or her scriptures theologically, yet

versity of South Africa, 1997).

While the majority of material on Pentecostal hermeneutics has been theoretical, there have been a few pieces which have focused primarily on reading a particular text, though the larger task of defining a Pentecostal style of reading has been on the horizon. I would like to highlight four such contributions. (1) R.O. Baker, 'Pentecostal Bible Reading: Toward a Model of Reading for the Formation of Christian Affections', *JPT* 7 (1995), pp. 34-48. Baker offers a reading of the death of Jesus in the fourth Gospel which was influenced by his own experience of the death of his grandmother and the affections he was able to draw on because of his experience. (2) R.D. Moore, '"And Also Much Cattle?!": Prophetic Passions and the End of Jonah', *JPT* 11 (1997), pp. 35-48. Moore offers a reading of the book of Jonah based on an assumption that consideration of Jonah's passions will get at the *heart* of the text and parallel the *heart* of the Pentecostal experience. (3) J.C. Thomas, 'Women, Pentecostals and the Bible', pp. 41-56. Thomas renders a reading of Acts 15 and its record of the Jerusalem Council, offering the practice of the early church as an exemplar for the contemporary church to use during theological deliberations. Thomas continues by testing his theory with the topic of women in ministry. (4) L.R. McQueen, *Joel and the Spirit: The Cry of a Prophetic Hermeneutic* (Sheffield: Sheffield Academic Press, 1995). This monograph may be the most extensive attempt to read an entire book of the Bible in a Pentecostal manner. McQueen delves into his own experience of 'praying through' in order to tap into the idea of lament which permeates the book of Joel.

[30] J. McKay, 'When the Veil is Taken Away: The Impact of Prophetic Experience on Biblical Interpretation', *JPT* 5 (1994), p. 25. McKay acknowledges the partiality of Tertullian for 'spiritual' Christians of his own Montanist church as opposed to 'natural' believers (*psychici*) in other churches. McKay, who also refers to similar sentiments in Irenaeus (*Adv. Her.* 5:6:1), pushes further back to the comments in the New Testament. Paul writes to the Corinthian church, 'The man without the Spirit (ψυχικο'ς) does not accept the things that come from the Spirit of God, for they are foolishness to him, and he cannot understand them, because they are spiritually discerned. The spiritual man (πνευματικός) makes judgments about all things' (1 Cor. 2:14-15 NIV translation, previously cited by McKay).

[31] *Prescription against Heretics,* 7 (*ANF,* 3:246).

on the other hand, there is nothing that is non-theological about the expectation maintained by the Pentecostal reader that God will unfailingly speak through the scriptures. Thus, it is with a somewhat latent effort to be faithful to the Spirit in which the biblical texts have been written that Pentecostals read the Bible theologically.

Approaching the Bible theologically is certainly not restricted to Pentecostals. Indeed, a good deal of recent hermeneutical work has argued that the Bible should be studied outside of a community of faith whose scripture it is. The debate over the development of a theological hermeneutic can be seen by contrasting the work of F. Watson[32] and P. Davies.[33] Watson, on the one hand, argues that every biblical scholar should pursue theological issues while critiquing a biblical text; Davies, on the other hand, argues that professional biblical studies should be free of all theological discussion, discussion which he would regulate to the church. I disagree with Watson that theological issues are the only appropriate pursuit for biblical scholars but I also disagree with Davies that the university has no place for theological inquiry.[34] The key to the issue is that a 'neutral' approach does not exist; therefore, the most responsible way forward is for scholars to acknowledge the subjectivity of their perspectives.[35]

The reluctance to integrate biblical studies and theology is not limited to biblical scholars. Theologians as well question whether the technical analysis of biblical scholars can be relevant for systematic theology. B.S. Childs has pioneered readings and interpretations that bridge the gap between biblical studies and theology caused by the professionalization of these respective disciplines. Childs calls into question the ability of historical criticism to begin with the neutral task of description. Childs writes, 'It is commonly assumed that the responsible exegete must start with the descriptive task and then establish a

[32] F. Watson, *Text, Church and World: Biblical Interpretation in Theological Perspective* (Grand Rapids: Eerdmans, 1994).

[33] P. Davies, *Whose Bible is it Anyway?* (Sheffield: Sheffield Academic Press, 1995).

[34] See also M.G. Brett, 'Four or Five Things To Do with Texts: A Taxonomy of Interpretative Interests', in *The Bible in Three Dimensions: Essays in Celebration of Forty Years of Biblical Studies in the University of Sheffield,* ed. D.J.A. Clines *et al.* (Sheffield: Sheffield Academic Press, 1990), pp. 356-377.

[35] See I. Paul, 'The Value of Paul Ricoeur's Hermeneutic of Metaphor in Interpreting the Symbolism of Revelation Chapters 12 and 13', Ph.D. thesis (Nottingham Trent University, 1998), p. 216.

bridge to the theological problem. It is felt that the real problem lies with the second task. Rather, the reverse is true.'[36]

Before proceeding with a possible profile of a theological hermeneutic, I should perhaps digress by offering a clarification of how the word 'theological' is being used in this context. When juxtaposing 'theological' with 'Pentecostal', I am suggesting, in agreement with Watson, that Christian scholars ought to read from a confessional point of view. The intended meaning of 'theological' in this context is more akin to 'spiritual' (Rev. 11 the witnesses saw the city 'spiritually' and called it Sodom and Egypt). Spiritual is not mystical because the reality of the spirituality is in a concrete context of love and passion, pain and pleasure, happiness and sorrow. Thus, for Pentecostals, a spiritual reading is not a head trip nor solely a heart trip but rather an exercise in imagination that is grounded by the contextual realism of the spirituality. Instead of subsuming 'theological' under an Enlightenment rationalistic model, I wish to circumvent such a dependence, preferring in its place a more Hebrew notion. 'Theology', which means 'study of God', is flipped on its head in Judaism because God is not the object of study but rather the subject. When reading scripture (the Word of God) theologically, the reader/believer is encountering the living God. Following R.D. Moore, I choose to understand 'Word of God' as an event (דבר). A theological reading is not merely a deduction but rather a revelation (ἀποκάλυψις). This revelatory idea may be complemented with an understanding of another Hebrew word, ידע. Traditionally translated 'to know', 'the Hebrew term resists such a subject–object dichotomy and points more to the actualization of a relationship between knower and known'.[37] Thus, a Pentecostal theological hermeneutic has less to do with Greek philosophy than with theophany, a divine encounter, a revelation, an experience with the living God.[38]

[36] B.S. Childs, 'Interpretation in Faith', *Int* 18 (1964), p. 260.

[37] R.D. Moore, 'Canon and Charisma', pp. 90-91. See the discussion of *yd'* in J.D. Johns and C. Bridges Johns, 'Yielding to the Spirit: A Pentecostal Approach to Group Bible Study', *JPT* 1 (1993), pp. 109-134. See also the comments of C.H. Pinnock, 'The Work of the Holy Spirit in Hermeneutics', *JPT* 2 (1995), p. 13. Pinnock writes, 'Interpretation is about more than retrieving information – it is also about the effects on readers that texts can set in motion'.

[38] Pentecostal readings, even of the Old Testament, will often exhibit a Christological accent owing in part to the strong Christological emphasis in the fivefold gospel. F. Watson addresses the issue of the Hebrew scriptures being read with a Christological twist. Watson acknowledges that the New Testament and the Old Testa-

Working with the above definition of 'theological', the discussion may now return to the delineation of a theological hermeneutic. Pentecostals are far more interested in the narrative of their spiritual experience than in the main concerns of modernity. Therefore, a theological reading will have some defining characteristics which reveal its recalcitrance toward not only the historical-critical method but modernity as well. The relationship between Pentecostalism and modernity is quite antithetical and yet the 'postmodern' label does not quite fit either. S.E. Fowl has suggested the use of the neologism, 'non-modern'.[39] Fowl lists four defining characteristics of a non-modern interpretation:

> First, it will be interested in premodern biblical interpretation. Second, it will shape and be shaped by the concerns of Christian communities seeking to live faithfully before the triune God rather than by the concerns of a discipline whose primary allegiance is to the academy. Third, theological interpretation of scripture will try to reject and resist the fragmentation of theology into a set of discrete disciplines that was a result of the conceptual aims of modernity and the practical result of professionalization. Finally, theological interpretation of scripture will be pluralistic in its interpretative methods; it will even use the interpretative methods of modernity to its own ends.[40]

ment are 'distinct' but 'inseparable', being mutually shaped by the other. He writes, 'Either the Hebrew scriptures are the sole property of the Jewish community, in which case the Christian church should denounce all claim on them; or they can also be read as the Christian Old Testament'. Watson is insightful to point out that tension with his conclusion is more often levied from the historical-critical approach than from the Jewish community (F. Watson, *Text Church and World*, p. 3).

Again Pinnock is helpful. He writes, 'The Old Testament is being read in the light of the new situation created by the coming of Jesus Christ and the Spirit is indicating meanings that do not correspond to the grammatical–historical meaning of the text'. He continues, the early theologians 'employed spiritual reading which allowed them to move in the midst of a kaleidoscope of biblical imagery... They knew that texts can cause dynamic things as the Spirit actualizes their message in our consciousness' (C.H. Pinnock, 'The Work of the Holy Spirit in Hermeneutics', p. 13).

[39] S.E. Fowl, ed., *The Theological Interpretation of Scripture,* p. xvi. The term 'non-modern' is preferred over the more popular 'postmodern'. For the precarious relationship between Pentecostalism and postmodernity see J.D. Johns, 'Pentecostalism and the Postmodern Worldview', *JPT* 7 (1995), pp. 73-96. Johns may also be credited with the trope, 'para-modern', as an alternative to 'postmodern'.

[40] S.E. Fowl, ed., *The Theological Interpretation of Scripture,* p. xvi.

Each of these characteristics of a non-modern approach finds substantial parallels within the ethos of Pentecostalism. An examination of these connections will provide the needed light to envision the contours of a Pentecostal theological hermeneutic.

The granting of a significant amount of credence to premodern interpretations and methods is easily justifiable in a postmodern society.[41] The decline of the theory that meaning is singular and the consequential crescendo of the voices from the fringe has deconstructed the historical-critical goal of discovering *the* meaning of a text.[42] Biblical scholarship by and large has treated premodern interpretations as a failure to obtain the single meaning of the text; however, the acceptance of a plurality of meaning rejects any such condemnation. Normally, Pentecostals read with an eye open towards the plain meaning of scripture; however, they are open to the multiple meanings in the texts which the Spirit can and does afford them when they read, a common testimony being 'every time I read, the Lord shows me something new'. Discovering the testimony of the early church will be a new experience for some Pentecostals. The restorationist theme so prominent in the movement has allotted little room for any acknowledgement of church history other than the New Testament stories. The lesson which may be learned from an acquaintance with premodern interpretation is that others too have struggled with the interpretation of scripture before God. The emphasis which Pentecostals have placed on testimonies may provide the vehicle needed with which our churches can learn to appreciate the premodern interpretations. In a post-critical society, nonmodern and reassessed premodern interpretations will determine not only the future of the church but perhaps the academy as well.

Historically, Pentecostalism has been suspicious of the academy. Anti-educational sentiments within the movement have been fueled by the rarity with which the concerns of the academy have paralleled the concerns of the community of faith. In a modern age, a scholar could claim to be pursuing objective truth so that concern (either academic or ecclesiastical) played little or no role in the pursuit. No

[41] D.C. Steinmetz, 'The Superiority of Pre-Critical Exegesis', *Theology Today*, 37, 1 (1980), pp. 27-38.

[42] See the comments of C.S. Lewis on his novel *Till We Have Faces*, where he says 'an author doesn't necessarily understand the meaning of his own story better than anyone else' (W.H. Lewis, ed., *Letters of C.S. Lewis* [New York: Harcourt, Brace and World, 1966], p. 273).

longer may claims of objectivity hide the latent presuppositions which had already been shaping the scholar's vision of the truth, which lacked the intellectual honesty of the contextual nature of his or her perceived truth. Reading the text in the light of a present experience of the community may provide an opportunity for the modern critic to cast the ultimate (historical) judgment against contextual reading (the charge of anachronism). However, inasmuch as it is in continuity with the testimony of the early church, the community continues to be a living organism and not merely an organization, thereby muting the perceived criticism.[43]

As mentioned above Pentecostalism is at its very heart an apocalyptic movement. The expectation of the return of Christ is paramount in Pentecostal theology. This eschatological theme resonates with Fowl's statement that the community in which a non-modern theological reading may take place must be living before the triune God.[44] Throughout history there have been segments of Christianity which have had a strong eschatological emphasis. It is with these groups that Pentecostalism will have the most continuity.

There are many contextual readings of scripture representing various segments of different communities of faith that are vying for the attention of the reader. The most popular readings which explicitly identify their contextual location have been feminist readings and African American readings.[45] Similar to these readings which contain sounds reminiscent of liberation theology,[46] Pentecostal readings will

[43] M. Cartledge, 'Empirical Theology: Towards an Evangelical-Charismatic Hermeneutic', *JPT* 9 (1996), pp. 115-126. Cartledge discusses the relationship of the current church with the testimony of scripture as a dialectic between consistency and innovation which allows room for both the idea that Spirit can speak fresh in today's church but also that the testimony from the past will not be violated.

[44] S.J. Land, 'The Triune Center: Wesleyans and Pentecostals Together in Mission', *WTJ* 34:1 (1999), pp. 83-100. Land defines the Pentecostal-Holiness community with five primary characteristics all of which are framed with the general idea of being trinitarian eschatologically.

[45] F.F. Segovia and M.A. Tolbert, *Reading from This Place: Social Location and Biblical Interpretation in the United States* (Minneapolis: Fortress, 1994).

[46] Liberation theology has many points of contact with Pentecostalism. See C. Bridges Johns, *Pentecostal Formation: A Pedagogy among the Oppressed* (Sheffield: Sheffield Academic Press, 1993). For the relationship of biblical studies to liberation motifs see G. West, *Biblical Hermeneutics of Liberation* (Pietermaritzburg: Cluster, 1991); idem, 'Reading the Bible and Doing Theology in the New South Africa', in *The Bible and Human Society*, ed. D. Carroll, D. Clines and P. Davies (Sheffield: Sheffield

also be from the bottom or from the margins. Pentecostal readings are sympathetic to feminist readings for the majority of Pentecostals are female and although the political climate has digressed into a more chauvinistic model the original Pentecostal movement was able to blur the gender lines in relation to authority and leadership that mirrored the early church. Likewise the majority of Pentecostals are non-white, which places a Pentecostal interpretation in a sympathetic relationship to African American reading as well. The extent to which African spirituality has influenced Pentecostalism can hardly be overstated.[47]

Resisting the temptation to fragment theology into various subdisciplines has been a challenge for Pentecostalism owing to the overwhelming influence of the modern academy. One paramount exception is the work S.J. Land has done on the integral relationship between spirituality and theology. According to Land, spirituality is not separate from theology as a sort of appendix, but is the essence of theology in theory and practice. Spirituality shapes an epistemology and permeates through theology into an ethic that goes out into the world (missionary) because Christ is returning (apocalyptic). In agreement with Land, I see a connection not only between spirituality and the academic discipline of theology but the academic discipline of biblical studies as well. Land fuses together the responses of worship, prayer and witness, responses that correlate with the central affections of gratitude, compassion and courage (respectively). I also have found this fusion of affections and erasure of traditional lines between academic disciplines in the work of R.D. Moore and C. Bridges Johns.

R.D. Moore explains that the caricature of the Pentecostal faith as experienced-based is faulty. Pentecostal worship, albeit ardent, maintains 'an inseparable interplay between knowledge and lived-experience, where knowing about God and directly experiencing God perpetually inform and depend on one another'.[48] Knowledge is here

Academic Press, 1995), pp. 445-58; R.S. Sugirtharajah, ed., *Voices from the Margin: Interpreting the Bible in the Third World* (Maryknoll: Orbis, 1991); J. Levison and P. Pope-Levison, 'Global Perspectives on New Testament Interpretation', in *Hearing the New Testament,* ed. J.B. Green, pp. 329-48; C. Rowland and M. Corner, *Liberating Exegesis: The Challenge of Liberation Theology to Biblical Studies* (Louisville: John Knox Press, 1989).

[47] See W.J. Hollenweger, *The Pentecostals,* pp. 21-28; idem, *Pentecostalism: Origins and Developments Worldwide* (Peabody: Hendrickson, 1997), pp. 18-40; S.J. Land, *Pentecostal Spirituality,* pp. 21-22; H. Cox, *Fire From Heaven,* pp. 139-160, 243-262.

[48] R.D. Moore, 'Pentecostal Approach to Scripture', *The Seminary Viewpoint* 8:1

understood as pointing 'beyond the conceptualization of an object to the actualization of a relationship'.[49] C. Bridges Johns has appropriated postmodern theorizing and deconstruction to the ministries of homiletics and catechesis, emasculating Enlightenment constructs which formed the basis of evangelical models of preaching and teaching, whose 'whole paradigm has served to domesticate the mystery of faith'.[50]

The future relationship between the postmodern world and Pentecostalism is ambiguous. As C. Bridges Johns writes, '[c]ontemporary Christianity seems caught between a past life governed by institutional certitude and a future *seemingly* without instruments of control' (italics mine).[51] She adopts an understanding of time as 'carnival time', a contribution from Mikhail Bakhtin, who described life as a fusion of binary opposites such as sacred/profane, lofty/low, great/insignificant, and wise/stupid. The deconstruction of modern theology will not be replaced by another monolithic system, but rather, a carnival sideshow, where various systems exist in tension.[52]

The ramifications for biblical studies of R.D. Moore's and C. Bridges Johns' observations are multiple, but I would like to note three. First, the difference between subject and object becomes blurred. In a time of carnival, the subject/object becomes a clown constantly changing masks but never surfacing unmasked. Deconstructing the modern notion of presence, the festival of Pentecost offers a presence which comes 'from the wilderness, from "otherness" itself. It comes from the margin and then marginalizes all who claim it,

(1987), p. 4.

49 Moore, 'Pentecostal Approach to Scripture', p. 4.

50 C. Bridges Johns, 'Meeting God in the Margins, Ministry among Modernity's Refugees', in *The Papers of the Henry Luce III Fellows in Theology,* ed. M. Zyniewicz (Atlanta: Scholars Press, 1999), p. 20.

51 Bridges Johns, 'Meeting God in the Margins, Ministry among Modernity's Refugees', p. 7.

52 Another helpful definition of the theological significance of deconstruction comes from F. Watson, *Text, Church, and World,* p. 80. Watson writes that 'from a deconstructive perspective, the assertion that a text has a meaning, or meanings, tacitly assumes the transparency of language to that which lies behind it and which generates it; that is, it assumes that one can transcend language, eventually arriving at the reality to which the language is merely a helpful sign post... Once it is written the meaning never fully exists... The overt logic of the text will always already have been subverted by a covert logic or anti-logic, and the role of deconstructive analysis is to bring this paradoxical situation to light.'

who are claimed by it.'[53] Secondly, C. Bridges Johns highlights the necessity of participation in the Spirit within the teaching/learning process. According to C. Bridges Johns, teaching 'involves an understanding that while critical reflection and dialogue are involved in learning, what is primary is not the critical side but the participatory side'.[54]

Finally, C. Bridges Johns questions the ontological status of the text. Given the nature of text/textus, how are Pentecostals going to articulate their theology of scripture? She writes that 'the biblical text must be approached as an avenue for personal and corporate engagement with God... The written text has an objective, historical reality which cannot properly be understood outside of the bounds of reason. Yet, it is a personal subjective word that is carried along by the Spirit.'[55]

Pentecostals have traditionally maintained a very high view of scripture, albeit vaguely defined. In the August issue of the *Evangel* in 1910, The Church of God published its earliest official statement about scripture: 'The Church of God stands for the whole Bible rightly divided. The New Testament is the only rule for government and discipline.' Later, the Church of God adopted a more evangelical terminology when writing its Declaration of Faith: 'We believe in the verbal inspiration of the Bible.' In a postmodern world where the ontological status of the text has been questioned, evangelical models are being deconstructed.[56] However, the Pentecostal understanding of the relationship between the Spirit and the written text does not suffer the same fate as the fundamentalist doctrines. S.J. Land has discussed the relationship between the Spirit and the text as a dynamic interaction of 'Spirit-Word'.

> The Spirit who inspired and preserved the Scriptures illuminates, teaches, guides, convicts and transforms through the Word today. The Word is

[53] R.D. Moore, 'Deuteronomy and the Fire of God', p. 33.

[54] Bridges Johns, 'Meeting God in the Margins, Ministry among Modernity's Refugees', p. 23.

[55] Bridges Johns, 'Meeting God in the Margins, Ministry among Modernity's Refugees', p. 24.

[56] Cf. the comments of S.A. Ellington: '[t]he Bible is not simply a text about whose propositions we can debate, it is the authoritative word of God *because* the same Holy Spirit who inspired its writers meets us today in its pages. For Pentecostals, biblical authority does not rest in the text we can justify, but in the God that we know in and through the text' (S.A. Ellington, 'Pentecostalism and the Authority of Scripture', p. 24).

alive, quick and powerful, because of the Holy Spirit's ministry. The relation of the Spirit to Scripture is based on that of Spirit to Christ. Even as the Spirit formed Christ in Mary, so the Spirit uses Scripture to form Christ in believers and vice-versa.[57]

Musing about the work of these Pentecostal scholars has demonstrated Fowl's final point that the method of a theological hermeneutic will be pluralistic. Indeed there is not so much a single Pentecostal method but rather multiple strategies which are faithful to the tradition without doing violence to the text.[58] In Pentecostalism, the hermeneutics of suspicion gives way to an open heart which is longing to be formed by God via the Spirit into the image of Christ. Understanding the Word of God requires a local hermeneutic that is sensitive to the spiritual context. Fowl's concluding comments in his introduction to his reader are insightful. Proficiency in performing theological interpretations of biblical texts 'is not simply reflected in increased intellectual capacities. Rather, for Christians proficiency in reading scripture theologically is ultimately reflected in a life that is transformed to conform more nearly to the image of Christ.'[59]

It is possible to sum up a Pentecostal hermeneutic with the following motto: 'Unless we believe, we shall not understand.' These words are adapted from the works of Anselm who writes, 'For I do not seek to understand so that I may believe; but I believe so that I may understand. For I believe this also, that unless I believe, I shall not understand.'[60] I modified the words to read with a more communal tone for I have become increasingly convinced that only in the community will we hear the voice of God,[61] or in other words, 'hear what the Spirit is saying to the churches'.

[57] Land, *Pentecostal Spirituality*, p. 100.

[58] I owe this idea of multiple strategies as opposed to a singular method to K.J. Archer. Cf. K.J. Archer, *Forging a New Path, A Contemporary Pentecostal Hermeneutical Strategy for the 21st Century* (London: T. & T. Clark, 2004).

[59] S.E. Fowl, ed., *The Theological Interpretation of Scripture: Classic and Contemporary Readings*, p. xxvi.

[60] *Proslog*. 1 (trans. M.J. Charlesworth, *St. Anselm's Proslogion*, Oxford: Clarendon, 1965), p. 115.

[61] Jack Deere offers his powerful testimony about how he learned to tell the difference between reading the Bible and hearing from God, in his book, *Surprised by the Power of the Spirit*. Deere writes: 'In the process of getting theologically trained and becoming a seminary professor, I developed an intense passion for studying God's Word. I found myself loving the Bible more than I loved the Author of the Bible. I was caught in this trap for more years than I would like to remember... It took me

4. Pentecostal Scholars and the Spirit of the Apocalypse

Now that the Pentecostal ethos has been defined along with a possible hermeneutic, attention can be shifted toward two new questions. First, what contributions have been offered by Pentecostal scholars concerning the role of the Spirit in the Apocalypse? Second, do their interpretations fit the preceding description of the tradition? Three pieces of scholarship have been selected to represent Pentecostalism.[62]

4.1. *S.M. Horton.* Although Horton's work is not solely on the role of the Spirit in the Apocalypse, his thoughts are of importance to a history of interpretation of Pentecostal scholars owing to the magnitude of his influence in the tradition. In reference to the image of the seven spirits, Horton can easily be aligned with Victorinus of Pettau and the others after him who identified the seven spirits as a reference to the seven-fold Spirit of Isaiah 11, which was to rest on the Messiah.[63] Horton places the majority of his discussion of the Spirit in the Apocalypse in a chapter titled, 'The Spirit in the Ministry of the Church', where he sees a close relationship first between the Spirit and Jesus Christ and then between the Spirit and the church. However, given that his primary emphasis in the aforementioned chapter is on Paul's letters, there is little else to glean from Horton's work on this topic.

4.2. *R.H. Gause.* Similar to most commentaries on Revelation, Gause's work does not allot special attention to the role of the Spirit. Thus, his position on the Spirit's role must be extracted by giving attention to the texts which refer to the Spirit. Gause understands the

too long to learn that knowing the Bible is not the same thing as knowing God, loving the Bible is not the same thing as loving God, and reading the Bible is not the same thing as hearing God' (J. Deere, *Surprised by the Power of the Spirit* [Grand Rapids: Zondervan, 1993], p. 187, previously cited in J.K.A. Smith, 'The Closing of the Book: Pentecostals, Evangelicals, and the Sacred Writings', *JPT* 11 [1997], pp. 49-71). Smith argues that Pentecostalism, like the early church, is a 'people of the Spirit' rather than a 'people of the Book'. Smith warns Pentecostals that a certain understanding of the Bible can lead to a textualization that circumvents the present involvement of the Spirit in interpretation of the Biblical texts.

[62] S.M. Horton, *What the Bible Says about the Holy Spirit* (Springfield: Gospel Publishing House, 1976); R.H. Gause, *Revelation: God's Stamp of Sovereignty on History* (Cleveland: Pathway Press, 1983); F. Martin, 'Book of the Apocalypse', *DPCM,* pp. 11-13.

[63] Horton, *What the Bible Says About the Holy Spirit,* p. 61.

symbol of the 'seven spirits' to be a reference to the Spirit of God. Likewise, he sees the phrase ἐν πνεύματι as a description of John's experience with the Holy Spirit. In regard to the hearing formula, Gause writes, 'The Lord's relationship to the Holy Spirit is fundamental to the Church. He forms His Church by the presence of the Holy Spirit in it.'[64] Furthermore, he states that the hearing formula is directed to all churches of all times as the Spirit continues to speak the words of Christ. Gause's work is helpful but somewhat limited given the popular nature of the commentary.

4.3. *F. Martin.* In the *DPCM,* Martin offers a succinct analysis of the Apocalypse focusing on two points that are of special interest to Pentecostals, namely the book's pneumatology and the millennium.[65] With regard to the pneumatology Martin discusses three aspects: (1) the role of the Spirit in the Act of Revelation; (2) the Spirit of Prophecy; and (3) the Spirit and the Church.

Under his first rubric, Martin addresses the phrase ἐν πνεύματι, arguing that the Spirit is the agent of revelation. Martin correctly sees John's appeal to the Spirit as a claim of prophetic authority. He also notes the close relationship between the Spirit in Christ evidenced by the hearing formula in the seven messages which instructs those in the church to hear what the Spirit is saying, despite the fact that Christ is identified as the speaker of the messages. Martin cites John 16:15, 'the Spirit will take from what is mine and make it known to you', as support that the Spirit and Christ are especially close in the Johannine literature.

Commenting on Rev. 19:10, he writes:

> Given the frequency with which the early rabbinic tradition designated the Spirit of God as the 'Spirit of Prophecy', it is clear that Revelation is asserting two things: (1) the role of the Holy Spirit is linked to the witness of Jesus, and (2) this witness is prophecy.[66]

According to Martin, when John identifies his work as 'prophecy', he is avowing dependence on the Spirit.

[64] Gause, *Revelation: God's Stamp of Sovereignty on History* (Cleveland, TN: Pathway Press, 1983), p. 46.

[65] Martin, 'Apocalypse, Book of the', *DPCM,* pp. 11-13.

[66] Martin, 'Apocalypse, Book of the', *DPCM,* pp. 12.

Finally, Martin addresses the Spirit and the Church. Focusing on the direct discourse of the Spirit in Rev. 14:13; 22:17, he asserts that the Spirit is closely related to the life of the church and is indeed the source of life in the resurrection (Rev. 11:11). He concludes the section on the Spirit with a brief discussion on the 'seven spirits', which he identifies as the Spirit, who possesses both the power and the knowledge of the Lamb (cf. Rev. 5:6).

4.4. *Summary*. The contribution of these scholars may best be explained within the context of the history of Pentecostal scholarship. Pentecostal scholarship has been outlined in three distinct phases by the editors of the *Journal of Pentecostal Theology,* in the editorial of the journal's inaugural issue. The first generation includes the earliest Pentecostal scholars who completed post-graduate work despite 'an environment which did not encourage nor even perceive the viability of interaction between Pentecostal faith and critical theological scholarship'.[67] Within the theological subdisciplines of descriptive historical study and social-scientific analysis, a second generation of scholars experienced the 'opportunity for the first time to bring their Pentecostalism to bear upon their graduate research'.[68] With the rise of a third generation, Pentecostal scholars have been given the opportunity to integrate the distinctives of Pentecostal faith with their critical theological research. In the 1998 SPS presidential address, J.C. Thomas suggests that perhaps the rise of a fourth generation of Pentecostal scholarship is being experienced. This generation, according to Thomas, will benefit from the increasing number of Pentecostals within academia and the attention that accompanies any group with such extensive demographics, but more importantly this generation will have the 'opportunity to read, assess, and critique academic works by Pentecostal scholars, an opportunity largely impossible just a few short years ago'.[69] If this assessment of the history of Pentecostal scholarship is accurate, then I would most likely be identified as a member of the fourth generation.

The previous work, while being consistent with the ethos of the movement, has been the labor of earlier generations. Martin's work is

[67] R.D. Moore, J.C. Thomas, & S.J. Land, 'Editorial', *JPT* 1 (1992), p. 3.

[68] Moore, Thomas, & Land, 'Editorial', p. 3.

[69] J.C. Thomas, 'Pentecostal Theology in the Twenty-First Century', *Pneuma* 20 (1998), p. 5.

somewhat of an exception as it shows tremendous foresight, hindered only by its brevity. The time has arrived for a new inquiry by a more recent generation which has the opportunity to integrate more deliberately the Pentecostal ethos and theology into an examination of the biblical texts. At times, Pentecostal scholars have avoided this more difficult task of developing a constructive theology, perhaps owing to an academic inferiority complex.[70] Although Pentecostalism has been historically dubbed as an anti-intellectual movement, W.J. Hollenweger suggests that 'anti-intellectual' is a critique of Pentecostalism 'which can no longer be accepted without qualification'.[71] Hollenweger cites *EPTA Bulletin, Pneuma,* the conference papers from SPS and the European Pentecostal Research Conferences as proof of the scores of first-rate Pentecostal scholarship. The generations of Pentecostal scholars which have gone before me are a rich heritage which I am happy to claim; however, a problem persists, according to Hollenweger, because the scholarly Pentecostal publications 'are not read by Pentecostal leaders (not to speak of the rank and file) who in general have no idea what a mine of insight and dedicated scholarship they are missing'.[72] I regret that Hollenweger's final assessment concerning the minimal impact of Pentecostal scholarship on the leaders and the laity of Pentecostal denominations continues to ring true; however, as the creative and helpful work produced by Pentecostal scholars continues to increase, there are signs that the scholarship is beginning to have an effect. Nevertheless, the chasm between the scholar's study and the church pew is nowhere more evident than in the interpretation of the book of Revelation.

5. A Pentecostal Hermeneutic for Revelation

When the word 'revelation' is used in the title of this section it has a double meaning, for it refers not only to the Apocalypse but also to the event of revelation. Pentecostals would claim that the ability to

[70] C. Bridges Johns has suggested that '[t]here is inherent within the ranks of Pentecostal believers an inferiority complex which assumes that non-Pentecostals know more than we do and do things better than we can' (C. Bridges Johns, *Pentecostal Formation: A Pedagogy among the Oppressed* [Sheffield: Sheffield Academic Press, 1993], p. 7; idem, 'The Adolescence of Pentecostalism: In Search of a Legitimate Sectarian Identity', pp. 3-17).

[71] W.J. Hollenweger, 'The Critical Tradition of Pentecostalism', *JPT* 1 (1992), p. 7.

[72] Hollenweger, 'The Critical Tradition of Pentecostalism', p. 7.

interpret *a* revelation is prerequisite for a valid interpretation of *the* Revelation. Further, the Apocalypse seems to be a good place to pursue the development of a Pentecostal hermeneutic owing to the apocalyptic nature of the movement's ethos. Thus, attention is now turned toward the Revelation with an expectation that not only will the text be unveiled but a hermeneutic may be unveiled as well.

5.1. Apocalypse or Revelation?

The book of Revelation is the first piece of literature included in the apocalyptic genre to use the word 'apocalypse'. The Jewish apocalypses which predate the book of Revelation do not even contain the word. It was not until after the Apocalypse of John that writers of apocalyptic literature began categorizing their works as apocalypses.[73] Therefore, my reading of Revelation takes its first pause after the initial phrase Ἀποκάλυψις Ἰησοῦ Χριστοῦ (the revelation of Jesus Christ), which stands in stark contrast to the title commonly given to the book, ΑΠΟΚΑΛΥΨΙΣ ΙΩΑΝΝΟΥ. Ironically, John is not using the word ἀποκάλυψις to identify his literary work with a particular genre but rather as a description of his experience. The extent to which experience should play a role in interpretation has been a hotly debated topic. Traditionally, Pentecostals have adopted an epistemology that was heavily influenced by their experience in the Spirit; and therefore, Pentecostals may easily identify with the experience of John recorded in the text (i.e. the experience of receiving a revelation).

[73] See J.J. Collins, ed., 'Apocalypse: The Morphology of a Genre', *Semeia* 14 (1979), pp.1-214; D.E. Aune, *The New Testament in its Literary Environment* (Philadelphia: Westminster, 1987), p. 242. and idem, 'The Apocalypse of John and the Problem of Genre', *Semeia* 36 (1986), pp. 65-96. The production of apocalyptic literature experienced a long and prolific climax from the second century BCE to the second century CE. The writers of the apocalypses wrote with pseudonyms, chosen strategically in order to give the literature more authority (e.g. Daniel, Baruch, Ezra, Isaiah, and Abraham). The genre is characterized by its eschatological outlook, which is fixed from an otherworldly perspective. The genre also contains an anti-establishment tone. Cf. L. Alexander, ed., *Images of Empire* (Sheffield: Sheffield Academic Press, 1991). The Jewish apocalypses claim to be in the tradition of their prophets but include concepts of demonology and dualism. Apocalyptic sections can be found in many NT texts (e.g. Mark 13; 1 Thess. 4:15-17; 2 Thess. 2:1-12; 1 Cor. 15:20-28; 2 Cor. 5:1-5; Heb. 12:22-25). Some of the Jewish apocalypses seem to have been edited with a Christian flavor (e.g. 4 Esdras, *Testaments of the Twelve Patriarchs*, *Ascension of Isaiah*, the Christian Sibyllines) and some Christian apocalypses were written (e.g. *Didache* 16, the *Apocalypse of Peter*, and the *Shepherd of Hermas*).

'Apocalypse', which is a transliteration of ἀποκάλυψις, means 'unveiling or revelation', whence the popular title, the 'Book of Revelation'. When John wishes to identify the literary genre of his work, he refers to it as a prophecy, an identification he makes at least five times (Rev. 1:3; 22:7, 10, 18-19), possibly six (Rev. 19:10).[74] Furthermore, John refers to the prophets as his brothers. Since the Apocalypse of John plays such a vital role in defining the apocalyptic genre perhaps it should be included in the list of apocalyptic literature.[75] Nevertheless, the theological significance of the opening phrase cannot be overstated. When reading the Apocalypse or any other passage of scripture, the Pentecostal reader expects to experience a revelation of Jesus Christ as Jesus unveils the meaning of the text for the reader. In a similar fashion, the Pentecostal reader also expects to experience the presence of the Spirit. Therefore, the reader is not surprised when the words of Christ are attributed to the Spirit in the closing endorsement of each letter to the seven churches (i.e. 'let anyone who has an ear, hear what the Spirit is saying to the churches').

Pentecostals accept the Bible by faith as the Word of God which will speak directly to their lives. The Bible is not merely an object to be studied but the Bible is used by Jesus to reveal to the believer personal insight so that as a Pentecostal reader I am apt to find out as much about myself as I am about the text. To put it in theoretical terms, the binary opposites of subject and object are deconstructed in a Pentecostal reading so that, at times, the interpreter of the text will be interpreted by the text.[76]

[74] M.W. Wilson, 'Revelation 19:10 and Contemporary Interpretation', in *Spirit and Renewal: Essays in Honor of J. Rodman Williams,* ed. M.W. Wilson (Sheffield: Sheffield Academic Press, 1994), pp. 191-202.

[75] According to D.E. Aune, the form, content, and function of the Apocalypse of John solidly places the book in the apocalyptic genre. Aune suggests that no ancient revelatory literature was considered to be unequivocal. The intentional ambiguity necessitates an interpretation, therefore perpetuating further revelations. According to Aune, 'the hearers must use their imaginations to understand [the visions] ... [and] experience for themselves the revelatory experience narrated by John' (D.E. Aune, *The New Testament in its Literary Environment,* p. 231). Cf. C. Rowland, *The Open Heaven: A Study of Apocalyptic in Judaism and Early Christianity* (New York: Crossland, 1982), pp.403-441. Against this, F.D. Mazzaferri argues that on the basis of generic definition Revelation fails to qualify as classical apocalyptic literature (F.D. Mazzaferri, *The Genre of the Book of Revelation from a Source-Critical Perspective* [New York: de Gruyter, 1989], pp. 223-258).

[76] R.D. Moore, 'Pentecostal Approach to Scripture', p. 4.

As for the genitive construction of Ἰησοῦ Χριστοῦ, the Pentecostal interpreter need not decide between objective and subjective genitive but rather understand the construction to be both objective *and* subjective. Jesus is certainly the subject as the revealer of the mysteries of God, yet He is also the object in that He reveals himself to John and to those who believe. The initial vision that John receives in Rev. 1:10-16 is a vision in which Christ reveals himself to John. I am proposing that the only interpretation of the biblical texts that a Pentecostal community will endorse is an interpretation which is centered on Jesus Christ.[77] Thus, I suggest that ἀποκάλυψις should be translated instead of being transliterated so that the experiential nature of the word might be emphasized and thereby shared with the reader. Acknowledging the necessity of revelation within the interpretative process of reading the Bible raises additional questions concerning the objective and subjective nature of the text and of interpretation.[78]

5.2. The Status of Scripture

The status of scripture is addressed early in the first chapter of Revelation, where John declares in the first beatitude, 'Blessed is the one who reads and those who hear the words of the prophecy and keep what is written therein, for the time is near' (Rev. 1:3). In Rev. 1:11, John records Jesus' instruction for him to 'write in a book what you are seeing and send it to the seven churches'. These two statements concerning John's own written work raise three questions concerning my understanding of scripture. First, what is the relationship between the written dimension of the text and the oral/aural dimension of the text? Second, what is the relationship between properly interpreting the words of the prophecy and the admonition to keep the words of the prophecy? Third, what role do the seven churches play as the recipients of the prophecy in the task of interpretation?

[77] The Christocentric theology of Pentecostals baffles outsiders who would think that the movement is obsessed with the Spirit only. Ironically, one of the major divisions of the Pentecostal movement which is centered on the nature of the Godhead does not revolve around the role of the Spirit but rather the identity of Jesus Christ: Oneness Pentecostals (Jesus Only) baptize in the name of Jesus (the formula found in Acts), while Pentecostal Trinitarians baptize in the name of the Father and of the Son and of the Holy Ghost (the formula found in Matthew).

[78] Bridges Johns, 'Meeting God in the Margins, Ministry among Modernity's Refugees', pp. 24-25.

Although Pentecostals are a 'people of the Book', they are foremost a 'people of the Spirit',[79] who expect the Spirit to speak an *inspired* message to the congregation which is relevant for the time.[80] S.J. Land describes the Spirit as 'the Spirit of Christ who speaks scripturally but also has more to say than scripture'.[81] Pentecostals place in high regard the oral Word of God spoken in the worship services which comes in the form of tongues, interpretation of tongues, prophecies, preaching, and testimonies.[82] The community's role in discerning the interpretation of the oral Word mirrors the community's involvement in discerning the proper interpretation of the written Word.[83]

The blessing of the beatitude is not only for reading and hearing but for *keeping* the words of the prophecy. John seems to be proposing an

[79] I am in agreement with J.K.A. Smith's proposal that Pentecostals (who are an oral community rather than a textual community) are primarily a 'people of the Spirit'. This understanding of Pentecostalism as an oral community does not preclude the use of scripture in the Pentecostal community, indeed it affirms the use of scripture; rather, it places scripture in a subservient relationship to the Spirit. Furthermore, Smith's emphasis on orality does not sanction all spoken word but he acknowledges the authority of the Spirit of Christ who 'resides and abides within the community of the faithful' (J.K.A. Smith, 'The Closing of the Book', p. 68, n. 68).

[80] Traditional doctrines of scripture include an understanding of *inspiration* which is regulated to the writing of scripture; conversely, the act of reading is described as an *illumination*, suggesting that there is a qualitative difference between the divine participation in the act of writing scripture and the divine participation in the act of reading scripture. I agree with Clark Pinnock that the word 'inspiration' serves well to describe both dynamic experiences of writing and reading (cf. C.H. Pinnock, 'The Work of the Holy Spirit in Hermeneutics', p. 3). See also the comment by J.C. Thomas, who writes, 'Scripture cannot be properly appreciated apart from divine inspiration' (J.C. Thomas, *Ministry & Theology: Studies for the Church and Its Leaders* [Cleveland: Pathway Press, 1996], p. 16). Cf. J. Goldingay, *Models for Scripture* (Carlisle: Paternoster, 1994), pp. 257-260.

[81] Land, *Pentecostal Spirituality*, p. 100.

[82] The preference towards speech over writing is a characteristic which Pentecostals share with the early church. Cf. L. Alexander, 'The Living Voice: Scepticism towards the Written Word in Early Christianity and in Graeco-Roman Texts', in *The Bible in Three Dimensions*, ed. D.J.A. Clines *et al.* (Sheffield: Sheffield Academic Press, 1990), pp. 221-247.

[83] The Bible for Pentecostals is not a history book which is free of errors, but rather a testimony of believers who have experienced the provision of God. There is also a sacramental use of the Bible in Pentecostal services. Pentecostal preachers have used their Bibles sacramentally as a sign of the power which is represented within the pages by either raising the book over their heads as if they are wielding a literal sword or by placing their Bibles on the chest or forehead of someone in the altar who has come forward for a prayer of healing.

integration of belief and practice (orthodoxy and orthopraxis). To this integration of belief and practice, Pentecostals would add passion (orthopathy).[84] The ethic derived from the beatitude prepares the believer for the eschatological return of Christ. Keeping the Word of God also has implications for catechesis. Pentecostal children (and students) learn not only to read and hear scripture, but to keep the words as well.[85]

Jesus' command to John to write (Rev. 1:11) was accompanied with the instruction to send his writing to the seven churches. These churches served as communities in which the words of the prophecy could be interpreted. The task of discerning the proper interpretation of the prophecy resides in the community of believers.[86] In Rev. 2:2b, the church at Ephesus is commended for its previous acts of discernment; 'you have tested those who claim to be apostles but are not, and have found them to be false'. It is at this point that the significance of my title comes into play, 'hearing what the Spirit says to the churches'. The title is an adaptation of a repeated endorsement which is recorded in every letter to the individual churches (Rev. 2–3). Although Christ is the speaker of the letters, the churches are admonished to hear the words of the Spirit.

5.3. A Community in the Spirit

In a postmodern world, Pentecostals no longer need to acquiesce to the evangelical doctrine *sola scriptura,* because the revelation of God is not transmitted to new generations by scripture alone but by the work of the Holy Spirit. The Protestant doctrine of *sola scriptura* in its original form contained a connotation that scripture was accompanied by the Spirit. However, American Evangelical theologians have often not maintained such a prominent place for the Spirit. R.D. Moore has proposed that it may be more beneficial for Pentecostals to adhere to

[84] Land has proposed that Pentecostal spirituality is an integration of these three elements, belief, passion, and praxis (S.J. Land, *Pentecostal Spirituality,* p. 44).

[85] The close connection between word and action is repeated in Rev. 12.17 where the children are identified as keeping the commandments of God and holding the testimony of Jesus. C. Bridges Johns has stressed the necessity of ethical praxis accompanying catechesis (C. Bridges Johns, 'Meeting God in the Margins, Ministry among Modernity's Refugees', pp. 22-23).

[86] Cf. J.C. Thomas's emphasis on the current and future need for community and accountability within Pentecostal theology (J.C. Thomas, 'Pentecostal Theology in the Twenty-First Century', pp. 3-19). See also S. Fish, *Is There a Text in This Class? The Authority of Interpretative Communities,* pp. 303-371.

solus spiritus (with the Scripture) as opposed to *sola scriptura* (with the Spirit). According to Moore, the former is far less susceptible to overstatement than the latter.[87] In response to Moore, F.D. Macchia writes:

> I would only want to qualify "Spirit alone" with "Word and Spirit alone" in order to make this fully trinitarian. But I would hasten to add that "Word" here is primarily the *living Christ* who was anointed and directed by the Spirit and now bestows the same Spirit upon us to serve God in Christ-like ways. In this light, "Word" is not simply *identifiable* with "Scripture", but Scripture is *subordinate* to Word and participates in Word *only* through the Spirit (hence a place for (Moore's) "Spirit alone").[88]

Interpretation of the scriptures continues for Pentecostals as it always has 'not by might nor by power' nor by educational level, social status or economic success, but by the Spirit of the living God. This view will require a new emphasis on the doctrine of the priesthood (1 Pet. 2:5, 9) and prophethood[89] of all believers (Num. 11:27-29; Joel 2:28-32; Acts 2:16-20).

John describes his own experience as being 'in the Spirit' (Rev. 1:10, ἐν πνεύματι). It is the Spirit that enables John to receive the revelation of Jesus Christ. Pentecostals easily identify with John's testimony of being in the Spirit.[90] The communal dimension of the Spirit enables the churches to share in John's experience. Within Pentecostalism, the Spirit is not limited to the leaders but is for all who believe experience the presence and the power of the Spirit. In addition to enabling the revelation and inspiring the reading of scripture, the Spirit also plays a vital role in inspiring the testimonies of the believers. The central challenge placed before the seven churches in Revelation is to

[87] R.D. Moore, 'A Letter to Frank Macchia', *JPT* 17 (2000), p. 13.

[88] F.D. Macchia, 'A Reply to Rickie Moore', *JPT* 17 (2000), p. 18.

[89] R. Stronstad, *The Charismatic Theology of St. Luke* (Peabody: Hendrickson, 1984), p. 77; idem, *The Prophethood of All Believers* (Sheffield: Sheffield Academic Press, 1999). See also Eduard Schweizer's proposal that according to Rev. 19:10 all members of the community (at least potentially) are prophets. E. Schweizer, 'Πνεῦμα', *TDNT* 6 (1968), p. 449. R.J. Bauckham is willing to agree that prophecy in the Apocalypse is equivalent with the testimony of Jesus and that the churches function prophetically in their witness to Jesus; however (*contra* Stronstad and Schweizer), he disagrees that every believer can therefore be identified as a prophet (R.J. Bauckham, 'The Role of the Spirit', p. 166).

[90] Cf. R.L. Jeske, 'Spirit and Community in the Johannine Apocalypse', *NTS* 31 (1985), pp. 452-466.

be faithful witnesses to Jesus Christ in spite of the power of the beast which would have them do otherwise.

In Rev. 1:5, Jesus is identified as *the* faithful witness, yet the followers of Jesus who were being assaulted by the dragon were able to 'conquer him by the blood of the Lamb and by the word of their testimony, for they loved not their lives even unto death' (Rev. 12:11). F.F. Bruce argues that 'no doubt their Lord was bearing *his* testimony in theirs, and suffering in them, but it is through their own testimony that they conquer, and their own testimony is that which they bear to Jesus and his redeeming power.'[91] The provision of God is paramount in the historical context of the Asian churches, as they face the possibility of martyrdom for their faithful witness of Jesus Christ. Pentecostal theology, which is often a theology from the bottom, also shares the need for reliance on the provision of God with the Asian churches in Revelation. Moreover, the definition of μάρτυς took on new meaning with the death of Antipas from the church in Pergamum. Although being a witness might not mean an immediate physical death, a type of death does occur when a believer becomes a faithful witness (μάρτυς). The faithful witness receives a new life in Christ, and therefore, has no reason to fear the beast.

5.4. Fearing God in Worship and in Bible Reading

John experiences fear when he sees the vision of Christ and falls at his feet as though dead. In this encounter with Christ, Jesus instructs John not to be afraid and offers him comfort saying, 'Do not fear, I am the First and the Last, the living One. I was dead, and behold I am alive forever and ever. And I have the keys of death and Hades' (Rev. 1:17-18). John's act of falling is not only a result of fear but it is also identified as an act of worship. On two occasions he fell down and attempted to worship an angel (Rev. 19:10; 22:8).[92] In both cases, John is instructed to worship God and not the angel who is a fellow servant

[91] F.F. Bruce, 'The Spirit in the Apocalypse', in *Christ and Spirit in the New Testament: In Honour of Charles Francis Digby Moule,* ed. B. Lindars and S.S. Smalley (Cambridge: Cambridge University Press, 1973), p. 338.

[92] *Contra* R.W. Wall, who argues that John was worshiping God in the presence of the angel. Wall notes that John does not explicitly state an intention to worship the angel and he argues that angel worship would be uncharacteristic of an apostolic figure such as John. Wall suggests that John is using the angel as a mouthpiece to endorse worship of God, the only one deserving of worship (R.W. Wall, *Revelation* [Peabody: Hendrickson, 1991], pp. 223, 264).

of God. The angel identifies John's fear as an act of worship. Jesus' instruction for him to stop being afraid is echoed in Rev. 2:10, where Jesus admonishes the church at Smyrna not to fear what they are about to suffer at the hands of the devil. The close relationship between fear and worship intensifies the necessity for the churches to avoid fearing the devil or the beast, which would thereby be an act of worship.

John's fearful reaction to the vision of Christ is a common reaction to theophanies found in scripture. Although Jesus subsequently tells John not to be afraid, I suggest that Jesus is not prohibiting the fear of the Lord but rather encouraging John not to fear his circumstances or 'what is now and what will take place later' (Rev. 1:19b).[93] The identification of Christ at the end of the vision affirms Him as the figure worthy of worship and fear. Furthermore, I want to propose that the fear of the Lord is at least an initial requirement in the interpretation of scripture for the Pentecostal. Pentecostals believe they will encounter God when they read the Bible, and I have proposed that a revelation of Jesus is necessary in order to interpret scripture properly. Therefore, a reading of the biblical text, not unlike the christophany experienced by John, should involve a certain amount of fear and worship.

6. Conclusion: Intertextuality and Pentecostalism

In my reading of Revelation, I have juxtaposed the experiences of John as a seer, a prophet, and a witness to Jesus with the experiences of contemporary Pentecostalism. I suggest that Pentecostals (and perhaps others as well) should follow the example in the text and rely on Jesus to reveal, in the Spirit, the meaning of the Word of God which is both oral and written. Further, I have emphasized the necessity of a community in which discernment must take place. I am committed to the Pentecostal interpretation of scripture which endorses the prophethood of all believers. The entire world is called by the Spirit to engage in testimony to Jesus which is a participation in the prophecy of Revelation. The scripture truly becomes an intertext for the

[93] *Contra* Aune, who classifies Jesus' exhortation to 'fear not' as 'a comfort formula meant to allay the reaction of fear at the experience of a divine epiphany', rather than an 'oracle of assurance... spoken to allay the fears which motivated the recipient of the revelation to address a lament to God (as in the case of the OT oracles of assurance)' (D.E. Aune, *Prophecy in Early Christianity and the Ancient Mediterranean World* [Grand Rapids: Eerdmans, 1983], p. 281).

reader/believer. The text becomes the words which the churches use to define themselves. Their experience intersects and is integrated with the texts that they read as they continually testify to the presence of God in their midst. As Christ is revealed, the church adopts an identity that reflects the image of Christ that has been revealed.

In addition to being avowedly Pentecostal, I have also been heavily influenced by the academic context in the University of Sheffield, where biblical studies often partners with various other disciplines in the examination of literary texts. In this setting, I have been introduced to a particular literary theory which seems to fit quite nicely with Pentecostalism (i.e. intertextuality). The integration of orthodoxy, orthopraxis and orthopathy within Pentecostalism finds resonance with the multiple intersections of literary and cultural (con)texts within the theory of intertextuality. The next chapter turns more directly toward the text of Revelation and analyses Rev. 11:1-13, which I argue is the intertextual center of the book. In keeping with the model of a non-modern hermeneutic which is multiple in method, the analysis will portray characteristics of a multilevel hermeneutic.

4

The Faithful Witness of a Pneumatic Church: The Spirit of Prophecy and the People of God

1. Introduction

Perhaps it would be helpful at this point to take a step back and review the flow of the argument. After a programmatic introduction, the study begins in Chapter 1 with a survey of literature on what is comparatively a neglected topic, namely the role of the Spirit in the Apocalypse. As the survey reveals a variety of views on the role of the Spirit, it becomes obvious that the opposing opinions are at least partially due to the variety of methods which are employed during the analysis of the text. In addition to the various methods, one of the common themes among scholars is an acknowledgment that allusions to the Old Testament play a pivotal role in interpreting the references to the Spirit. However, the manner in which these allusions should be interpreted is highly debated.[1] One of the methods being utilized to navigate the topic of allusions is intertextuality, yet intertextuality seems to be as enigmatic as the symbols in the Apocalypse. Therefore, following the survey of literature, Chapter 2 explores the method of intertextuality both in theory and in practice. As defined in this study, intertextuality seeks on the one hand to integrate literary allusions in the creation of meaning and on the other hand it emphasizes the role of the reader as a valid (con)text in an intertextual analysis. Attempting to articulate the context of the reader, Chapter 3 seeks to define a

[1] For a discussion of the effect of certain Old Testament passages on the interpretation of the Spirit in Revelation see the survey of literature above, especially Bruce, 'The Spirit in the Apocalypse', pp. 333-344; R.J. Bauckham, *The Climax of Prophecy,* pp. 150-173; J. Fekkes, *Isaiah and Prophetic Tradition in the Book of Revelation,* pp. 107-110. See also the chapter on intertextuality, especially section 3 on intertextuality and Revelation studies.

Pentecostal theological viewpoint and the effects such a stance may have on the interpretation of the role of the Spirit in Revelation.

In this chapter the study comes to a climax by integrating biblical studies and literary studies within the context of a Pentecostal community. I have chosen to focus on the prophecy concerning the temple and the two witnesses in Rev. 11:1-13. This passage sits at the center of the book literarily and I believe theologically as well,[2] forming the intertextual center of the role of the Spirit in the Apocalypse. Ironically, most commentators do not acknowledge the presence of the Spirit in these verses. Although πνεῦμα appears in v. 11, the English versions disagree on how to translate the term, compare for example 'breath' (RSV, NIV, NRSV,[3] REB, NKJV, NASB), 'spirit' (NLT), and 'Spirit' (KJV). Furthermore, there is even greater dispute over the translation of the cognate πνευματικῶς in v. 8, for instance, 'allegorically' (RSV), 'prophetically' (NRSV), 'prophetic language' (REB), 'mystically' (NASB), 'figuratively' (NIV), and 'spiritually' (KJV, NKJV). The NTL does not even attempt to translate πνευματικῶς, omitting the term altogether.

While the presence and significance of Old Testament allusions are important for understanding many aspects of Revelation, in relation to the role of the Spirit Zechariah 4 is considered the key intertext. In Zechariah's vision he sees a lampstand, seven flames of fire, seven eyes of the LORD, and two olive trees. The seven flames of fire appear as a symbol for the seven spirits in Rev. 4:5. In Rev. 5:6, John expands the imagery of the seven eyes to include seven horns and ascribes the expanded imagery to the Lamb rather than the LORD. After using the image of the lampstand in chs. 1–3, he reuses it in ch. 11 coupled with the symbol of the two olive trees. The intention of this chapter is to demonstrate that the double imagery of the two olive trees and the two lampstands complemented by the use of πνεῦμα and πνευματικῶς creates a textual fabric that enables John to express richly the role of the Spirit in the prophetic ministry of the church, whose primary task is to bear witness to Jesus in the world.

The chapter begins with a literary contextualization examining the significance of Rev. 11.1-13 within the larger structure of the book. Following the literary contextualization, an intertextual analysis of this key passage is offered which leads in all directions from the Apocalypse

[2] Cf. Bauckham, *The Climax of Prophecy*, pp. 266-283.

[3] The NRSV offers 'spirit' in a footnote as an alternative translation.

to Zechariah (and Ezekiel), only to move back to the Apocalypse and finally forward to the contemporary reader. At key points the analysis diverges in order to explore allusions and intratextual connections.

2. Literary Contextualization

It should come as no surprise that a book as complex as Revelation continues to inspire a plethora of possible outlines. The proposals offered by the commentators have been described by one scholar as 'a maze of interpretative confusion'.[4] According to R. Bauckham, 'the major literary study of Revelation which will do justice to it has yet to be written'.[5] Despite the recent monumental work of G.K. Beale and D. Aune, not to mention Bauckham's own contribution,[6] this statement continues to ring true. Rather than attempting to fill this vacuum, this section has a modest goal, to offer a discussion on the significance of Rev. 11:1-13 and the role the passage plays in the larger argument of the book.

Discussions on the structure of Revelation are always affected by the scholar's opinion concerning the unity (or disunity) of the text. Even a casual reading of the Apocalypse reveals 'repetitions, doublets, and artificial constructions'.[7] Many of the older commentaries and a few more recent ones propose source-critical theories which seek to explain the existence of such discrepancies. G.R. Osborne offers a helpful categorization dividing the source-critical theories into three types:[8] (1) compilation theories which suppose that Revelation is a combination of earlier Jewish and/or Christian apocalypses;[9] (2) theories of

[4] Bauckham, *The Climax of Prophecy,* p. 1.

[5] Bauckham, *The Climax of Prophecy,* p. 1.

[6] Beale, *The Book of Revelation,* pp. 108-170; Aune, *Revelation 1–5,* pp. xc-cxxxiv; Bauckham, *The Climax of Prophecy,* pp. 1-37.

[7] E. Schüssler Fiorenza, *The Book of Revelation, Justice and Judgment* (Philadelphia: Fortress, 1985), p. 160.

[8] Osborne, *Revelation* (Grand Rapids: Baker Academic, 2002), pp. 27-28.

[9] W.G.J. Weyland, *Omwerkings en Compilatie-Hypothesen toegepast op de Apokalypse van Johannes* (Groningen: Wolters, 1888); F. Spitta, *Die Offenbarung des Johannes* (Halle: Waisenhaus, 1889); J. Weiss, *Die Offenbarung des Johannes* (Göttingen: Vandenhoeck & Ruprecht, 1904); M.-E. Boismard, 'Notes sur L'Apocalypse', *Revue Biblique* 59 (1952), pp. 161-181; J.M. Ford, *Revelation,* pp. 22-37. Perhaps the most esoteric, Ford's compilation theory has found few supporters. She proposes that chs. 4–11 were written by John the Baptist and that chs. 12–19 were added later by a disciple of John. The final form of Revelation, including chs. 1–3 and 20–22, was finished still later by a Jewish-

revision which argue that a single apocalyptic work evolved through various stages;[10] and (3) theories which assume that fragments of Jewish apocalypses were incorporated into the original text.[11]

The most extensive attempt to develop a comprehensive source-critical theory is the work of D. Aune, whose proposal combines all three of Osborne's categories.[12] Aune divides the writing of the Apocalypse into three stages produced for a variety of reasons over a period of twenty to thirty years. The author, according to Aune, later combined the separate tracts into a single document. The first stage included twelve independent sections written in the 50's and 60's (7:1-17; 10:1-11; 11:1-13; 12:1-17; 13:1-18; 14:1-20; 17:1-18; 18:1-24; 19:11-16; 20:1-10). Aune believes most of this material was written after the author had converted to Christianity from Judaism with the possible exception of 7:1-17 and 11:1-13 (ironically these two passages are central in the following delineation of the role of the Spirit). Aune dates stage two somewhere between AD 69 and 74 when the separate segments of stage one were combined with the addition of an introduction (1:7-12a). Stage two was held together by an overarching eschatological framework (e.g. 20:4-6) with additional transitional supplements (1:20; 4:1, 5; 5:6; 9:4; 10:7; 11:7, 14a). This second stage would have also included the Christianization of Jewish texts with the additions of 12:11; 14:13; 16:6 and 17:6. The final stage completed after the end of the first century provided further material to frame the

Christian disciple.

[10] E. Vischer, *Die Offenbarung Johannis: Eine jüdische Apokalypse in christlicher Bearbeitung* (Leipzig: Hinrichs, 1886); R.H. Charles, *A Critical and Exegetical Commentary on the Revelation of St. John* 2 vols. (Edinburgh: Clark, 1920), pp. xxix-lxi, Charles argues that the original author died after completing 20:3 and the book was finished by an inept disciple who also included a number of interpolations, including several key texts concerning the Spirit (e.g. 1:4c; 4:5); P. Prigent, *Apocalypse et liturgie* (Paris: Delachaux et Niestle, 1964); H. Kraft, *Die Offenbarung des Johannes* (Tübingen; Mohr, 1974); J.F. Whealen, 'New Patches on an Old Garment: The Book of Revelation', *BTB* 11 (1981), pp. 54-59. Whealen argues that Revelation has been transformed into a Christian apocalypse from its original Jewish form by the addition of Christian interpolations (11:8; 12:17; 13:8; 14:12b; 16:15; 17:6; 18:13, 20; 19:9b-10, 13; 20:4, 6; 21:14; 22:7).

[11] W. Bousset, *Die Offenbarung Johannes* (Göttingen: Vandenhoeck & Ruprecht, 1906). Bousset suggests that the author incorporated 7:1-8; 11:1-13; 12:1-7; 13:11-18; 14:14-20; 17:1-18-24; 21:9–22:5.

[12] Aune, *Revelation 1–5,* pp. cxviii-cxxxiv.

book as a whole and stress the exaltation of Christ into the unity of God (1:1-6; 1:12b–3:22; 22:6-21).

Despite the possibility of such source-critical theories, most recent commentators have written with the assumption that the text contains a high level of literary unity.[13] Although the redactional theories which have been applied to the text are helpful to a certain degree,[14] I agree with those who choose to see unity within the text in which case the 'repetitions, doublets, and artificial constructions' are understood as being deliberate. There are simply too many possible ways of structuring the text that make sense without having to develop elaborate theories of editorial activity. G.R. Osborne notes five types of outlines:[15] (1) chiastic structures;[16] (2) structures patterned after a seven act Greek play;[17] (3) structures based on multiple series of seven;[18] (4) structures

[13] E.g. G.R. Beasley-Murray, *The Book of Revelation* (London: Marshall, Morgan & Scott, 1974); R.H. Mounce, *The Book of Revelation* (Grand Rapids: Eerdmans, 1977); G.A. Krodel, *Revelation* (Minneapolis: Augsburg, 1989); M.R. Mulholland, *Revelation: Holy Living in an Unholy World* (Grand Rapids: Zondervan, 1990); R. Wall, *Revelation* (Peabody, MA: Hendrickson, 1991); J. Roloff, *Revelation* trans. by J.E. Alsup (Minneapolis, Fortress, 1993); Bauckham, *The Climax of Prophecy,* and Beale, *The Book of Revelation.*

[14] There are certain red flags which may signal redactional activity. For a discussion of these signals see Schüssler Fiorenza, *The Book of Revelation,* pp. 160-164; D. Guthrie, *New Testament Introduction* (4th edn; Downers Grove: InterVarsity Press, 1990), pp. 967-69; Aune, *Revelation 1–5,* pp. cxviii-cxxxiv.

[15] The first four types of outlines have been previously noted in S.L. Waechter, 'An Analysis of the Literary Structure of the Book of Revelation according to Textlinguistic Methods', Ph.D. thesis (Mid-America Baptist Theological Seminary, 1994), pp. 173-82.

[16] N.W. Lund, *Chiasmus in the New Testament* (Chapel Hill: University of North Carolina, 1942), pp. 323-330; idem, *Studies in the Book of Revelation* (Chicago: Covenant, 1955), pp. 34-37; K.A. Strand, 'Chiastic Structure and Some Motifs in the Book of Revelation', *AUSS* 16 (1978), pp. 401-408; J. Moffatt, 'The Revelation of St. John the Divine', vol. 5 in *The Expositor's Greek Testament* (Grand Rapids: Eerdmans, 1983), pp. 279-494; Schüssler Fiorenza, *The Book of Revelation,* pp. 159-180; M.V. Lee, 'A Call to Martyrdom: Function as Method and Message in Revelation', *Nov Test* 40 (1998), pp. 174-175.

[17] R.R. Brewer, 'The Influence of Greek Drama on the Apocalypse of John', *Anglican Theological Review* 71 (1936), pp. 74-92; J.W. Bowman, 'The Revelation to John: Its Dramatic Structure and Message', *Int* 9 (1955), pp. 436-453; L.C. Spinks, 'A Critical Examination of J.W. Bowman's Proposed Structure of the Revelation', *EQ* 50 (1978), pp. 211-222; J.L. Blevins, *Revelation as Drama* (Nashville: Broadman, 1984). See also D.L. Barr, 'The Apocalypse of John as Oral Enactment', *Int* 38 (1984) 243-256 for a structure devised as a three-act play.

based on liturgical patterns;[19] and (5) outlines which center around the notion of recapitulation.[20]

In addition to this surplus of outlines other theories of structure have been proposed which identify repetitive phrases as literary markers which divide the text. Given the length and the intended oral presentation of the book (Rev. 1:3), the repetitive phrases serve as vital signifiers helping to orient the hearers/readers.[21] G.K. Beale identifies ἅ δεῖ γενέσθαι μετὰ ταῦτα in 1:19 and 4:1 as a key literary marker which John used to divide the text into its two major sections (1:19–3:22; 4:1–22:5).[22] This twofold division of the book may be expanded to a fourfold division by noting the similar phrase ἅ δεῖ γενέσθαι ἐν τάχει appearing in 1:1 and 22:6. This second phrase serves as an introductory statement for both the prologue and the epilogue.[23] Various other phrases play minor roles in the structure of the book,[24] but the most significant is perhaps John's reference to being 'in the Spirit'.

[18] E. Lohmeyer, *Die Offenbarung des Johannes* (Tübingen: Mohr, 1926); A.M. Farrer, *The Revelation of St. John the Divine* (Oxford; Clarendon, 1964); J.M. Ford, *Revelation,* pp. 46-50; A. Yarbro Collins, *Crisis and Catharsis: The Power of the Apocalypse* (Philadelphia: Westminster, 1984).

[19] M.H. Shepherd, *The Pascal Liturgy and the Apocalypse* (Richmond: John Knox, 1960); J.J. O'Rourke, 'The Hymns of the Apocalypse', *CBQ* 30 (1968), pp. 399-409.

[20] G. Bornkamm, 'Die Komposition der apokalyptischen Visionen in der Offenbarung Johannes', *ZNW* 36 (1937), pp. 132-149; W. Hendricksen, *More Than Conquerors: An Interpretation of the Book of Revelation* (2nd edn; Grand Rapids: Baker, 1967), pp. 22-31; C.H. Giblin, 'Recapitulation and the Literary Coherence of John's Apocalypse', *CBQ* 56 (1994), pp. 94-95.

[21] Bauckham, *The Climax of Prophecy,* p. 23; D.L. Barr, 'The Apocalypse of John as Oral Enactment', pp. 243; Beale, *The Book of Revelation,* p. 111.

[22] The phrase is not exactly the same in these two verses because 1:19 the δεῖ has been substituted by μέλλει. This variation of the verb is surprisingly overlooked by Beale; however, the variation may have no real significance as John tends to vary phrases slightly when he repeats them.

[23] Cf. Bauckham, *The Climax of Prophecy,* p. 23.

[24] For instance, Yarbro Collins argues that John uses the phrase 'and I saw' (καὶ εἶδον) and the verb 'appeared' (ὤφθη) in order to divide Rev. 12:1–15:4 into a series of seven unnumbered visions. Likewise, she identifies καὶ εἶδον again as marking another unnumbered series of seven in Rev. 19:10–21:8. In both situations, construing seven elements in the series is a bit artificial and ultimately fails to convince (A. Yarbro Collins, *The Combat Myth in the Book of Revelation* [Missoula: Scholars Press, 1976], pp. 14-16, dependent on A. Farrer, *A Rebirth of Images: The Making of St. John's Apocalypse* [Westminster: Dacre Press, 1949], pp. 47-57).

2.1. ἐν πνεύματι and the Structure of Revelation

Four times John writes that he was 'in the Spirit' (1:10; 4:2; 17:3; 21:10). The anarthrous construction of ἐν πνεύματι has led some scholars to argue that John is not referring to the Spirit but rather an ecstatic state or trance as opposed to being in the flesh.[25] Although I argue below that John is ascribing his visionary experience to the agency of the Spirit, at this point the translation is irrelevant. My objective is to show how ἐν πνεύματι serves as a major marker within the structure.[26] Despite whatever redactional activity has taken place with the text, in its final form the text may be divided into six major sections based on John's use of the phrase ἐν πνεύματι: (1) a prologue (1:1-8); (2) a vision of Christ and his ensuing prophetic messages to the seven churches in Asia (1:9–3:22); (3) a lengthy drama of the Lamb and the opening of the seven-sealed scroll (4:1–16:21); (4) the judgment of the harlot/Babylon (17:1-21:8); (5) the description of the bride/New Jerusalem (21:9–22:9); and (6) an epilogue (22:6-21).[27]

This basic outline is not intended to exhaust the complexity of Revelation but rather serves as an initial step in understanding the structure. The lines of demarcation between these sections are fuzzy, owing to a good deal of foreshadowing and recapitulation. At times a group of verses may play a dual role, concluding one section while introducing another.[28] In regard to the structure, the first section intro-

[25] G.B. Caird, *A Commentary on the Revelation of St. John the Divine* (London: A. & C. Black, 1966), p. 19. Caird translates each occurrence of ἐν πνεύματι as 'falling into a trance'.

[26] For similar arguments, see E.-B. Allo, *L'Apocalypse de Saint Jean* (Paris: Gabalda, 1933), pp. lxxxv-xcvi; M.C. Tenney, *Interpreting Revelation* (Grand Rapids: Eerdmans, 1958), pp. 32-34; G.E. Ladd, *A Commentary on the Revelation of John* (Grand Rapids: Eerdmans, 1972), pp. 14-17; W.R. Kempson, 'Theology in the Revelation of John', Ph.D. thesis (Louisville: Southern Baptist Theological Seminary, 1982), pp. 38-142; F.D. Mazzaferri, *The Genre of the Book of Revelation from a Source-Critical Perspective* (New York: de Gruyter, 1989), pp. 302-303, 338-243; Bauckham, *The Climax of Prophecy,* p. 3; C.R. Smith, 'The Structure of the Book of Revelation in Light of Apocalyptic Literary Conventions', *NovT* 36 (1994), pp. 373-393. Against this view see P. Prigent, *Commentary on the Apocalypse of St. John* (trans. W. Pradels; Tübingen: Mohr Siebeck, 2001), pp. 94-97.

[27] Rev. 22:6-9 represents one of the transitional sections which function with the dual role of concluding the vision of the new Jerusalem as well as serving as an introduction to the epilogue.

[28] Bauckham refers to this as overlapping or interweaving (Bauckham, *The Climax of Prophecy,* pp. 8-9). See also Yarbro Collins on this phenomenon, which she calls 'interlocking' (Yarbro Collins, *The Combat Myth in the Book of Revelation,* pp. 16-18).

duced by ἐν πνεύματι is fairly straightforward. The characteristics of Christ described in the initial vision (1:12-16) are referenced and at times expanded in each of the introductions to the seven prophetic messages (2:1–3:22). In contrast to the following section, where the series of sevens are enumerated, the seven prophetic messages are not numbered. Perhaps the lack of enumeration points to structural independence of the seven messages from the other series of seven (seals, trumpets, and bowls) all of which fall under the second section introduced by ἐν πνεύματι (4:1–16:21). In addition to the lack of enumeration, R.J. Bauckham has identified an intricate numbering pattern in the series of seven. The seven messages follow a 3+4 pattern instead of the pattern 4+3 of the seals, trumpets, and bowls. The prophetic messages fall into this pattern based on the location of the admonition to conquer, which comes after the hearing formula in the first three messages and before the hearing formula in the last four messages. As for the three numerated series: (1) the first four seals consist of a horse and a rider dividing the series into 4+3; (2) the final three trumpets are categorized as 'woes', thus giving this series the 4+3; and (3) less distinctly but nevertheless in the 4+3 pattern the first four bowls parallel the first four trumpets in that they share common objects of judgment (earth, sea, fresh waters, heavens).[29]

When John repeats that he was in the Spirit (4:2), he introduces a long and complex portion of the vision which runs from the throne room (4:1–5:14) to the pouring out of the seventh bowl of judgment (16:17-21). Chapters 4 and 5 contain John's vision of the throne room, which serves as a general introduction for the rest of the section.[30] Initially in the throne room John witnesses the worship of God (the one seated on the throne). In 5:1, John notices the seven-sealed

[29] Bauckham, *The Climax of Prophecy,* pp. 10-15. For an alternative view that all four series fall into a 4+3 pattern see A.M. Farrer, *The Revelation of St. John the Divine,* pp. 70-83.

[30] Especially within the futurist camp, chs. 4–5 serve as an introduction to the rest of the book. This is one of the structural systems based on 1:19, where 'what you have seen' refers to 1:9-18; 'what is' refers to 2:1-3:22; and 'what must happen after these things' refers to 4:1-22:5. For instance: J.F. Walvoord, *The Revelation of Jesus Christ* (London: Marshall, Morgan, & Scott, 1966), pp. 47-49; R.L. Thomas, 'John's Apocalyptic Outline', *Bibliotheca Sacra* 126 (1969), pp. 334-341. See also Bousset, *Die Offenbarung Johannes*; H.B. Swete, *The Apocalypse of St. John* (London: Macmillan, 1906), pp. xxxiii-xlv; Charles, *A Critical and Exegetical Commentary on the Revelation,* pp. xxiii-xxviii.

scroll in the hand of God and later learns that only the Lion/Lamb is capable of opening the scroll and breaking the seals. When the Lamb takes the scroll the heavenly inhabitants proceed in their worship but, this time, in addition to God the Lamb is included as a recipient of worship (5:13).

Chapter 6 records the opening of the first six seals, which increase in length and escalate with intensity. However, before the seventh seal is opened (8:1), John includes a description of those sealed by God (7:1-17). The identity of those with the seal of God may be answering the concluding question of ch. 6, 'who can stand before the wrath of the Lamb?'[31] While at first the identity of those sealed by God in ch. 7 may seem enigmatic, close attention to John's testimony reveals a possible solution. Chapter 7 describes two groups, 144,000 Jews (12,000 from each tribe) and a multitude greater than anyone can number from every nation, from all tribes and peoples and tongues. In Bauckham's words, the key is noticing what John *hears* versus what he *sees.*[32] John hears that the number of those sealed by God is 144,000 (7:4); however, what he sees is the great multitude (7:9). The contrasting images between what he hears and what he sees can be compared to a similar construction in ch. 5, where John hears that the Lion of Judah can open the scroll and the seven seals, but upon turning he sees a Lamb rather than a Lion. Like the dual image of the Lion of Judah and the Lamb representing a single referent (Jesus Christ), my contention is that the 144,000 and the great multitude are dual images for a single reality, namely the people of God.[33] In the next series of seven, John

[31] 'Standing' plays a prominent role in ch. 7. The four angels stand at the four corners of the earth, and more importantly the great multitude stands before the throne and before the Lamb (7:9).

[32] Bauckham, *The Climax of Prophecy,* pp. 215-229.

[33] Commentators are divided over the identity of the 144,000 and the great multitude. Some commentators see the 144,000 as a literal number of ethnic Jews who are sealed as last day remnant, e.g. J.A. Seiss, *The Apocalypse: A Series of Special Lectures on the Revelation of Jesus Christ* (Grand Rapids, Eerdmans, 1966), pp. 160-169; J.F. Walvoord, *The Revelation of Jesus Christ,* pp. 140-141; R.L. Thomas, *Revelation 1-7: An Exegetical Commentary* (Chicago: Moody, 1992), pp. 473-482. See also H. Kraft, *Die Offenbarung des Johannes,* pp. 126-128, who does not understand the number to be literal but does maintain that the symbol refers to an eschatological Jewish group. A. Feuillet, 'Les 144,000 Israelites marques d'un sceau', *NovT* 9 (1967), pp. 191-224, sees the group as a remnant of Jews in the first century who emerged after the destruction of the Temple in AD 70. For those who understand the symbols to represent a single group see G.B. Caird, *A Commentary on the Revelation,* p. 96; J.P.M. Sweet, *Revelation*

will again pause after the sixth element to include a fuller, albeit more symbolic, description of the people of God (cf. 10:1–11:13).

After the interlude in ch. 7, the seventh seal is opened (8:1). The contents of the seventh seal are debatable;[34] however I agree with those who identify the seven trumpets as the contents of the seventh seal.[35] The descriptions of the trumpet blasts increase in length as the judgments intensify much like the progression of the seals. The series of trumpets follows the same pattern as the series of seals with a break (or literary pause) between the sixth and seventh elements. The interlude separating the sixth and seventh trumpets serves a similar role to the interlude separating the sixth and seven seals. Both passages create a literary delay postponing (at least in the narrative) the final judgment in the series. Thematically, the interludes are also linked together because they both provide information concerning the protection and activity of the people of God in relation to the judgments.[36]

In the second interlude, John sees 'another mighty angel' (ἄλλον ἄγγελον ἰσχυρόν) who is holding in his hand a little scroll. The angel calls out, and this results in another series of seven, the seven thunders.[37] However, John is instructed not to write the account of this series in order to avoid further delay (10:6) and to expedite the coming time of the seventh trumpet (10:7). In 10:9, the angel instructs

(London: SCM, 1979), pp. 150-151; Bauckham, *The Climax of Prophecy,* pp. 215-229.

[34] For a list of various opinions of the commentators on the meaning and significance of the silence produced by the opening of the seventh seal, see Osborne, *Revelation,* pp. 336-337.

[35] E.g. Bauckham, *The Climax of Prophecy,* p. 8.

[36] Avoiding the notion of interludes, J.R. Michaels identifies the sealing of the people of God in ch. 7 as part of the sixth seal and likewise he identifies the eating of the scroll and the prophecy concerning the two witnesses in 10:1–11:14 as part of the sixth trumpet (J.R. Michaels, *Interpreting the Book of Revelation* [Grand Rapids: Baker Books, 1992], pp. 55-60).

[37] If the series of seven thunders is included in the numbering of the series of sevens in this section then the total comes to four (seals, trumpets, *thunders,* and bowls). Four series of seven elements each (4+7), according to Bauckham's calculations, would suggest universal and complete judgment. Noticing the seals affected a quarter of the earth and the trumpets affected a third of the earth, one might expect the thunders to affect a still larger percentage (perhaps one half, so Farrer, *The Revelation of St. John the Divine,* p. 125). The final series (bowls) seems to have no limitations, leading to the ultimate and final destruction. Cf. I.T. Beckwith, *The Apocalypse of John* (Grand Rapids: Baker Book House, 1967, repr. of 1919 edition), pp. 574-578. The seven thunders most likely are an allusion to Psalm 29, where the voice of the Lord, which is depicted as thunder, is mentioned seven times.

John to take a scroll from its hand and eat it.[38] The eating of the scroll implies the seer's consumption of the revelation. Following the digestion of the scroll, the angel commands John to prophesy (again). John's subsequent prophecy is the vision of the temple and the two witnesses in Rev. 11. In other words, Rev. 11:1-13 is the content of the scroll which John received from the angel. Although later chapters of Revelation will greatly expand on it, according to R.J. Bauckham, 'the central and essential message of the scroll is given most clearly here (11:1-13)'.[39] Thus, G.K. Beale is not far off the mark when he identifies the contents of the scroll as chs. 11–16, possibly including chs. 17–22 as well.[40] The identity of the little scroll and the significance of recognizing 11:1-13 as its central (albeit condensed) message is discussed further below.[41]

The end of this longer interlude is clearly marked by 11:14 which announces that the second woe has passed but the third woe is soon to come. The seventh trumpet (11:15-19), foreshadowed in 10:7, is the final eschatological trumpet which announces the coming of 'our Lord and his Christ'. The relationship between the seventh trumpet and the final series of seven bowls is analogous to the relationship between the seventh seal and the seven trumpets. In other words, the content of the seventh trumpet is the seven bowl judgments. Thus, the throne room vision and the three enumerated series (seals, trumpets and bowls) along with their perspective interludes form the content of the second major division in the Apocalypse (4:1–16:21). However, unlike the overlapping that takes place in 8:1-5 between the seals and the trumpets, the series of trumpets and bowls are separated by 12:1–15:4. Nevertheless, the connection between the seventh trumpet and the seven bowls can be seen in a number of literary links.

[38] An allusion to Ezek. 3:1-3.

[39] Bauckham, *The Climax of Prophecy,* p. 266. See also G. Schrenk, 'βιβλίον' *TDNT* 1, p. 619. Other commentators have identified 11:1-13 as the contents of the little scroll based partly on the faulty assumption that the contents of the (larger) scroll in 5:1 has already been revealed in 6:1-8:5. E.g. Charles, *A Critical and Exegetical Commentary on the Revelation of St. John,* vol. 1, pp. 260-269; H. Lilje, *The Last Book of the Bible: The Meaning of the Revelation of St. John* (Philadelphia: Muhlenberg, 1957), p. 158; E. Lohmeyer, *Die Offenbarung des Johannes,* p. 87; E. Lohse, *Die Offenbarung des Johannes* (Göttingen: Vandenhoek & Ruprecht, 1960), p. 56; A. Satake, *Die Gemeindeordnung in der Johannesapokalypse* (Neukirchen: Neukirchener Verlag, 1966), p. 73; M. Rissi, *Zeit und Geschichte in der Offenbarung der Johannesapokalypse* (Zurich: Zwingli, 1965), p. 43.

[40] Beale, *The Book of Revelation,* p. 527.

[41] See section 2.2. *The Identity of the Little Scroll.*

Each of the three series in this section (seals, trumpets, and bowls) ends with a similar yet expanded formula that appears to be an allusion to the Sinai theophany. The first instance of the phrase occurs as part of the throne room introduction (4:5 ἀστραπαὶ καὶ φωναὶ καὶ βρονταί). With each subsequent occurrence the phrase expands either by adding an extra item or in the case of 16:18-21 lengthening the description of the final two items:[42]

4:5	ἀστραπαὶ καὶ φωναὶ καὶ βρονταί
8:5	βρονταὶ καὶ φωναὶ καὶ ἀστραπαὶ καὶ σεισμός
11:19	ἀστραπαὶ καὶ φωναὶ καὶ βρονταί καὶ σεισμὸς καὶ χάλαζα μεγάλη
16:18-21	ἀστραπαὶ καὶ φωναὶ καὶ βρονταί καὶ σεισμὸς· μέγας καὶ χάλαζα μεγάλη

John's use of repetition may be the result of a Rabbinical exegetical method known as גזירה שוה (equivalence of expression).[43] The method was a form of elaborate cross-referencing where the use of a term or phrase in two separate texts was considered to be sufficient justification for using the texts to interpret each other. As a common form of interpretation, it is reasonable to conclude that John both employed this method and expected the readers of the Apocalypse to employ it is well.[44] In any case, the repetition of these words marks a definite literary link between the throne room and the final item of each series. In

[42] See Bauckham, *The Climax of Prophecy*, pp. 8, 202-204.

[43] גזירה שוה is a form of *Peshat* perhaps best represented by Hillel. For a summary of this form of exegesis see B. Rosenzswig, 'The Hermeneutic Principles and Their Application', *Tradition* 13 (1972), pp. 49-76; J. Weingreen, 'The Rabbinic Approach to the Study of the Old Testament', *BJRLM* 34 (1951-52), pp. 166-190; B.S. Childs, 'Midrash and the Old Testament', in *Understanding the Sacred Text: Essays in Honor of Morton S. Enslin on the Hebrew Bible and Christian Beginnings,* ed. J. Reumann (Valley Forge: Judson, 1972), pp. 45-49.

[44] Bauckham, *The Climax of Prophecy*, pp. 296-326. Bauckham argues convincingly that John employs the method. Beale's understanding of John's use of σημαίνω in Rev. 1:1 is a perfect example of a modern utilization of גזירה שוה. Beale rightly understands Rev. 1:1 to be an allusion to Dan. 2:28-30, 45. 'The clauses "revelation... God showed... what must come to pass... and he *made known* (σημαίνω)" occur together only in Daniel 2 and Rev. 1:1.' In this passage Daniel is interpreting the king's dream, which is best understood as a form of symbolic communication. Having identified this verbal coincidence, Beale concludes that John has intentionally used σημαίνω in order to identify his writing as a form of symbolic communication. Hermeneutically, this has far-reaching implications, indicating that the text is intended not to be read literally but rather symbolically (Beale, *The Book of Revelation,* pp. 50-52).

addition to the repetition of the Sinai language, the seventh trumpet and the series of bowls is further connected by the first part of 11:19 (Καὶ ἠνοίγη ὁ ναὸς τοῦ θεοῦ ὁ ἐν τῷ οὐρανῷ καὶ ὤφθη ἡ κιβωτὸς τῆς διαθήκης αὐτοῦ ἐν τῷ ναῷ αὐτοῦ) being echoed in 15:5-6 (καὶ ἠνοίγη ὁ ναὸς τῆς σκηνῆς τοῦ μαρτυρίου ἐν τῷ οὐρανῷ, καὶ ἐξῆθον οἱ ἑπτὰ ἄγγελοι οἱ ἔχοντες τὰς ἑπτὰ πληγὰς ἐκ τοῦ ναοῦ). 'Thus, despite the intervention of chapters 12-14, the whole sequence of bowls is clearly marked as a development of the seventh trumpet.'[45]

The subtlety and complexity of the interconnections within the Apocalypse makes the break beginning in 12:1 all the more abrupt. John utilizes a completely new introductory formula (καὶ σημεῖον μέγα ὤφθη ἐν τῷ οὐράῷ· καὶ ὤφθη ἄλλο σημεῖον ἐν τῷ οὐρανῷ [12:1; 12:3, respectively]). The necessity of such a new beginning may best be described by noticing the way in which the seventh trumpet has announced the ultimate end. It is indicative of this finale that the threefold description of God (the one who is and who was and who is to come) has been reduced to a twofold description: simply 'the one who is and who was' (11:17). No longer is God described with the phrase 'is to come', because now he has taken his power and begun to reign.[46] Having announced the end, John regresses to retell the story from a cosmic perspective. Beginning chronologically far before the rest of the Apocalypse, John alludes to the conflict between the woman and the dragon but focuses on the struggle of the people of God who must face the threat of the beast.

Although the beginning of this section may have no visible links to the earlier portions of the book, John does weave the end of this section into the final series of seven bowls in at least two ways. First, reusing the method of overlapping similar to the integration of the seals and the trumpets in 8:1-5, John places the story of the victory celebration of the people of God who have conquered the beast (15:2-4) between an introduction of the seven angels with the seven plagues (15:1) and the account of their preparation for pouring their bowls out on the earth (15:5-8).[47] Secondly, John links the introduction of the

[45] Bauckham, *The Climax of Prophecy,* p. 9.
[46] Cf. Rev. 16:8 'the one who is and who was'.
[47] Bauckham, *The Climax of Prophecy,* p. 16.

seven angels with the seven plagues with 12:1-3 by using similar descriptive language (καὶ εἶδον ἄλλο σημεῖον ἐν τῷ οὐρανῷ).[48]

In addition to the structural connections, chs. 12–15 also bear significant thematic links to the other two interludes (7:1-15; 10:1–11:13). The topic of each of these sections is the people of God and their conflict with the forces that are opposed to God. R.J. Bauckham mentions several of these links:

> the 144,000 (7:4) reappear in 14:1, the apocalyptic period of the church's suffering and witness (11:2-3) reappears in 12:6, 14; 13:5, the beast who appears enigmatically in 11:7 is properly introduced in chapter 13, where he makes war on the saints and conquers them (13:7) as he already had in 11:7.[49]

Another significant link between chs. 12–15 and the earlier parts of the book is the reference to the conquering of the beast by the people of God (12:11). This verse not only helps to link this section with the previous portions of the text but it also prepares the readers proleptically for future sections as well. The reference to conquering echoes the promises in the seven messages for those who conquer. Indeed, 12:11 provides the paradigm for conquering in triplicate: (1) 12:11a (διὰ τὸ αἷμα τοῦ ἀρνίου), which echoes the sacrificial death of the lamb in 5:6; (2) 12:11b (διὰ τὸν λόγον τῆς μαρτυρίας αὐτῶν), which not only alludes to the testimony of John and the witnesses previously mentioned (1:9; 6:9) but also foreshadows later depictions of the church bearing witness (12:17; 19:10; 20:4);[50] and (3) 12:11c (οὐκ ἠγάπησαν τὴν ψυχὴν αὐτῶν ἄχρι θανάτου), which links to those who have been martyred including the group described in the fifth seal opening (6:9-11) and perhaps the death of the witnesses in 11:7 described more fully in 13:7a.[51] The significance of the death and martyrdom is explored more fully below in the analysis of 11:1-13.

[48] John's first use of σημεῖον occurs in 12:1 and although he uses it later in the plural σημεῖα the only appearance of the singular is in 12:1, 3; 15:1.

[49] Bauckham, *The Climax of Prophecy*, p. 17.

[50] Mounce, *The Book of Revelation*, p. 247. Mounce also understands the phrase, 'by the word of their testimony', as a circumlocution for proclamation (*contra* Mazzaferri, *The Genre of the Book of Revelation*, p. 313).

[51] Although most of the best mss. omit the clause καὶ ἐδόθη αὐτῷ ποιῆσαι πόλεμον μετὰ τῶν ἁγίων καὶ νικῆσαι αὐτούς (𝔭[47] A C 2053 𝔐[A]) the preferred reading includes the clause assuming an early scribal error skipping from the καὶ ἐδόθη αὐτῷ in the first clause to the identical phrase in 13:7b.

In summary, the second occurrence of ἐν πνεύματι introduces the lengthiest and most complex vision (4:1–16:21). Commencing with the throne room vision (4:1–5:14), the drama consists of three series of seven (seals, trumpets and bowls). The series of seals is interrupted with the sealing of the people of God (7:1-17). Likewise the series of trumpets is interrupted by the delivery of the 'little scroll' and resultant prophecy (10:1–11:13). The seventh trumpet is separated from the bowls with chs. 12–14 which rehearse the conflict between evil and the people of God. Not unlike the customary 'The End' at the close of a movie, the final bowl judgment concludes the vision with a single word, γέγονεν, followed only by the grand finale in 16:18-21 (i.e. the final and most elaborate Sinai allusion).[52]

Based solely on the literary marker ἐν πνεύματι, the remainder of the book (17:1–22:21) consists of two final visions (17:1–21:8; 21:9–22:5).[53] However, additional literary parallels suggest that the vision of the harlot/Babylon (17:1–19:10) and the vision of the bride/New Jerusalem (21:9–22:9) form parallel scenes which are connected by a transitional passage (19:11–21:8).[54] These visions contain significant verbal parallels. They both begin with an expanded form of the literary marker καὶ ἀπήνεγκέν με ... ἐν πνεύματι (17:3 and 21:10, respectively). In addition to the expanded literary marker, both visions share broader parallel introductions and conclusions:

17:1a Then came one of the seven angels who had the seven bowls and it spoke with me, saying, "Come, I will show you...

21:9a Then came one of the seven angels who had the seven bowls ... and it spoke with me, saying, "Come, I will show you...

19:10 I fell down before his feet to worship him, but he said to me, "Do not do that, I am a fellow servant of you and your brothers... Worship God".

[52] An initial hearer might have expected the story to end here. However, in retrospect an actual hearer (or reader) should recognize that the reference in Rev. 16:19 to Babylon, the great city, serves as a literary link, relating the vision of the lamb and the scroll with the following vision of the harlot/Babylon (cf. 17:18; 18:10, 16, 18, 19, 20). The only previous reference to 'the great city' is in 11:8.

[53] An abundance of possible outlines exist for these final chapters. For a representative list of the lack of consensus, see Beale, *The Book of Revelation,* p. 109.

[54] Proposed by C.H. Giblin, 'Structural and Thematic Correlations in the Theology of Revelation 16-22', *NTS* 30 (1984), pp. 433-459 and later endorsed by Bauckham, *The Climax of Prophecy,* pp. 4-5, and Beale, *The Book of Revelation,* pp. 109-110.

22:8b-9 I fell down to worship before the feet of the angel who showed to me these things, and he said to me, "Do not do that, I am a fellow servant of you and your brothers... Worship God".

Furthermore, the conclusion to each vision includes a beatitude (cf. 19:9b; 22:7b). Each of the final visions also contains thematic parallels contrasting the dual images of a woman and a city (the harlot/Babylon vs. the bride/New Jerusalem).[55]

The section between the final two visions provides far more than a simple transition. Indeed, 19:11–21:8 contains the climax of the story, namely the apocalypse of Jesus Christ (the parousia [19:11-21], the millennium [20:1-10], the final judgment [20:11-15], and the new creation [21:1-8]). The initial reader may find it difficult to recognize this section as a transition but in retrospect the bounds of this segment are clearly delimited by the close parallels between Babylon (17:1–19:10) and Jerusalem (21:9–22:9).[56] Although this section begins rather abruptly, John has been foreshadowing these events. The final eschatological judgment alluded to in 6:17, though previously delayed, is narrated at last (19:11-20). Likewise, the depiction of final judgment in 14:14-20 points forward to 19:15. The description of one like the Son of Man (14:14-20) is clearly a reference to Christ; and although the reaping is accomplished by a pair of angels (14:15-19), the subject who treads out the wine press is only enigmatically identified (14:20).[57] However, in 19:15 John unambiguously identifies the treader of the wine press as Jesus Christ.

Numerous other descriptions of Jesus exist which link ch. 19 to earlier portions of the text (cf. 19:11//3:14: he is faithful and true; 19:12//1:14; 2:18: eyes like a flame of fire; 19:15//1:16; 2:12, 16: sharp sword from his mouth; 19:15//2:26-27; 12:5: rule all the nations with a rod of iron: 19:16//17:14: king of kings and lord of lords). Furthermore, the exact title 'God the Almighty' occurs only in 16:14

[55] It is possible to conceive the final two visions as alternative endings to the larger story. John's readers may choose to be unfaithful and thereby face judgment as citizens of Babylon or they may remain faithful and receive rewards as citizens of the new Jerusalem.

[56] As mentioned above, A. Yarbro Collins attempts to divide 19:11–21:8 into an unnumbered series of seven visions based on John's use of καὶ εἶδον. Although her theory is not totally convincing, it successfully highlights a significant structural feature. On two occasions (12:1–15:4; 19:11–21:8), John uses καὶ εἶδον repetitively, which helps to move the narrative forward.

[57] A case of the divine passive.

and 19:15. Each of these texts is juxtaposed to a reference to the kings of the earth gathering their armies (16:16; 19:19, respectively).[58]

Two final ways in which this section is integrated into the structure of the book should be mentioned. First, the transition ends with a reference to the new Jerusalem (21:2). This prepares the reader for the final vision of the bride/Jerusalem not unlike the proleptic reference to Babylon after the pouring of the sixth bowl (16:19), which prepares the reader for the following vision. Secondly, the transition ends with God announcing, γέγοναν (21:6), an end which is strikingly similar to the end of the vision of the lamb and the scroll (16:17).

In summary, the structure of the Apocalypse which has been presented relies primarily on the observation of John's four uses of the phrase ἐν πνεῦματι, and on the inference that Revelation is a literary unit. On the one hand, the complexity of the book along with the subtle interlinking of different sections defies attempts to produce an outline that will do justice to the book. On the other hand, even an imperfect outline may be helpful in order to guide the reader's journey into the Apocalypse. Notwithstanding the challenges of outlining the text, the following outline is offered based on the above observations:

- I. Prologue (1:1-8)
- II. Vision of Christ and the Churches (1:9–3:22)
- III. Vision of the Lamb and the Scroll (4:1–16:21)
  - A. The Throne Room: God, Lamb and Scroll (4:1–5:14)
  - B. Seven Seal Openings (6:1–8:1; 8:3-5)
    - 1. Seal Openings 1-6 (6:1-17)
    - 2. Interlude: Sealing the People of God (7:1-17)
    - 3. Seal Opening No. 7 (8:1, 3-5)
  - C. Seven Trumpet Blasts (8:2; 8:6–11:19)
    - 1. Introduction of the Seven Angels with the Seven Trumpets (8:2)
    - 2. Trumpet Blasts 1-6 (8:6–9:21; 11:14)
    - 3. Interlude: Receiving and Delivering (the) Prophecy (10:1–11:13)
    - 4. Trumpet Blast No. 7 (11:15-19)
  - D. Cosmic Recapitulation: Interpreting the Scroll (12:1–14:20; 15:2-4)

[58] Bauckham, *The Climax of Prophecy*, pp. 18-21. Bauckham highlights all of these connections between 19:11–21:8 and the rest of the book and he adds two conjectures concerning possible chiasms in the text as a whole. If the chiastic structure could be thoroughly demonstrated it would further illustrate the links between this passage and the rest of the book as well as strengthen the notion that the text is a literary unit. However, the chiasms which Bauckham proposes can only be construed by intentionally overlooking certain other references.

E. Seven Bowl Pourings (15:1; 15:5–16:21)
1. Introduction of the Seven Angels with the Seven Plagues (15:1; 5-8)
2. Bowl Pourings 1-6 (16:1-14; 16)
3. Compensatory Beatitude: in lieu of an interlude (16:15)
4. Bowl Pouring No. 7 (16:17-21)

IV. Vision of the harlot, Babylon (17:1–19:10)
V. The Climax of the Story: Between Babylon and Jerusalem (19:11–21:8)
VI. Vision of the bride, Jerusalem (21:9–22:9)
VII. Epilogue (22:6-21)

This outline has several things to commend it. The prologue and epilogue are easily identifiable.[59] The four uses of ἐν πνεύματι clearly mark the four major visionary sections of the Apocalypse. The transition between Babylon and the new Jerusalem serves not only as the climax of the story but also as an intercalation within the macro-structure of the book separating the third and fourth ἐν πνεύματι visions. While other intercalations exist, they divide series within the substructure of Revelation (for instance, 12:1–15:4 serves as an intercalation between the second and third series of seven). Likewise, within the micro-structure of the book, 7:1-17 serves as an intercalation between the sixth and seventh seal openings, and 10:1–11:13 serves as an intercalation between the sixth and seventh trumpet blasts.[60]

The intercalations which interrupt the series of seals and the series of trumpets have long been recognized and are often described as interludes. These interludes clearly interrupt the numerated series within the second major vision (4:1–16:21). However, the three numerated series also form their own progression (seals, trumpets, and bowls) which is interrupted between the penult and the ultima by 12:1–15:4. In a similar fashion, the series of the four ἐν πνεύματι visions is interrupted between the last and next to last vision by 19:11–21:8, the watershed of the whole book, where Christ returns in full force to deal with evil and reward the saints. 'Thereafter all is bliss in paradise.'[61]

[59] As stated above the prologue and the epilogue have parallel introductions (cf. 1:1; 22:6), δεῖξαι τοῖς δούλοις αὐτοῦ ἅ δεῖ γενέσθαι ἐν τάχει.

[60] The structure can be envisioned as folders on a computer desktop, allowing the different levels of the structure to be visualized. For example, each seal could be represented with a folder. By clicking on the folder marked 'seal number one' a horse and rider would be revealed and so on until the seventh seal which would then reveal seven additional folders titled trumpet blast one, trumpet blast two, etc.

[61] Mazzaferri, *The Genre of the Book of Revelation*, p. 245.

Not unlike the chorus of a Greek drama, all of these intercalations highlight a recurring theme, namely the people of God and their polemical relationship with evil. In 7:1-17, John recounts the story of the sealing of the people of God, a symbol of their spiritual protection. The next intercalation (10:1–11:13) reveals the contents of the 'little scroll' which John receives from the angel, divulging more about the protection of God's people (11:1-2) as well as the prophetic ministry in which they are called to engage (11:3-13). 12:1–15:4 provides a broader yet more detailed perspective of the revelation found in 11:1-13. Cast in the language of a cosmic struggle, this section can be read historically as a critique of the Roman economic system.[62] However, limiting the economic critique to Rome alone would be unnecessarily narrow as the beast can be seen as Babylon, Rome or any other system that attempts to control the kingdom of this world. The final intercalation (19:11–21:8) brings closure to the others: Christ returns; the saints are rewarded; Satan is defeated; the unrighteous are judged; and God reigns in the new heaven and the new earth.

In the light of the proposed structure, the significance of 11:1-13 can hardly be overstated. The first half of the book points forward to this prophecy and the remainder of the book seeks to explicate it. In order to appreciate fully the centrality of 11:1-13, the identity of the little scroll and its relationship to the seven-sealed scroll must be comprehended.

2.2. The Identity of the Little Scroll

Determining the identity of the little scroll has been problematic for scholars owing in large part to the ambiguity concerning the interpretation of βιβλαρίδιον (Rev. 10:2, 9-10). Although the manuscript evidence is muddled,[63] most scholars will agree that John uses βιβ-

[62] E.g. Aune, *Revelation 6–16,* pp. 679-693.

[63] The numerous variants in the mss. perpetuates the interpretative confusion. The text of the UBS Fourth Revised Edition contains βιβλαρίδιον in 10:2, 9, 10, and βιβλίον in 10:8, yet all four references describe the same item (a scroll that is held by an angel and subsequently eaten by John). Furthermore, the UBS text fails to list the ms. variants in its textual apparatus. The variants listed in the Nestle-Aland 27th edition are as follows: (1) 10:2 *txt* א* A C^2 P 1.2351 *al* | βιβλίον 𝔓$^{47\text{vid}}$ 𝔐 gig vg^{mss}; Vic Tyc Prim | βιβλιδάριον (א^1) C* 1006 1611 1841 2053 2344 *al* | βιβλάριον 2339 *pc*; (2) 10:8 *txt* A C 1006 1611 1841 1854 2053 *pc* lat | βιβλαρίδιον א P 1.2344 2351 *al* | βιβλιδάριον 𝔐 | βιβλάριον 2339; (3) 10.9 *txt* A^c C P 1.2351 *al* | βιβλίον 𝔓^{47} א

λαρίδιον in 10:2; 9-10 and βιβλίον in 10:8. Thus the vocabulary utilized by John is rarely debated.[64] However, scholars continue to disagree whether the (little) scroll that was eaten in 10:10 should be equated with the seven-sealed scroll of Rev. 5 or rather be understood as a new scroll. At first look the scrolls appear to be different. In ch. 5, the scroll (βιβλίον) rests in the right hand of God and is sealed with seven seals. Conversely, the little scroll (βιβλαρίδιον) sits open in the hand of the mighty angel.[65] The scroll in ch. 5 is taken by the Lamb, who alone can open the scroll and its seven seals. In ch. 10, John takes the scroll out of the hand of the angel and eats it. These discrepancies serve for many as sufficient proof that the two scrolls are different.[66] Be that as it may, dissimilarity between the two scrolls requires further investigation.

First, the use of the diminutive (βιβλαρίδιον)[67] does not in itself rule out the possibility that these two scrolls are one and the same.[68] As

1006 1841 1854 2053 *pc* lat | βιβλαριον A* 2339 | βιβλιδάριον 𝔐; and (4) 10:10 *txt* A C 2344 2351 𝔐^{A} | βιβλίον ℵ 1854 𝔐^{K} lat | βιβλίδιον 𝔭^{47} *pc* | βιβλιδάριον 1006 1611 1841 2053 *al* | βιβλαριον 2339.

The only clear conclusion of a review of the variants is that the ambiguity concerning βιβλαρίδιον is not new. If the decision of the editors of the GNT is followed, then in Rev. 10 John uses βιβλαρίδιον and βιβλίον as synonyms.

[64] Some scholars argue for βιβλαρίδιον as the original reading in 10:8 as well, e.g. Bousset, *Die Offenbarung Johannes,* p. 312; K. Elliott, 'Nouns with Diminutive Endings in the New Testament', *NovT* 12 (1970), p. 396. The external evidence certainly does not point in this direction. Only the uncial P, which is relatively late, contains βιβλαρίδιον in all four verses.

[65] Aune offers a further distinction suggesting that the little scroll in ch. 10 sits in the *left* hand of the angel because the angel raises its right hand (10:5) to swear an oath. While this is possible and certainly resembles a modern court room (placing the left hand on the book and raising the right hand), it is not necessarily the case. The angel may have raised its right hand while holding the scroll.

[66] E.g. Charles, *A Critical and Exegetical Commentary on the Revelation,* vol. 1 p. 260; Mounce, *The Book of Revelation,* p. 208.

[67] βιβλαρίδιον is a diminutive of βίβλος, so Aune, *Revelation 6–16,* p. 558. Cf. BAGD *in loc.* Against this view, some see βιβλαρίδιον as a diminutive of βιβλάριον. Charles, *A Critical and Exegetical Commentary on the Revelation,* vol. 1 p. 269, H.B. Swete, *The Apocalypse of St. John,* p. 127. Prigent goes even further, 'Βιβλαρίδιον est un hapax, mais il est clair qu'il s'agit d'un diminutif de βιβλάριον qui est lui-même un diminutif de βιβλίον. C'est donc un tout petit livre' (Prigent, *Apocalypse et Liturgie,* p. 151). Cf. Osborne, *Revelation,* p. 394.

[68] E.g. M.E. Boring, 'The Theology of Revelation: "The Lord Our God the Almighty Reigns"', *Int* 40 (1986), pp. 257-269; Mazzaferri, *The Genre of the Book of Revelation,* pp. 350-357; Wall, *Revelation,* pp. 136-137; Bauckham, *The Climax of*

F.D. Mazzaferri has demonstrated, John employs diminutive forms without diminutive force.[69] For example,

> βιβλίον can hardly be distinguished from βίβλος. John's pointless pendulation between τὸ βιβλίον τῆς ζωῆς and ἡ βίβλος τῆς ζωῆς is sufficient evidence. Again, though θηρίον is formally a diminutive of θήρ, it has certainly lost all such sense by now. For example, John has no diminutive tyrant in mind in 13. Likewise, ποτήριον has merged fully with ποτήρ, and it is no demitasse from which God's wrath is poured out. Furthermore, χρυσίον and χρυσός are hard to separate.[70]

Notwithstanding Mazzaferri's astute observation, D. Aune proposes that βιβλαρίδιον is a true diminutive unlike the faded diminutives cited above. Thus, the question remains, 'How does John utilize these terms?' As mentioned above, John uses τὸ βιβλίον in 10:8 referring to the little scroll introduced in 10:2 as βιβλαρίδιον, indicating that the words can be used as synonyms. The evidence supports two possible conclusions. On the one hand, a reader could infer that βιβλαρίδιον has lost its diminutive force and should be equated with βιβλίον (so Mazzaferri and Bauckham). On the other hand, it is possible that βιβλίον in 10:8 has retained its original diminutive sense (so Aune) or that John simply refers to the 'little book' as a 'book' (so Beale).

An analogous employment of this wording is found in the *Shepherd of Hermas,* which is the only other ancient attestation of βιβλαρίδιον. Hermas seems to use βιβλίον, βιβλαρίδιον, and βιβλίδιον all interchangeably (2:1:3; 2:4:1). As Bauckham has pointed out, the similar use of the vocabulary by Hermas is further paralleled by a common theme of receiving a prophetic message which is intended to be communicated to the church.[71] Demonstration of the synonymous character of βιβλίον and βιβλαρίδιον does not prove the two scrolls are

Prophecy, pp. 243-257. Cf. G.R. Beasley-Murray, *The Book of Revelation,* pp. 171-172; J.P.M. Sweet, *Revelation,* p. 176.

[69] Mazzaferri, *The Genre of the Book of Revelation,* pp. 268-269, endorsed by Bauckham, *The Climax of Prophecy,* pp. 243-245. On the other hand, Beale discredits the value of Mazzaferri's observation concerning faded diminutives because he cites only four examples (Beale, *The Book of Revelation,* p. 531). However, every diminutive form in Revelation is considered faded save βιβλαρίδιον.

[70] Mazzaferri, *The Genre of the Book of Revelation,* p. 268.

[71] Bauckham, *The Climax of Prophecy,* pp. 244-245.

identical but it does remove 'the obstacle which has prevented the vast majority of scholars from even considering this possibility.'[72]

Regardless of the debate over the vocabulary, several literary links exist which suggest that the scrolls are closely related if not identical.[73] The most important is the parallel between the prophetic call narrative of Ezekiel (Ezek. 1:1–3:11) and John's own call narrative. Few would disagree that John's vision of the throne room resembles the initial vision of Ezekiel. While the details are by no means exact, the similarities are striking. The throne seen by John is encircled with a rainbow (Rev. 4:2; cf. Ezek. 1:26; 28). In both visions lightning flashes from the throne (Rev. 4:5; Ezek. 1:13). John sees four living creatures which resemble in some ways the seraphim from Isaiah's call narrative, who sing 'holy, holy, holy' and have six wings (as opposed to Ezekiel's four winged creatures). However, like Ezekiel, the creatures in John's vision are covered with eyes and possess the same four faces in turn (a lion, an ox, a man, and an eagle), though Ezekiel's creatures possessed four faces listed in a different order.

All of these similarities are noteworthy, yet the most consequential parallel comes in the description of the prophets' scrolls. Compare Rev. 5:1 with Ezek. 2:9-10:

> Rev. 5:1 And I saw in the right hand of him who was seated on the throne a scroll written within and on the back, sealed with seven seals.

> Ezek. 2:9-10 I looked, and a hand was stretched out to me, and a written scroll was in it. He spread it before me; it had writing on the front and on the back.

Both scrolls are opisthographs[74] and are initially seen in the hand of God. At this point the accounts differ somewhat, leading many commentators to miss the true significance. On the one hand, once the

[72] Bauckham, *The Climax of Prophecy,* p. 245.

[73] See Mazzaferri, *The Genre of the Book of Revelation,* pp. 264-279 and Bauckham, *The Climax of Prophecy,* pp. 243-261 for the most cogent arguments in favor of equating the scrolls.

[74] Based on the allusion to Ezekiel's scroll (Ezek. 2:10 LXX καὶ ἐν γεγραμμένα ἦν τὰ ὄπισθεν καὶ τὰ ἔμπροσθεν) and the preferred reading of ὄπισθεν in Rev. 5:1, John's scroll should be viewed as an opisthograph. So Charles, *A Critical and Exegetical Commentary on the Revelation,* vol. 1, pp. 136-137; Beckwith, *The Apocalypse of John,* p. 506; H.B. Swete, *The Apocalypse of St. John,* p. 75; W.R. Kempson, *Theology in the Revelation of John,* p. 127 n. 270. For other options see Aune, *Revelation 1–5,* pp. 341-343.

scroll is opened for Ezekiel by God, the prophet is instructed to eat the scroll, which is sweet as honey in his mouth. John, on the other hand, does not eat his scroll until 10:10. This discrepancy is best understood in light of the fact that John's scroll is sealed with seven seals. As in Ezekiel's experience, John must have his scroll opened for him; however, only the lamb is able to open the scroll and break its seals.[75] Therefore, once John sees the scroll he first records the events related to its opening (the breaking of the seals). Subsequent to the seals being broken, John receives the scroll so that he may consume it, much like the experience of his exemplar Ezekiel.[76]

Several details further support this interpretation. The angel who delivers the scroll to John is described as another (ἄλλον) mighty angel

[75] Granting the clear allusion to Ezekiel's call narrative, Bauckham argues that John has interwoven texts from the book of Daniel with the call narrative of Ezekiel in order to produce his own symbol of a divinely given *sealed* scroll (cf. Dan. 8:26; 12:4, 9). Special attention is required of Dan. 12:4-9, where Daniel is instructed to close up and seal the words of his scroll until the time of the end (12:4). Daniel then witnesses a conversation between two angelic beings (12:5-7). One of the angels inquires as to the duration of time before the fulfillment of Daniel's visions (cf. Rev. 6:10). In response, the other angelic being swears an oath by him who lives forever, saying, 'It will be for a time, times and half a time' (cf. Rev. 10:5-7). Perplexed by the response, Daniel questions, 'what will the outcome of all this be?' (12:8). The angelic being retorts, 'Go your way, Daniel, because the words are closed up and sealed until the time of the end' (12:9).

In light of Dan. 12:4-9 and Ezek. 2:9–3:3, Bauckham interprets the evidence thus: (1) the scroll which John initially sees is 'in the hand of God' (Rev. 5:1a // Ezek. 2:9), but it is also sealed (Rev. 5:1b // Dan. 12:4); (2) before recounting his eating of the scroll (Rev. 10:8-10 // Ezek. 3:1-3), John hears his revelatory angel swear an oath that closely parallels the angelic oath heard by Daniel (Rev. 10:5-7 // Dan. 12:7). Therefore, the scroll which John eats should be understood as a scroll that was once sealed but now opened. 'The combination of Ezekiel and Daniel enables John to characterize the scroll both as a prophetic revelation of the divine purpose ... and also as, more specifically, a revelation of God's purpose for the final period of world history' (Bauckham, *The Climax of Prophecy,* pp. 251-253).

[76] Consonant with Ezekiel's experience, John's scroll tastes as sweet as honey in his mouth though he adds that it is bitter in his stomach, yet, as Bauckham notes, 'even this additional detail turns out to be inspired by Ezekiel, for Ezekiel is told to digest the scroll in his stomach (3:2) and the content of the scroll is said to be "words of lamentation and mourning and woe"' (Ezek. 2:10; Bauckham, *The Climax of Prophecy,* p. 247). Furthermore, having heard from God that his message would be rejected, Ezekiel leaves in 'bitterness and in the anger of (his) spirit' (Ezek. 3:14). The scroll is sweet because it is God's word of provision but it is bitter because the provision involves keeping the church *during* suffering and persecution as opposed to keeping it *from* such troubles. Cf. Osborne, *Revelation,* p. 405.

(10:1). At this point in the narrative the only mighty angel previously mentioned appears in 5:2 in close relation to the sealed scroll. Indeed, the first mighty angel proclaims, 'Who is worthy to open the scroll and break its seals?' Most commentators acknowledge the link between these two mighty angels but offer no further comment about the connection of the two pericopes. However, this angel is exceptionally remarkable, possessing divine characteristics. Like Christ (1:7), he is wrapped in a cloud (10:1). Reminiscent of God's throne (4:3), a rainbow is over the angel's head (10:1); his face is like the sun (10:1; cf. 1:16); his feet are pillars of fire (10:1; cf. 1:15); and his voice is like a roaring lion (10:3; cf. 5:5). This mighty angel is described in singularly resplendent terms.

The fact that John receives his scroll from an angel, as opposed to Ezekiel who receives his scroll from God, presents the interpreter with a hermeneutical conundrum. Although some scholars are content to identify this revelatory agent with simply 'another mighty angel',[77] the evidence supports a more precise identification. Two worthy attempts have been made to establish the identity of this mighty angel. According to the first theory, the answer is found in the chain of revelation described in Rev. 1:1. 'The revelation of Jesus Christ which God gave him to show his servants what must soon take place; and he made it known by sending *his angel* to his servant John.' The opening verse of the Apocalypse provides a summary of the revelatory process narrated in the book. In other words, the message comes from God to Christ, from Christ to his angel, and from the angel to John. Consequently, the mighty angel in 10:1f is Jesus' angel referred to in 1:1 and 22:16, who is responsible for delivering the revelation to John.[78]

[77] So A. Feuillet, 'Les 144,000 Israelites marques d'un sceau', *NovT* 9 (1967), p. 210; Osborne, *Revelation,* p. 393. On two other occasions John uses the adjective ἰσχυρός to describe an angel (5:2; 18:21), whence the conclusion of Feuillet and Osborne that the angel in 10:1 is simply an angel within this special category. Other commentators have identified the mighty angel in 10:1 as Gabriel on the basis of Gabriel's name (mighty one of God) and the parallel with Dan. 12:7, where a man makes an oath similar to the one heard by John in 10:6. However, this hypothesis fails to convince in light of the fact that the speaker in Dan. 12:7 is anonymous! Cf. e.g. Charles, *A Critical and Exegetical Commentary on the Revelation,* vol. 1, pp. 258-259; J.P.M. Sweet, *Revelation,* p. 177; Farrer, *The Revelation of St. John the Divine,* p. 123; Beasley-Murray, *The Book of Revelation,* p. 170.

[78] Mazzaferri, *The Genre of the Book of Revelation,* pp. 264-267; Bauckham, *The Climax of Prophecy,* pp. 253-257, endorsed by Aune, *Revelation 6–16,* p. 557. See also R. Bergmeier, 'Die Buchrolle und das Lamm (Apk 5 und 10)', *ZNW* 76 (1985), pp.

It is assumed that Christ serves as his own visionary liaison in the first two visions, thereby transmitting his revelation without the employment of his angel, contrary to the chain of revelation in 1:1.[79] Defending what appears to be John's delay in narrating the reception of the revelation from an angel, Mazzaferri declares, 'no charge of imprecision should be laid at John's feet. He is far more the master of his craft than most critics are of theirs.'[80] Accordingly, Mazzaferri argues that John intentionally avoids portraying Jesus' angel in his mediating role until after the dramatic portrayal in 10:1-11. Henceforth, John's visions are mediated by his angel guide, who shows (δείξω; cf. 1:1) him the visions of the harlot/Babylon (17:1) and the bride/Jerusalem (21:9).

While evocative, Mazzaferri's conclusions raise some concerns. First, it is difficult to equate the resplendent angel of 10:1 with the revelatory angel in the final two visions, who is described in very different terms (15:6). Bauckham, who otherwise follows Mazzaferri very closely, also resists identifying John's revelatory angel with the angel who shows John his final two visions, namely one of the seven angels who had the seven bowls (17:1; 21:9).[81] However, Bauckham's solution, while plausible, ultimately fails to convince. Despite the clear parallel between 19:10 and 22:8-9, Bauckham argues that in the latter text John is not trying to worship the angel who has shown him the vision of the new Jerusalem, but rather the singular revelatory angel from 1:1.[82]

A more natural reading of 22:6-9 would conclude that the angel whom John tries to worship (22:8-9) is identical with the angel who has recently spoken to him (22:6); however, this would equate Jesus' angel in 1:1 and 22:16 with the angel who accompanied John in his visionary transports (17:1; 21:9). This perplexity can only be solved if the resplendent angel from 10:1-11 is something (or someone) other

230-241. Cf. Farrer, *The Revelation of St. John the Divine,* p. 19.

[79] Mazzaferri, *The Genre of the Book of Revelation,* p. 278; Bauckham, *The Climax of Prophecy,* p. 255.

[80] Mazzaferri, *The Genre of the Book of Revelation,* p. 278.

[81] So Bauckham, *The Climax of Prophecy,* p. 256.

[82] Bauckham's interpretation is governed too strictly by his prior conclusion that the mighty angel in 10:1 can be equated with Jesus' angel in 1:1; 22:16. For the sake of argument, if this assumption is suspended, 22:6-9 reads very differently. See my comments below.

than Jesus' angel. Before exploring another option, the chain of revelation requires attention.

If, as I will argue, the angel in 10:1-11 is not the angel listed within the revelatory hierarchy (1:1), then is John guilty of imprecision by failing to narrate a process of revelation which would include all of the characters listed in 1:1? The evidence says no. Mazzaferri and Bauckham are correct in that John discloses a chain of revelation in 1:1; however, they err by overlooking the subtlety which John uses to introduce his angelic messenger. 1:10 opens the first vision revealing that John was in the Spirit on the Lord's day when he *heard* a great voice as a trumpet (ὡς σάλπιγγος). Once again, attention must be given to what John *hears* versus what John *sees*. I contend John's initial vision does not fail to reflect the chain of revelation in 1:1. The angel speaks to John, but upon turning John sees a vision of Christ whose voice (ὡς φωνὴ ὑδάτων πολλῶν) is clearly distinguishable from that of the angel's (ὡς σάλπιγγος). Likewise, in his second vision John begins: 'the first voice which I had heard speaking to me like a trumpet, said, "Come up here, and I will show (δείξω) you..."' (4:1).

Consequently, I agree that John truly is a master of his craft. While recording his vision, he does not deviate from the hierarchy of his prologue (God →Christ →Angel →John). Initially John only hears the angel of Jesus, however, in the final two visions John is carried away in the Spirit and shown by the angel the harlot/Babylon and the bride/Jerusalem. It is not altogether clear that the angel of the final two visions, whom John attempts to worship (19:9-10; 22:8-9), is identical with the voice as a trumpet in 1:10; 4:1. However, given the chain of revelation in 1:1 the inference can be made. On a side note, John parallels the experience of Zechariah, who also received his visions via the assistance of a singular visionary guide.[83]

Regarding the identity of the mighty angel, a noteworthy alternative focuses intently on the godly traits ascribed to the angel. Most commentators explain these divine characteristics as a representation of the angel's origin; however, a few scholars have given greater weight to these allusions, concluding that 10:1-11 is a Christophany.[84] The

[83] Mazzaferri, *The Genre of the Book of Revelation,* p. 186. Cf. Zech. 1:9, 11, 12, 13, 14; 2:2, 7; 4:1, 4, 5; 5:5, 10; 6:4, 5.

[84] Moffatt, 'The Revelation of St. John the Divine', pp. 279-494; Seiss, *The Apocalypse,* pp. 223-225; M.G. Kline, *Images of the Spirit* (Grand Rapids: Baker, 1980), pp. 70-75; Kraft, *Die Offenbarung des Johannes,* p. 147.

most thorough treatment of this possibility has been offered by G.K. Beale.[85] Beyond the obvious parallels within Revelation, Beale excavates a variety of Old Testament texts where he finds further support that this angel must be divine. Indeed, descending in a cloud is exclusively a divine mode of transport (e.g. Exod. 19:9) with the lone exception of the one like a son of man (Dan. 7:13). However, this signal deviation does not provide a problem since John describes Jesus both 'as coming with the clouds' (1:7) and 'as one like a son of man' (1:13).

While it is true that the term 'rainbow' (ἶρις) occurs only twice in the New Testament, above the angel's head (10:1) and around the throne of God (4:2), the rainbow also echoes Ezekiel's vision, where he sees on the throne 'a figure like that of a man ... whose appearance was like that of a (rain)bow in the clouds on a rainy day' (Ezek. 1:26-28). This allusion carries additional weight given the context of John's call narrative which correlates so thoroughly with Ezek. 2:9–3:3.

Finally, John describes the angel's face (ὡς ὁ ἥλιος) and his feet (ὡς στῦλοι πυρός). In 1:15-16, John depicts Jesus in similar though not identical terms.[86] Although not Christological, the pillar of fire echoes a plethora of Old Testament texts which describe the presence of God. Consequently, Beale's arguments are certainly compelling that the mighty angel of 10:1 is divine,[87] yet further evidence suggests that the angel conceivably serves as a symbol for the Spirit rather than Christ.

To begin, the divine traits ascribed to the angel are associated not with Christ alone but with God as well. In Revelation the cloud is linked more with Christ but the rainbow is certainly related to the throne of God, and although the angel's face resembles Christ's, the angel's feet are distinct from the feet of Christ, which are ὅμοιοι χαλκολιβάνῳ ὡς ἐν καμίνῳ πεπυρωμένης. Furthermore, as I argue

[85] Beale, *The Book of Revelation,* pp. 522-526.

[86] Conversely, Bauckham notes that the phrase, 'a face shining like the sun', is a common description of heavenly beings in apocalyptic literature. Furthermore, Christ's face is distinguished as being 'like the sun shining *in full strength*'. Bauckham ignores the other parallels to Christ, citing the angel's face as its only common feature with Christ (Bauckham, *The Climax of Prophecy,* p. 253).

[87] Beale compliments the discussion of the angel's godlike features by highlighting the parallel between the actions of the angel in 10:2-6 with the actions of 'one like the son of man' in Dan. 10–12 (Beale, *The Book of Revelation,* p. 524). See also Beasley-Murray, *The Book of Revelation,* p. 170. Bauckham rejects the connection between Dan. 10 and Rev. 10 on the basis of a stronger parallel of Dan. 10 in Rev. 1:3-16 (Bauckham, *The Climax of Prophecy,* p. 253). However, it is more likely that all three texts form an intertextual connection, which is the argument of Beale.

below, the Spirit (i.e. the seven spirits) is connected intimately both with God 'as seven flames of fire before the throne' (4:5) and with the Lamb 'as seven horns and seven eyes sent out into all the earth' (5:6). As in the Fourth Gospel, the Spirit serves as another (ἄλλο) divine representative (cf. John 14:16).

An additional indication of the angel's divinity may be the sound of its voice. The angel roars like a lion (10:3, cf. 5:3), and its voice is associated with the sound of thunder. In the Old Testament, the voice of the Lord is described time and again as the roar of a lion.[88] In this case, Amos is perhaps the clearest echo given that he associates the voice of the Lord with a lion's roar and the sound of thunder. He writes, 'The LORD roars from Zion and thunders from Jerusalem' (Amos 1:2), and 'the lion has roared, who will not fear? The LORD God has spoken, who can but prophesy?' (Amos 3:8).

As regards the sound of thunder, John sees the Lamb and the 144,000 standing on Mount Zion, when he hears a voice from heaven 'like the sound of many waters and like the sound of loud thunder' (14:1-2). The voice of Christ is described in the opening vision 'as the sound of many waters' (1:15). At first this might seem to further Beale's position that 10:1-11 is a Christophany. Yet, if it is not too much of a strain on the spatial imagery, the Lamb is *on* Mount Zion when the voice *from* heaven is heard by John, suggesting that the voice from heaven sounds like the voice of Christ and the mighty angel from 10:1-11. In any case, this close association between the voice of the Lamb and the voice of the Spirit is best understood in light of the seven prophetic messages. While the messages to the churches are clearly the words of Christ as attested by the opening identification of each letter, the churches are encouraged to hear what the Spirit is saying.

As a representative of divine revelation, the Spirit is a perfect candidate. Often overlooked owing to her absence in the hierarchy, the Spirit serves as John's primary agent of revelation evidenced in the phrase ἐν πνεύματι.[89] As argued above, ἐν πνεύματι serves as a literary marker in the Apocalypse but the allusion to Ezekiel suggests a deeper theological significance is intended. Similar to his prophetic protégé, Ezekiel is the only Old Testament prophet who identifies the Spirit of

[88] Cf. Hos. 11:10; Joel 3:16; Amos 1:2; 3:8.

[89] Mazzaferri, *The Genre of the Book of Revelation,* pp. 300-303; Bauckham, *The Climax of Prophecy,* pp. 149-159.

God as his revelatory agent (Ezek. 2:2; 3:12, 14, 24; 11:1; 43:5). Likewise, the Spirit is defined for John as the Spirit of prophecy (19:10). By identifying the mighty angel with the Spirit (or at least with Christ), John maintains a closer parallel with Ezekiel's call narrative. As Ezekiel received his scroll from the hand of God, John receives his scroll from the hand of the Spirit (or Christ).[90] Within the rich symbolism of the Apocalypse, the attempt to differentiate Christ and the Spirit completely may be futile. Certainly, one would not want to separate the Lamb from his eyes. In any case, the suggestion that John personifies the Spirit via the symbol of the divine angel (10:1) is possible, but conjectural. This alternative should not distract from the preponderance of evidence which points to the divinity of the angel.

Some problems remain, above all the fact that the entity in 10:1 is called another mighty 'angel', which leads even the best of scholars to conclude this is a 'quasi-divine' representative of Christ.[91] Even Beale has to admit, 'It is possible that the angelic figure in 10:1 is merely an angelic representative of Christ who therefore possesses Christ's traits.'[92] However, if this angel with all of his extraordinary and unique attributes fails to qualify as a theophany, then one wonders if all supposed angelic theophanies are merely quasi-divine angels. To dismiss automatically the possibility of an angelic theophany seems to be unwarranted in light of the Old Testament notion of the Angel of the LORD. Nonetheless, judgment at this point must be suspended owing to a lack of sufficient evidence; yet, as I demonstrate below, identification of the angel with the Spirit solves certain narrative-critical issues in the story of the temple and the two witnesses (11:1-13).

One final comparison to Ezekiel is helpful. As Bauckham has sagely noted, Ezekiel alters his terminology concerning his scroll in a manner that might explain John's use of βιβλαρίδιον. When Ezekiel first sees the scroll in the hand of God he describes it as מגלת־ספר (2:9); however he subsequently refers to it as מגלה (3:1-3). Bauckham concludes, 'It is possible that John used βιβλίον for Ezekiel's מגלת־ספר and βιβλαρίδιον for Ezekiel's מגלה'[93] (cf. Ezek. 2:9–3:3 LXX, where the translators use κεφαλὶς βιβλίου for מגלת־ספר and κεφαλίς for מגלה).

In summary, sufficient evidence exists to conclude that the open scroll which John receives from the (divine) angel is one and the same

[90] The divine identification of the mighty angel contains significant theological import. Although Jesus sends his angel as John's visionary guide, the role of revelation is ultimately divine. The angel is merely a messenger, the revelation belongs to Jesus Christ. Like Ezekiel, John can only receive the word of the Lord by the agency of the Spirit.

[91] E.g. Mazzaferri, *The Genre of the Book of Revelation*, p. 266.

[92] Beale, *The Book of Revelation*, p. 526.

[93] Bauckham, *The Climax of Prophecy*, p. 247.

as the seven-sealed scroll which the Lamb has opened. A few scholars admit the identity between the scrolls but stop short of endorsing absolute unity.[94] If this latter hypothesis is correct, then the scroll which Jesus takes from God is shared only in part at this point. Yet the evidence better supports the conclusion that John suspends his call narrative which he began in 4:1–5:14 in order to record the breaking of the seals. Once the seals have been broken, the divine angel of the Lord, distinct from John's visionary guide, delivers the opened scroll to John. What follows on the heels of the call narrative is the prophecy, or better put, *the* revelation (11:1-13).[95] The brevity of 11:1-13 presents a hurdle for most scholars, preventing them from identifying these verses as the content of the sealed scroll. Yet Bauckham is exactly right, '11:1-13 contains the revelation of the scroll *in nuce*'.[96]

[94] J.P.M. Sweet, *Revelation*, p. 176; G. Brütsch, *Die Offenbarung Jesu Christi: Johannes-Apokalypse*, vol. 1 (Zurich: Zwingli-Verlag, 1970), pp. 401-408; J.R. Michaels, *Revelation* (Downers Grove: InterVarsity Press, 1997), pp. 133-34; Beale, *The Book of Revelation*, pp. 530-32; Osborne, *Revelation*, p. 395.

[95] Contra Yarbro Collins, *The Combat Myth*, p. 27; A.J.P. Garrow, *Revelation* (New York: Routledge, 1997), p. 32.

[96] Bauckham, *The Climax of Prophecy*, p. 266.

3. The Contents of the Scroll: The Intertextual Center of the Prophecy

Focusing on the prophecy of the temple and the two witnesses may at first appear to be a strange starting point for a pneumatology of the Apocalypse. However, closer examination reveals this to be an ideal place to begin. As stated above, Zechariah 4 serves as the primary intertext for John in regard to the role of the Spirit. Two of the four symbols which John borrows from Zechariah are placed together in Rev. 11:4, specifically the two olive trees and the (two) lampstand(s). The fact that John describes two lampstands rather than one demonstrates that he is not bound by the Old Testament texts to which he alludes. In other words, John's revelation may be similar to Zechariah's vision but it is certainly not identical with it. In addition to the olive trees and the lampstand, Zechariah also sees seven flames of fire and seven eyes. Both of these images are used in Revelation to represent the seven spirits (4:5; 5:6). Thus, the largest concentration of allusions to Zechariah 4 proves to be 11:1-13. Moreover, the use of πνεῦμα (11:11) and πνευματικῶς (11:8) further escalates the importance of this key pericope. Finally, the theme of prophecy which pervades this story is closely related to the role of the Spirit in Revelation.

11:1-13 commences abruptly with little transition from the previous passage,[97] further supporting the theory that this section is a fulfillment of the commission in 10:11. John begins with the use of the passive voice (ἐδόθη), indicating to most commentators an unequivocal reference to God and/or Christ, thereby emphasizing the origin of his prophecy.[98] However, attention to the flow of the narrative suggests another conclusion. Given the lack of transition, as noted above, the natural reading of the text implies that John receives the measuring rod from the angel with whom he has been speaking (10:8-11).[99] In spite of the flow of the narrative, identifying the speaker as an angel is very difficult in light of 11:3, where the speaker declares, 'I will give to *my* two witnesses and they will prophesy 1260 days clothed in sackcloth.'

[97] If John were introducing a new section, the reader would expect John's customary καὶ εἶδον.

[98] So T. Zahn, *Die Offenbarung des Johannes* (Leipzig: Deichert, 1924), p. 419; H. Giesen, *Die Offenbarung des Johannes* (Regensburg: Pustet, 1997), pp. 241-242. Others see here a reference to Christ alone, e.g. A. Loisy, *L'Apocalypse de Jean* (Paris: Nourry, 1923), p. 204.

[99] So Kraft, *Die Offenbarung des Johannes*, p. 152.

The text appears convoluted, first pointing to the angel as the narrator but shifting to a divine voice without notice. Most commentators overlook the apparent lacuna by simply assuming the speaker in 11:1-3 is God or Christ, ignoring the clear connection with the previous passage. Indeed, Aune highlights these discrepancies as a sign of poor editing on the part of the author.[100]

In any case, it can be agreed that the speaker in 11:3 is divine, yet this raises another query, 'Where does the initial narration of the prophecy end?' All commentators divide this passage between the measuring of the temple (11:1-2) and the story of the two witnesses (11:3-13).[101] However, the English translations agree, as evidenced by the quotation marks, that the spokesperson in 11:1 does not stop speaking until the end of 11:3 (so RSV, NRSV, NIV, REB, NLT). Thus, the introduction of the two witnesses (11:3) is inseparable from the measuring of the temple (11:1-2). Although the text in no way indicates a change in speaker, it is assumed on the basis of 11:8, where Jesus is referenced in the third person, that the divine speech must have ended; but where?

If the mighty angel in 10:1-11 is recognized as the Spirit, most of the problems dissolve. The Spirit becomes the unspoken subject of the divine passives in 11:1-2. The possessive (μου) qualifying the witnesses signals that they belong to and are commissioned by the Spirit (11:3). Indeed, the Spirit can be seen as the narrator of the complete prophecy 11:1-13. The Spirit may even speak of the death of Christ in the third person without difficulty (11:8).[102] No other character qualifies. Only

[100] Aune, *Revelation 6–16,* p. 610.

[101] Many commentators have argued that Rev. 11:1-13 consists of two originally separate Jewish oracles which have been combined and augmented with a Christian interpolation in v. 8, e.g. Charles, *A Critical and Exegetical Commentary on the Revelation,* vol. 1, p. 270; Beasley-Murray, *The Book of Revelation,* pp. 37-38; M. Black, 'The "Two Witnesses" of Rev. 11:3f in Jewish and Christian Apocalyptic Tradition', in *Donum Gentilicum: New Testament Studies in Honour of David Daube,* ed. E. Bammel, *et al.* (Oxford: Claredndon, 1978), pp. 227-237. Cf. Aune, *Revelation 6–16,* pp. 585-586. Aune defines Rev. 11:1-13 as 'a coherent literary unit'. Moreover, Aune observes, 'With regard to vocabulary, it is quite remarkable that *none* of the 107 *hapax legomena* in Revelation ... occurs in 11:1-13'.

[102] So C.H. Giblin, 'Revelation 11:1-13: Its Form, Function and Contextual Integration', *NTS* 30 (1984), p. 458 n. 58. Giblin's observation is based on his narrative assumption that 11:1-13 should be read as a literary unit and not *a priori* dissected, attributing segments to disparate sources. Although Giblin claims sensitivity to the contextual placement of 11:1-13, he ironically separates the 'little scroll' from the

the Spirit can possess attributes otherwise ascribed to God and Christ while at the same time narrating the prophecy in its entirety. With no indication of a change in speaker, the Spirit becomes the best solution providing corroborative evidence that the mighty angel is a theophany of the Spirit.

Not a vision per se nor a prediction, 11:1-13 is a narrative prophecy which John delivers in compliance with his commission in 10:11, καὶ λέγουσίν[103] μοι·, Δεῖ σε πάλιν προφητεῦσαι ἐπὶ λαοῖς καὶ ἔθνεσιν καὶ γλώσσαις καὶ βασιλεῦσιν πολλοῖς.[104] On the basis of content, the prophecy is divided into two parts, the measuring of the temple (11:1-2) and the story of the two witnesses (11:3-13). The two sections are clearly connected by a common allusion to Daniel's eschatological time period of three and half years (Dan. 7:25; 9:27; 12:7, 11-12), represented by the forty-two months of persecution in 11:2 and the 1260 days of prophesying in 11:3.[105]

prophecy in 11:1-13.

[103] John's use of the third person plural baffles many interpreters. Some understand this to be a case in point of the 'plural of indefinite statement' ('they say...'), e.g. Charles, *A Critical and Exegetical Commentary on the Revelation,* vol. 1, p. 269. Aune identifies the indefinite plural as a substitute for the passive (Aune, *Revelation 6–16,* p. 573). The RSV and NIV thus translate 'I was told'. However, the best interpretation understands the plural to refer to both the angel and the voice from heaven which has been speaking to John (10:4, 8), so B. Weiss, *Die Johannes-Apocalypse: Textkritische Untersuchungen und Textherstellung* (Leipzig: Hinrichs, 1892), p. 184. In this case, the voice of the angel (i.e. the Spirit) speaks in tandem with the heavenly voice.

[104] The best understanding of again (πάλιν) in 10:11 appears to be a comparison with 1:19 where John receives the commission to write what he sees, what is and what is to take place hereafter. The initial vision seems to contain several of the major elements of a classical call narrative, including the divine confrontation (1:12-16), the introductory word (1:17b-18), and the commission (1:19). The seven prophetic messages are the initial fulfillment of this commission. Thus, the angel's instruction to prophesy again (10:11) parallels the command of Christ to write (1:19).

[105] An implicit connection between 11:1-2 and 11:3-13 may include the theme of prophecy. In 11:1, the measuring of the temple resembles the prophetic act in Ezek. 40–42 and Zech. 2:1-5. Accordingly in 11:3, the witnesses are granted the power to prophesy. See also the references to the holy city (11:2) and the great city (11:8). Although the identification of these cities is debated, the city of Christ's crucifixion (11:8) and the city in which the temple is located (11:1-2) shows a connection between these verses.

3.1. The Measuring of the Temple (11:1-2)

Verse 1. Καὶ ἐδόθη μοι κάλαμος ὅμοιος ῥάβδῳ, λέγων· Ἔγειρε καὶ μέτρησον τὸν ναὸν τοῦ θεοῦ καὶ τὸ θυσιαστήριον καὶ τοὺς προσκυνοῦντας ἐν αὐτῷ. ('And a measuring rod like a staff was given to me, saying, Get up and measure the sanctuary of God and the altar and those who worship in it.' The instruction to measure given by the divine voice recalls the Old Testament theme of protection.[106] The protection motif is strikingly parallel with the previous interlude between the sixth and seventh trumpets, represented by the sealing of the servants of God (Rev. 7:3-4; cf. 3:10).[107] Moreover, the symbolism of measuring the temple is an exact equivalent to Ezek. 40–42 and Zech. 2:1-5.[108] In both of these Old Testament texts, the image of measuring the temple represents divine protection of God's people. Indeed, the language in Ezek. 40:5 LXX is most similar, where Ezekiel sees a man measure the temple with a measuring rod (κάλαμος). The fact that 10:1-11 closely imitates Ezekiel's call narrative further supports the notion that 11:1 is an allusion to Ezekiel's vision.[109]

Be that as it may, Zech. 2:1-5 conceivably vies with Ezekiel to be the most resonant intertextual echo in v. 1. Unlike the vision of Ezekiel, both Zechariah and John omit the actual description of the measuring. Furthermore, the vision of Ezekiel is followed much more closely by John in Rev. 21:10-17, where John is carried away in the Spirit to a high mountain and shown a city which is measured by his angelic companion (cf. Ezek. 40:1-4). Nevertheless, defining the inter-

[106] Contrary to theme of protection, 'measuring' may also be used as a metaphor for destruction (2 Sam. 8:2a; 2 Kgs 21:13; Amos 7:7-9); however, this is unlikely here (Aune, *Revelation 6–16,* p. 604; cf. J.M. Ford, *Revelation,* p. 176).

[107] J.M. Court, *Myth and History in the Book of Revelation* (London: SPCK, 1979), pp. 82-83. Court notes that the sealing of the 144,000 and the story of the two witnesses share an initial common theme of protection.

[108] For an alternative interpretation that Lev. 16 stands behind this description of the temple see K.A. Strand, 'An Overlooked Old Testament Background to Revelation 11:1', *AUSS* 22 (1984), pp. 322-324.

[109] Aune identifies the act of measuring as a symbolic prophetic action, not unlike the actions of the Old Testament prophets (e.g. Isa. 8:1-4; Jer. 27:1–28:16; Ezek. 24:3), thereby providing corroborative evidence linking 11:1 with the prophetic commission in 10:11 (Aune, *Revelation 6–16,* pp. 603-604). The fact that John never actually measures the temple in 11:1f leads Mazzaferri to resist identifying John's measuring as a classical symbolic act. 'Nevertheless, it has almost the same force and import as a classical symbolic act for those with healthy imaginations, and clearly attests John's prophetic status' (Mazzaferri, *The Genre of the Book of Revelation,* pp. 319, 329).

textual echo need not mean an exclusive decision. Zechariah and Ezekiel are both heard, but in this case Zechariah's vision provides the melody while Ezekiel's supplies the harmony (and vice versa, the prophets switch parts in Rev. 21:10-17). For John, the prominence of Zechariah is carried through to 11:4, where echoes of Zechariah 4 resound in the description of the two witnesses.

John is instructed to measure three things: the temple, the altar, and the worshipers. Various identifications of the temple have been offered which are largely governed by whether the interpreter has taken a preterist, dispensationalist or idealist view. The preterist view sees this passage as a description of the destruction of Jerusalem in AD 70,[110] and the dispensationalist view understands the temple to be a literal temple in Jerusalem which has yet to be rebuilt.[111] The idealist view and the one argued for in this study is that the temple represents the heavenly temple and serves as a symbol for the people of God.[112] This latter interpretation correlates best with the allusions to Zechariah and Ezekiel as well as John's use of ναός elsewhere.[113] In Revelation, ναός is John's singular designation for the 'temple' (see 3:12; 7:15; 14:15, 17; 15:5-6, 8; 16:1, 17), yet the most significant parallel comes in 11:19, where the exact phrase 'the temple of God' is qualified with the modifying phrase ἐν τῷ οὐρανῷ. While ναός has a variety of meanings in the New Testament, it is most commonly used to designate the sanctuary or temple building and not the temple area (cf. ἱερόν).

In regard to the altar (τὸ θυσιαστήριον), scholarly opinion is divided between two identifications, the altar of incense[114] and the altar

[110] E.g. Roloff, *Revelation, in loc.*

[111] E.g. Walvoord, *The Revelation of Jesus Christ,* p. 175-177.

[112] E.g. Caird, *A Commentary on the Revelation,* p. 132. Likewise, Beale notes that the notion of the people of God forming a spiritual temple in which God's presence dwells is common to the New Testament (see 1 Cor. 3:16-17; 6; 19; 2 Cor. 6:16; Heb. 3:6; 1 Pet. 2:5; Beale, *The Book of Revelation,* p. 562). Cf. Aune, *Revelation 6–16,* p. 630. Contrary to Caird and Beale, who identify the symbolism in 11:1 as the church of all ages, Aune identifies the symbolism as representing the church at the eschaton. See also Osborne, *Revelation,* p. 410. Osborne takes a middle position, arguing that the symbolism points primarily to the church of the final age and secondarily to the church of all ages. I think John would have imagined it presented his church (!) but not at the exclusion of the church to come.

[113] If John is identifying the temple in 11:1 with a literal earthly building, then this represents a unique use of ναός, which on all other occasions refers to the heavenly temple of God's presence.

[114] Bauckham, *The Climax of Prophecy,* pp. 269-270; Osborne, *Revelation,* p. 410.

of burnt offering.[115] John makes repeated reference to an altar in his heavenly vision. At times it is clear that John is referring to the altar of incense [8:3 (2x), 5; 9:13]. A close look at the remaining references indicates the same altar is in view. For example, the altar in 6:9 under which the martyrs cry out is closely associated with the altar in 8:3-5, where their prayers are offered up before the throne (cf. 16:7, where the altar speaks in approval of what appears to be the judgment and vengeance requested by the martyrs for their blood). The only unaccounted-for reference appears in 14:18, where an angel coming out of the altar is described as ὁ ἔχων ἐξουσίαν ἐπὶ τοῦ πυρός, which parallels the action of the angel in 8:5 who throws fire from the golden altar on the earth. The altar of burnt sacrifice which was located in the court outside of the sanctuary is not measured thereby leaving it unprotected (see 11:2; cf. Heb. 10:18).

Finally, John is instructed to measure those who worship in it (τοὺς προσκυνοῦντας ἐν αὐτῷ). The qualifying phrase 'in it' may refer to the altar, meaning 'at the altar,' or perhaps, as Bauckham has suggested, 'in the sanctuary'.[116] In the temples of Solomon and Herod, only the priest worshiped in the sanctuary before the altar of incense. However, via the sacrifice of Christ all believers have become a kingdom and priests (1:6; 5:10). Thus, the worshipers represent the priestly aspect of the saints as they offer up their prayers as incense before God.

One last observation is called for concerning the exact meaning of 'protection' in this verse. The promise of preservation represented by the symbolism of measuring stands in stark contrast with the images of persecution in the remainder of the book. In 6:9-11, the number of the martyrs is not given but the implication of 20:4b is that the number is not few. Most commentators therefore interpret the preservation figuratively, representing protection from spiritual harm rather than physical harm.[117] Aune, however, sees the protection as a literal physical protection of the church until their witness is accomplished at the end

[115] Aune, *Revelation 6–16,* p. 606. Aune bases his conclusion on two points. First, θυσιαστήριον is used primarily in the New Testament as designation for the altar of burnt offering. Second, if ναός represents the temple building, then measuring the altar of incense would be redundant since this altar was housed in the sanctuary. Cf. Beale, *The Book of Revelation,* p. 563. Beale identifies the altar in 6:9-11 as the altar of burnt offering, representing the priestly act of sacrifice as the martyrs have sacrificed themselves to God.

[116] Bauckham, *The Climax of Prophecy,* p. 269.

[117] Aune, *Revelation 6–16,* p. 604.

of the eschatological three and a half years (cf. 11:7 where the witnesses are put to death once they have finished their testimony). This seems to be the best reading, allowing for both spiritual protection and (limited) physical protection during the time of persecution described in v. 2.

Verse 2. καὶ τὴν αὐλὴν τὴν ἔξωθεν τοῦ ναοῦ ἔκβαλε ἔξωθεν καὶ μὴ αὐτὴν μετρήσῃς ὅτι ἐδόθη τοις ἔθνεσιν, καὶ τὴν πόλιν τὴν ἁγίαν πατήσουσιν μῆνας τεσσεράκοντα καὶ δύο ('But cast outside the outside court of the temple and do not measure it, because it is given to the nations and they will trample the holy city forty-two months'). The outside court may refer to a variety locations, given the multiplicity of courts in Herod's temple. This conundrum is easily solved given the interpretation offered above, where ναός is understood as the sanctuary of Old Testament times. Thus, the singular court is simply outside of the sanctuary.

This explanation is strongly supported by the intertextual echo of Dan. 8:11-14. As Bauckham convincingly argues, John's curious use of ἔκβαλε is explained best as his translation of the ending of Dan. 8:11, והשלך מכון מקדשו (and the place of his sanctuary was cast down). Granted the association with Antiochus IV, the verb שׁלך, normally translated 'cast down', cannot refer to the temple itself; thus John understands the phrase to refer to the court of the temple. According to Bauckham, the verb ἐκβάλλω would be an appropriate translation because John understands the court of the temple to be 'cast out' owing to its defilement by the Gentiles.[118] Daniel's vision continues to echo as John hears that the court has been given to the nations, who will trample the holy city for forty-two months. Daniel conveys the same sense of a divine passive as he describes the giving over of the temple area and the host to be trampled (Dan. 8:13). Bauckham suggests that John may have extended the trampling city wide in order to express Daniel's reference to the host being trampled.

Notwithstanding the clear allusion to Dan. 8:11-14, a better explanation of the trampling of the city may be the echo of Zech. 12:3 LXX, which speaks of the nations 'trampling' Jerusalem.[119] Thus,

[118] Bauckham, *The Climax of Prophecy,* pp. 270-271, endorsed by Aune, *Revelation 6–16,* p. 607; Beale, *The Book of Revelation,* p. 569; Osborne, *Revelation,* p. 413.

[119] So Bauckham, *The Climax of Prophecy,* p. 271; cf. Osborne, *Revelation,* p. 413, following Bauckham.

Zechariah's text provides not only the extent of the persecution but also the means (i.e. unlike Zechariah, Daniel does not mention the involvement of the 'nations').[120] Despite this clear echo from the Old Testament, it is important to note that the 'holy city' in 11:2 does not refer directly to literal Jerusalem but rather the heavenly city which serves as a symbol for the people of God (21:2, 10; cf. 3:12).[121] As Beale notes, '11:2 must refer to the initial form of the heavenly city, part of which is identified with believers living on earth'.[122] In any case, while Zechariah continues to provide intertextual echoes, the primary intertext at this point remains Dan. 8, as Daniel's vision ends with a reference to his time of eschatological distress (Dan. 8:14: 2,300 evenings and mornings = Rev. 11:2: forty-two months).

Within the Apocalypse, John employs three separate ways to express the enigmatic time period, 'a time, times, and half a time' (Dan. 7:25; 12:7). Although this cryptic expression can refer to a variety of durations depending on the definition of 'time', the context in Daniel confirms the span to be three and a half years (cf. Dan. 12:11-12). The only exact parallel to Daniel comes in Rev. 12:14, where the woman is sequestered in the wilderness protecting her from the dragon for 'a time, times, and half a time'. Earlier in the text (12:6), the woman's reclusion is defined as 1260 days, the identical amount of time given to the two witnesses to prophesy (11:3).[123] In 11:2, John hears that the nations will trample the city for forty-two months. Likewise, the beast is allotted forty-two months to exercise authority (13:5).

The 1260 days and the forty-two months have at times been taken to refer to the two halves of the seven-year 'great tribulation' associated with Daniel's seventieth week (Dan. 9:27). However, this interpretation fails to appreciate that John describes the identical period of time, albeit from opposing perspectives. In other words, the span of three and a half years serves as symbolic amount of time in which the church will face the threat of the beast (forty-two months), yet throughout this same span of time, the church can trust that she will be protected by God (1260 days).[124] The juxtaposition of the variant expressions in 11:2-3 further supports this conclusion.[125]

[120] Many commentators have also noted the similarities with the Lucan apocalypse (Luke 21:24).

[121] Beale, *The Book of Revelation,* pp. 568-570.

[122] Beale, *The Book of Revelation,* p. 568.

[123] 1260 days equals forty-two months only if each month has exactly thirty days.

[124] Aune, *Revelation 6–16,* pp. 610-611; Beale, *The Book of Revelation,* pp. 565-568.

Recalling John's initial response to the prophecy, the reader can now understand why 'it was sweet as honey in (his) mouth, but when (he) had eaten it (his) stomach was made bitter' (10:10). The protection of the Lord is encouraging but the thought of persecution can leave one sick. John's reaction to the prophecy suggests another possible comparison with Daniel. After receiving his vision, which included an angelic interpretation, he exclaimed, 'I, Daniel, was exhausted and lay ill for several days' (Dan. 8:27).[126]

3.2. The Prophecy of the Witnesses (11:3-13)

The two witnesses appear on the scene of the Apocalypse unexpectedly (11:3) only to be killed post-haste when they have finished their testimony (11:7), and although they are resurrected shortly (11:11), they disappear from the story quickly, leaving those who dwell on the earth in awe (11:12). Who are these witnesses? Enoch and Elijah, Moses and Elijah, Joshua and Zerubbabel, the Law and the Prophets? Or are the witnesses to be understood as a symbol for the church(es), either the seven churches from Rev. 2–3, the paradigmatic church of all ages, or the church of the final eschaton?[127] Once again, the intertextual echoes from the Old Testament provide sufficient clues to establish an answer. However, the identity of the witnesses is not the only interpretative challenge presented by this narrative (for instance, the content of their testimony is not detailed).

The story of the witnesses can be divided into four sections: (1) the prophetic testimony of the witnesses (11:3-6); (2) the attack of the beast defined obscurely as τὸ θηρίον τὸ ἀναβαῖνον ἐκ τῆς ἀβύσσου and the death of the witnesses (11:7-10); (3) the resurrection and ascension of the witnesses (11:11-12); and (4) the earthquake judgment

See also Bauckham, *The Climax of Prophecy,* pp. 384-407. Bauckham presents an elaborate numbering scheme which accounts not only for the eschatological time period but also the number of the beast and the 144,000.

[125] I am inclined to agree with the commentators who understand the three and a half years symbolically to represent the church age (cf. e.g. Beale, *The Book of Revelation,* pp. 565-568). Be that as it may, I do not want to rule out a final eschatological fulfillment of the prophecy. So Osborne, *Revelation,* p. 414.

[126] See also Daniel's reaction to his dream: 'I, Daniel, was deeply troubled by my thoughts, and my face turned pale' (7:28). I am indebted to Rickie Moore for drawing my attention to these texts.

[127] For the most thorough survey of the proposed identifications of the witnesses, see Aune, *Revelation 6–16,* pp. 599-603.

(11:13). The consistent theme running through the narrative is prophecy, which is evidenced by a variety of factors. The witnesses are divinely granted time to prophesy (11:3); their ministry parallels the prophetic judgments of Elijah and Moses (11:5-6); like the prophets of the Old Testament they are rejected and put to death (11:7-10; cf. Rev. 18:24); and at the end of their ministry they ascend into heaven (11:12; cf. 2 Kgs 2:11, Elijah's ascension).[128]

Verse 3. Καὶ δώσω τοῖς δυσὶν μαρτυσίν μου καὶ προφητεύσουσιν ἡμέρας χιλίας διακοσίας ἑξήκοντα περιβεβλημένοι σάκκους ('And I will give to my two witnesses and they will prophesy one thousand two hundred and sixty days having been clothed in sackcloth'). Unlike the previous verses, the divine passive is abandoned in favor of a more direct statement (δώσω). While the unidentified antecedent of μου is certainly divine, the best choice seems to be the Spirit, but more significant than precise identification is the theological import that the witnesses are divinely commissioned.

Distinguishing *two* prophetic witnesses proves to be problematic given the prominence in Judaism of the expectation of a single eschatological prophet, Elijah. However, as Aune has noted, there was also 'an early Jewish expectation of *two* messianic figures, a priestly Messiah of Aaron and a Davidic lay Messiah of Israel, based on the two figures in Zech 3–4'.[129] The allusion to Zechariah becomes more apparent when the witnesses are further defined in 11:4. Others have suggested that the number of witnesses is related to the Old Testament notion that a legal testimony requires two witnesses (Num. 35:30; Deut. 17:6, 19:15; cf. Matt. 18:16; John 8:17).[130]

It might come as a surprise to the reader that the two witnesses will prophesy as opposed to testifying (cf. 11:7). However, as becomes clear, testifying and prophesying are synonymous in this narrative. The rare use of μάρτυς heightens the value of this designation. Serving as the ultimate exemplar, Jesus is described as the 'faithful witness' (1:5; 3:15). Jesus refers to Antipas as ὁ μάρτυς μου ὁ πιστός μου (2:13). The final reference to witnesses comes in the description of the harlot

[128] According to Jewish tradition, Moses also ascended into heaven (cf. Josephus, *Ant.* §§ 320-326).

[129] Aune, *Revelation 6–16,* p. 611.

[130] E.g. Bauckham, *The Climax of Prophecy,* p. 274; Osborne, *Revelation,* p. 419. See also Luke 10:1-12, where Jesus sent out seventy(-two) evangelists in groups of two.

who is 'drunk with the blood of the saints and the blood of the witnesses of Jesus (τῶν μαρτύρων Ἰησοῦ)' (17:6). Despite the fact that every witness in the book suffers a martyr's death, scholars universally agree that witness defines the proclamation and should not be understood exclusively as martyrdom.[131]

The clothing of the witnesses in sackcloth further supports the link between the witnesses and their prophetic role (cf. Elijah, 2 Kgs 1:8; John the Baptist, Mark 1:6). The wearing of sackcloth may express a variety of things, but in this case it appears to express two things simultaneously: mourning in anticipation of imminent judgment[132] and the hope of repentance.[133]

Verse 4. οὗτοί εἰσιν αἱ δύο ἐλαῖαι καὶ αἱ δύο λυχνίαι αἱ ἐνώπιον τοῦ κυρίου τῆς γῆς ἑστῶτες[134] ('These are the two olive trees and the two lampstands which stand before the Lord of the earth'). In this most strategic verse, the intertextual echoes from Zechariah converge to reveal the identity of the witnesses and the role of the Spirit in the Apocalypse. The primary intertextual echo comes from Zechariah 4. In a vision, Zechariah sees a golden lampstand which has seven burning lamps with two olive trees standing on either side of the lampstand. Clearly, the symbolism of the lampstand refers to the menorah, the sevenfold candelabrum which was kept in the tabernacle (Exod. 25:31-40; 40:4, 24-25). After seeing the vision, Zechariah queries his angelic messenger concerning the identity of the lampstand and the olive trees. The answer is postponed while the angel delivers the word of the LORD to Zerubbabel, which serves as the central message of the vision. 'Not by might nor by power but by my Spirit says the LORD of hosts. What are you, O great mountain? Before Zerubbabel you shall become a plain; and he shall bring forward the top stone amid shouts of "Grace, grace to it!"' (Zech. 4:6-7). The message indicates that Zerubbabel will complete the rebuilding of the temple despite

[131] Cf. H. Strathmann, 'μάρτυς, μαρτυρέω, μαρτυρία', *TDNT* 4 (1967), p. 495.

[132] Aune, *Revelation 6–16,* p. 611.

[133] Bauckham, *The Climax of Prophecy,* p. 278.

[134] ἑστῶτες, a masculine perfect participle, is problematic given that ἐλαῖαι and λυχνίαι are both feminine. Some manuscripts offer ἑστῶσαι as a corrective, e.g. א². The antecedent may be οὗτοι, so A.T. Robertson, *A Grammar of the Greek New Testament in the Light of Historical Research* (Nashville: Broadman, 1934), pp. 410, 704, or perhaps τοῖς δυσὶν μαρτυσίν (11:3).

opposition. Indeed, the work has begun as Zerubbabel already holds the plumb-line in his hand (Zech. 4:10).

With regard to the meaning of the two olive trees, Zechariah hears that they are the two anointed ones (literally 'sons of oil') who stand by the Lord of the whole earth (Zech. 4:14). It is widely accepted that the olive trees represent Joshua the high priest and Zerubbabel the governor. Within early Jewish literature, interpretations of this passage also exist which argue for two messianic figures (e.g. 1QS 9:11 '... until the prophet comes, and the Messiahs of Aaron and Israel').[135] The significance of the dual symbolism of a priest and a king reaches an intertextual climax when John associates the olive trees with two lampstands.

In his vision, Zechariah sees only a single lampstand which holds seven lamps. The seven lamps are further defined as 'the eyes of the LORD which look upon the whole earth' (Zech. 4:10b). John utilizes the symbol of the seven lamps and the seven eyes to describe his own symbol of the 'seven spirits'; however, before we explore the imagery of the seven spirits, the symbol of the lampstand requires further investigation. In Revelation, John initially sees Christ in the midst of the seven golden lampstands (1:12-13). Rarely does John receive explanations of his visions, yet the lampstands are defined by Christ as the seven churches. Given the fact that John uses the lampstand as a symbol for a church, many commentators have concluded that the two witnesses represent the church (or Christian witness).[136] With no attempt on John's part to redefine the symbol of the lampstand, the burden of proof will continue to lie with those who wish to identify the two lampstands as anything other than the church.[137]

[135] F.G. Martínez and E.J.C. Tigchelaar, eds., *The Dead Sea Scrolls: Study Edition*, vol. 1 (Leiden: Brill, 1997), p. 93.

[136] L. Goppelt, *Typos: The Typological Interpretation of the Old Testament in the New* (Grand Rapids: Eerdmans, 1982), p. 197; J.S. Considine, 'The Two Witnesses, Apoc. 11:3-13', *CBQ* 8 (1946), pp. 377-392; A. Satake, *Die Gemeindeordnung in der Johannes-apokalypse*, pp. 129-132; Beasley-Murray, *The Book of Revelation*, pp. 183-184; M. Wilcock, *I Saw Heaven Opened* (London: InterVarsity Press, 1975), pp. 105-106; Mounce, *The Book of Revelation*, pp. 222-224; Wall, *Revelation*, p. 144; H. Hailey, *Revelation* (Grand Rapids: Baker, 1979), pp. 253-261; G.A. Krodel, *Revelation*, pp. 222-224; Bauckham, *The Climax of Prophecy*, pp. 273-274; Beale, *The Book of Revelation*, p. 573; Aune, *Revelation 6–16*, p. 631; Prigent, *Commentary on the Apocalypse of St. John*, p. 350.

[137] A variety of Old Testament figures have been proposed as models for the two witnesses. See the survey in Aune, *Revelation 6–16*, pp. 599-601: (1) Enoch and Elijah,

It is important at this point to remember the genre of this passage (a narrative prophecy). John is not describing the historical churches in Asia Minor nor the eschatological church at the end of the ages, but rather 11:1-13 serves as a prophetic call to the people of God to be faithful witnesses. As discussed above, the purpose of having 'two' witnesses is related to the legal issue of a legitimate testimony, yet some interpreters have mistakenly attempted to identify only 'two' churches, perhaps Smyrna and Philadelphia; however, this is clearly wrong.[138] The witnesses serve as a synecdoche for the entire church,[139] not unlike the lampstand which serves as a synecdoche for the whole temple.[140] The church is to engage in prophecy as it bears the word of God and the testimony of Jesus before the world just as John has borne the word of God and the testimony of Jesus before the churches.

Represented as olive trees the church is anointed like the sons of oil, Joshua and Zerubbabel, to be priests and kings (cf. Rev. 1:6; 5:10; 20:6),[141] and not only priests and kings but also prophets (11:3, 5-6, 10). The notion that the Spirit of prophecy would be corporately

cf. Bauckham, 'Enoch and Elijah in the Coptic Apocalypse of Elijah', *StudP* 16 (1985), pp. 66-76; (2) Moses and Elijah; and (3) Elijah and Jeremiah, see J. Haussleiter, *Vicorinus Episcopi Petavionensis Opera* (Leipzig: Feytag, 1916), p. 85. In addition to the Old Testament models, a number of historical figures have been proposed as the source for the two witnesses. See again Aune, *Revelation 6–16,* pp. 601-602: (1) Peter and Paul; (2) Stephen and James the Just; (3) James and John, the sons of Zebedee; (4) John the Baptist and Jesus. Other interpretations include: (1) the Old Testament prophet message and the New Testament apostolic witness, K.A. Strand, 'The Two Witnesses of Rev. 11:3-12', *AUSS* 19 (1981), pp. 127-135; (2) despite the fact that John uses λυχνίαι to define the witnesses, Mazzaferri insists that the two witnesses 'constitute a self-portrait' of John. His decision is based on the fact that the two witnesses obviously engage in prophecy, which would imply that the community consists of prophets, a claim Mazzaferri is certain John does not make (Mazzaferri, *The Genre of the Book of Revelation,* p. 325).

138 Aune offers an alternative reason why the lampstands number 'two'. 'Though biblical tradition mentions but a single menorah in the wilderness tabernacle, and ten are mentioned in connection with the temple of Solomon (1 Kgs 7:49), ancient representations of the menorah often show *two* menorahs flanking the Torah shrine' (Aune, *Revelation 6–16,* p. 612).

139 So Wall, *Revelation,* p. 144. *Contra* the idea that the witnesses represent the church through the ages and also two individuals who are to came at the end of the age, so G.E. Ladd, *A Commentary on the Revelation of John,* p. 154; Osborne, *Revelation,* p. 418.

140 Beale, *John's Use of the Old Testament in Revelation,* p. 105.

141 Court, *Myth and History in the Book of Revelation,* p. 92; Giesen, *Die Offenbarung des Johannes,* p. 250.

available to the eschatological community of God's people can be traced through the Old Testament. Moses wished that 'all the LORD's people were prophets, and that the LORD would put his Spirit upon them' (Num. 11:29). Moreover, Joel prophesied that the Spirit of God would be poured out on all flesh (Joel 3:1-5 [English 2:28-32]).[142] Peter understood the events of the day of Pentecost to be a fulfillment of Joel's prophecy (Acts 2:16-21), which culminates in the great and awesome day of the LORD (Joel 3:4 [English 2:31]).

As in the story in Acts, the paradigmatic church represented by the two olive trees and the two lampstands is to be empowered by the Spirit to act as Jesus' witnesses to the end of the earth (Rev. 11:4b//Acts 1:8).[143] Thus, John is calling the church to engage in its prophetic role by bearing witness to Jesus via the power of the Spirit.[144] As a priesthood of all believers, the church offers worship to God, but

[142] See L.R. McQueen, *Joel and the Spirit: The Cry of a Prophetic Hermeneutic* (Sheffield: Sheffield Academic Press, 1995).

[143] Like the olive trees who stand before the lord of the whole earth, the witnesses occupy the same spot, indicating the service to God and also the universality of their testimony (cf. Acts 1:8). See Beale, *John's Use of the Old Testament in Revelation,* p. 106. Beale offers further support from early Jewish literature.

[144] Despite the fact that John places the entire community in the role of prophecy, many scholars resist the notion that all Christians were prophets, e.g. Mazzaferri, *The Genre of the Book of Revelation,* p. 325; Bauckham, *The Climax of Prophecy,* p. 160. In the Apocalypse, John appears to distinguish between prophets and saints in general (11:18; 16:6; 18:20, 24; 22:9). The other three occurrences of προφήτης appear in 10:7; 11:10; 22:6. The only clear reference to the church (i.e. the witnesses) as prophets comes in 11:10. It is not clear whether the other references refer to John's contemporaries or rather the Old Testament prophets (22:9 may be the exception). The activities of Christian prophets along with the form, content, and function of their prophecies have received considerable attention. See J. Panagopoulos, Prophetic Vocation in the New Testament and Today (Leiden: Brill, 1977); D. Hill, New Testament Prophecy (London: Marshall, Morgan & Scott, 1979); Aune, Prophecy in Early *Christianity and the Ancient Mediterranean World* (Grand Rapids: Eerdmans, 1983). Governed largely by 1 Cor. 14, majority opinion admits that any Christian may on occasion prophesy, but reserves the title of 'prophet' for those few 'who came to hold a recognized and authoritative position in a congregation by reason of their prominent and continuing exercise of the spiritual gift' (D. Hill, *New Testament Prophecy,* p. 121). Pentecostals would not disagree that a gifted individual may serve a community as a 'prophet'; however, the spiritual gifts are not be so statically conceived. In any case, the charismatic gift of prophesying as depicted in 1 Cor. 14 is not exactly the issue in Revelation. Faithful members of the church are prophetic not because they deliver a charismatic word for the community but rather because they bear a prophetic witness of Jesus to the world.

as a prophethood of all believers, the church bears the witness of God to the world.[145] The testimony of the witnesses produces judgment on the world (11:5-6), but not necessarily damnation, as salvation is available for those who give glory to God in heaven (11:13).

In addition to contributing to the meaning of the two witnesses, the echoes of Zechariah 4 also remind the reader dialogically of John's use of the symbols of the seven lamps and the seven eyes (Rev. 4:5; 5:6). As noted above, both of these symbols are employed by John to define his own symbol of the 'seven spirits'.[146] Four times John uses the symbol of the seven spirits. In each case, John depicts a close relationship between the Spirit and God and/or Christ.

God:	the seven spirits who are before his throne (1:4)
Christ/God:	the words of him who has the seven spirits of God (3:1)
God:	before the throne burn seven torches of fire which are the seven spirits of God (4:5)
Christ/God:	a Lamb...with seven horns and seven eyes which are the seven spirits of God sent out into all the earth (5:6)

Modified with the phrase ἅ ἐνώπιον τοῦ θρόνου αὐτοῦ, the seven spirits are introduced (1:4) in the threefold greeting located between 'the one who is and who was and who is to come' and 'Jesus Christ the faithful witness'. The second occurrence appears in the salutation of the message to Sardis (3:1), where Christ is depicted as having the seven spirits *of God* and the seven stars.[147]

[145] See R. Stronstad, *The Prophethood of All Believers: A Study in Luke's Charismatic Theology* (Sheffield: Sheffield Academic Press, 1999). Given the fact that so few New Testament prophets are known by name, Reiling argues that 'the ministry of the official prophet was the exception' and not the norm. J. Reiling, 'Prophecy, the Spirit and the Church', in *Prophetic Vocation in the New Testament and Today,* ed. J. Panagopoulos (Leiden: Brill, 1977), p. 67. Cf. W.H. Lampe, 'The Testimony of Jesus is the Spirit of Prophecy (Rev 19.10)', in *The New Testament Age: Essays in Honor of Bo Reicke,* ed. W.C. Weinrich (Macon: Mercer University Press, 1984), pp. 245-258. Lampe supports the suggestion that in Revelation the saints are represented as prophets.

[146] Various interpretations of the 'seven spirits' are offered above in the survey of literature, Chapter 2, section II. Bruce and Bauckham are especially helpful for a comparative literature analysis. Cf. Bruce, 'The Spirit in the Apocalypse', pp. 333-344; Bauckham, *The Climax of Prophecy,* pp. 150-173. While comparison with ancient literature is certainly enlightening, in this analysis focus remains on allusions to Old Testament texts (Zech. 4).

[147] 'The καί which links the seven spirits and the seven stars ... is probably copulative, not epexegetic' (Bruce, 'The Spirit in the Apocalypse', p. 335). So R.H. Charles,

Although the symbol of the seven spirits may seem to be ambiguous, the clear allusion to Zechariah's vision clarifies the symbolism. For Zechariah, the seven lamps from the lampstand are defined as the 'eyes of the LORD which range through the whole earth' (Zech. 4:10). When John describes the seven lamps before the throne (4:5) he omits a reference to a lampstand, perhaps because he has already employed that image as a symbol for the church. In other words, the seven flames which burn before the throne also inhabit the church(es), lighting up the lampstand(s),[148] making the caveat to Ephesus all the more severe (2:5b).

In the final reference to the seven spirits, John expands the imagery of the 'eyes of the LORD' in two ways. First, John ascribes the eyes of the LORD to the Lamb (5:6); however, this alteration may be explained by John's understanding of Zech. 3:9 where the branch (i.e. the Davidic Messiah figure) is pictured as having seven eyes.[149] Furthermore, John combines the image of seven horns with the image of seven eyes,[150] thereby implying the complete power and the complete knowledge of the Lamb. The horns of the Lamb may be contrasted in Revelation with the horns of the dragon and the beasts (Rev. 12:3; 13:1, 11; 17:12-13), however, the horns may also echo a contrast between Zerubbabel and his opposition symbolized by four horns (Zech 1:18-21).[151] As the horns and the eyes of the Lamb, 'the seven spirits are sent out into all the earth to make (the Lamb's) victory effective throughout the world'.[152]

As the primary location in which the Spirit operates, the church plays a vital role in the accomplishment of the Lamb's victory. As they stand before the Lord of the earth, the witnesses (i.e. lampstands) shine with the light of the Spirit.[153] Sharing a common echo from Zech. 4:1-13, the images of the seven spirits and the two witnesses are linked together. The role of the Spirit is to speak the words of Christ in the

A Critical and Exegetical Commentary on the Revelation, vol. 1, p. 13.

[148] So Bauckham, *The Climax of Prophecy,* pp. 165-166; R.L. Thomas, *Revelation 8–22: An Exegetical Commentary* (Chicago: Moody, 1995), p. 89; Beale, *The Book of Revelation,* p. 106.

[149] Bauckham, *The Climax of Prophecy,* p. 164.

[150] Cf. Bruce, 'The Spirit in the Apocalypse', p. 334; Bauckham, *The Climax of Prophecy,* p. 164.

[151] Bauckham, *The Climax of Prophecy,* pp. 164-165.

[152] Bauckham, *The Climax of Prophecy,* p. 165.

[153] Bauckham, *The Climax of Prophecy,* p. 165.

church and inspire the church to bear the testimony of Jesus to the world. In spite of the fact that John never directly cites Zech. 4:6, the word of the LORD to Zerubbabel echoes clearly as the church is encouraged that despite resistance in the world the people of God will complete their eschatological mission, 'not by might nor by power but by the Spirit of the LORD'.[154]

As noted above, the connection of the Spirit and the Lamb could not be closer, evidenced by the Spirit being the horns and eyes of the Lamb. Likewise, the hearing formula at the end of the seven prophetic messages suggests that the Spirit and Christ speak in tandem.[155] The speaker is clearly identified as the risen Christ and yet each church is admonished 'to hear what the Spirit is saying to the churches'. The hearing formula in Revelation echoes both the Old Testament prophets (e.g. Isa. 6:9-10; Ezek. 3:27) and the words of Jesus in the synoptic Gospels (e.g. Matt. 13:9, 43). Beale has demonstrated that John's use of the formula retains 'the idea of hardening or blinding which it had in the synoptics'.[156]

In regard to Old Testament allusions, the clearest echo comes from Ezek. 3:22-27 where the hearing formula not only contains similar wording but is also 'said to be the very words of the Spirit'.[157] As with the use of the hearing formula elsewhere, John is encouraging the churches not only to hear but also to heed the word of the Lord (cf. Rev. 1:3; 22:17).[158] On the one hand, the words of the Spirit are salvation for those who obey, hence the hearing formula in Rev. 2–3 is coupled with a promise for those who conquer. On the other hand, those who refuse to keep the words of the Spirit can expect only judgment.

Verses 5-6. καὶ εἴ τις αὐτοὺς θέλει ἀδικῆσαι πῦρ ἐκπορεύεται ἐκ τοῦ στόματος αὐτῶν καὶ κατεσθίει τοὺς ἐχθροὺς αὐτῶν· καὶ εἴ

[154] Bauckham, *The Climax of Prophecy*, pp. 163-164; Beale, *John's Use of the Old Testament in Revelation*, p. 105.

[155] *Contra* Schweizer, 'Πνεῦμα', pp. 449-450. See Chapter 2 for details.

[156] Beale, *John's Use of the Old Testament in Revelation*, pp. 298-317. So L.A. Vos, *The Synoptic Traditions in the Apocalypse*, pp. 73-75; *contra* A.-M. Enorth, 'The Hearing Formula in the Book of Revelation', *NTS* 36 (1990), pp. 598-608.

[157] Beale, *John's Use of the Old Testament in Revelation*, p. 309.

[158] The only other occurrence of the hearing formula outside of the seven prophetic messages appears in 13:9-10, where the theme of obedience and faithful endurance is again emphasized.

τις θελήσῃ αὐτοὺς ἀδικῆσαι, οὕτως δεῖ αὐτὸν ἀποκτανθῆναι. [6]οὗτοι ἔχουσιν τὴν ἐξουσίαν κλεῖσαι τὸν οὐρανόν, ἵνα μὴ ὑετὸς βρέχῃ τὰς ἡμέρας τῆς προφητείας αὐτῶν, καὶ ἐξουσίαν ἔχουσιν ἐπὶ τῶν ὑδάτων στρέφειν αὐτὰ εἰς αἷμα καὶ πατάξαι τὴν γῆν ἐν πάσῃ πληγῇ ὁσάκις ἐὰν θελήσωσιν ('And if anyone wishes to harm them, fire proceeds out of their mouth and destroys their enemies; and if anyone should wish to harm them, in the same way it is necessary for him to be killed. [6]These have the authority to shut up heaven, in order that rain may not fall during the days of their prophesying, and they have authority over the waters to turn them into blood and to strike the earth with every plague as often as they desire').

Although the testimony of the witnesses is not detailed, the punitive results of their prophecy alludes strongly to the ministries of Elijah and Moses.[159] As many commentators have noted, the two witnesses in Revelation share a common ministry, disallowing the possibility that they represent two literal figures.[160] Assuming the condition to be real, 11:5 opens with a first-class conditional sentence.[161] In other words, the witnesses are destined to be the objects of malice. The fire which proceeds out of their mouth (N.B. mouth is singular) may be understood as an allusion to Elijah's conflict with the soldiers of King Ahaziah (2 Kgs 1:10), where Elijah calls fire down from heaven which consumes his foes and confirms his prophetic identity.[162] Notwithstanding the overall allusion to Elijah, a clearer echo seems to be coming from Jer. 5:14b, 'I am making my words in your mouth a fire, and this people wood, and the fire shall devour them.'[163] 11:5b is a third-class conditional sentence, despite the atypical use of εἴ with the subjunctive,

[159] Elijah and Moses appear as witnesses in the transfiguration story of the synoptic Gospels. If the appearance of the mighty angel in 10:1-11 is identified as a Christophany, then 11:1-13 would serve as a Johannine transfiguration story with one primary alteration (i.e. Elijah and Moses serving as prophetic prototypes for the eschatological role of the church).

[160] So P.S. Minear, 'Ontology and Ecclesiology in the Apocalypse', *NTS* 12 (1966), pp. 96-97; C.H. Giblin, 'Revelation 11:1-13: Its Form, Function and Contextual Integration', p. 442; Bauckham, *The Climax of Prophecy,* pp. 275-276; Beale, *The Book of Revelation,* p. 575.

[161] *BDF* §§ 371-372. Cf. Aune, *Revelation 6-16,* p. 613.

[162] Beale, *The Book of Revelation,* pp. 580-581; Osborne, *Revelation,* p. 422.

[163] Aune, *Revelation 6–16,* p. 613. Aune *notes* that 'Victorinus regarded the fire that proceeded from their mouths to mean "the power of the word"'. See also Beale, *The Book of Revelation,* p. 580. Beale adds that expectation of an eschatological return of Jeremiah as evidenced in Matt. 16:14 may also be in mind.

indicating 'that the condition is assumed as possible of realization'.[164] Thus, the witnesses may retaliate in like manner (i.e. *lex talionis;* cf. Num. 35:30; Deut. 19:19).

The judgments listed in 11:6 clearly allude to both Elijah, shutting up the sky for three and a half years (1 Kgs 17:1), and Moses, turning water to blood (Exod. 7:14-24) and striking the earth with a variety of plagues (cf. 1 Sam. 4:8). The witnesses have the authority to affect the sky, the waters and the earth, suggesting a possible parallel with the trumpet and bowl judgments which affect the same areas in turn. It is even possible that the ministry of the witnesses is responsible for initiating the judgments.[165]

Verse 7. Καὶ ὅταν τελέσωσιν τὴν μαρτυρίαν αὐτῶν, τὸ θηρίον τὸ ἀναβαῖνον ἐκ τῆς ἀβύσσου ποιήσει μετ᾽ αὐτῶν πόλεμον καὶ νικήσει αὐτοὺς καὶ ἀποκτενεῖ αὐτούς ('And when they have finished their testimony, the beast that ascends out of the abyss will make war with them and will conquer them and will kill them'). The witnesses have been protected during the time of their prophesying (1260 days); however, the time of protection has ended. The relationship between bearing witness and martyrdom first appeared in the fifth seal opening (6:9) where the saints were told to wait until the number of their fellow servants is completed (6:11).[166] The end of the eschatological time period has finally been reached.

Introduced enigmatically, the beast which appears here for the first time in the book is articular, suggesting the readers should know this character (cf. 13:1-10; 17:8). Modified with the phrase τὸ ἀναβαῖνον ἐκ τῆς ἀβύσσου, the beast is certainly demonic.[167] The activity of the beast suggests that 11:7 is an allusion to the ten-horned beast in Daniel 7. In Daniel's dream, the beast 'was waging war against the saints and overpowering them' (Dan. 7:21).[168] This allusion further supports the interpretation that the witnesses are to be understood as the people of God. The phrase 'waging war' is very awkward if the witnesses were intended to be literal individuals. Moreover, as the story unfolds in

[164] Aune, *Revelation 6–16,* p. 614.

[165] J.R. Michaels, *Revelation,* pp. *139*-140, endorsed by Osborne, *Revelation,* p. 423. Cf. Beale, *The Book of Revelation,* pp. 585-586.

[166] Beale, *The Book of Revelation,* p. 587.

[167] Osborne, *Revelation,* p. 425.

[168] Beale, *The Book of Revelation,* p. 574.

chs. 12–13, the beast is allowed explicitly to make war on the saints and conquer them (13:7).

In spite of all the clear allusions to Elijah and Moses, the death of the witnesses ironically fails to parallel the ministries of these prophets in the most striking way. 'Elijah had not even died, and some Jewish traditions affirmed this also of Moses.'[169] Although the parallel between the witnesses and Elijah and Moses fails, a stronger parallel becomes more evident as the place where the witnesses die is identified with the location of Jesus' crucifixion (11:8). Indeed, the entire ministry of the witnesses can now be seen as a replica of the ministry of Christ. As the faithful witness and firstborn of the dead, Christ serves as prophet, priest and king. He represents the epitome of the persecuted servant who suffers before a rejoicing world (cf. John 16:20; Rev. 1:7). Yet, he was vindicated in his resurrection and ascension in a cloud, and the church can expect the same exoneration (Rev. 11:11-12).[170]

Verse 8. καὶ τὸ πτῶμα αὐτῶν ἐπὶ τῆς πλατείας τῆς πόλεως τῆς μεγάλης, ἥτις καλεῖται πνευματικῶς Σόδομα καὶ Αἴγυπτος, ὅπου καὶ ὁ κύριος αὐτῶν ἐσταυρώθη ('and their corpse[171] [will lie] upon the wide street[172] of the great city which is Spiritually called Sodom and Egypt, where also their[173] Lord was crucified'). The reference to the great city is problematic. The modifying phrase ὅπου καὶ ὁ κύριος αὐτῶν ἐσταυρώθη seems to point clearly to Jerusalem, yet the designation 'great city' is used consistently in Revelation to refer to Babylon (16:19; 17:18; 18:10, 16, 18, 19, 21). Be that as it may, the great city is spiritually (or prophetically) called neither Jerusalem nor Babylon but rather 'Sodom and Egypt'. In the Old Testament, apostate Jerusalem is

[169] Bauckham, *The Climax of Prophecy,* pp. 279-280.

[170] Bauckham, *The Climax of Prophecy,* p. 280; Beale, *The Book of Revelation,* pp. 567-568.

[171] Note the singular πτῶμα, which further emphasizes the corporate aspect of the witnesses (cf. 11:5, where the witnesses have a singular mouth).

[172] Given the articular construction of ἡ πλατεῖα, Aune attempts to identify the exact street in pre-AD-70 Jerusalem (Aune, *Revelation 6–16,* pp. 618-619). Any conclusion in this matter is suggestive at best, since the excavations of Jerusalem are incomplete and the identity of the great city is debatable.

[173] The antecedent of αὐτῶν is most likely the witnesses, in which case the second occurrence of αὐτῶν parallels the first. So Osborne, *Revelation,* p. 425. Alternatively, Beale argues that ὁ κυρίος αὐτῶν refers to the idea that Christ is the Lord of the whole earth including those who are responsible for the death of the witnesses, in which case the αὐτῶν modifies the understood subject of the preceding verb, βλέπουσιν.

associated at times with Sodom (Isa. 1:9-10; Jer. 23:14; Ezek. 16:46-49). Egypt serves as the epitome of oppression and slavery (Joel 3:19). The collage is further enhanced since Babylon is widely accepted as a symbol for Rome. Thus, five cities are woven into a grand intertextual image of the 'great city'.[174] Minear puts it aptly:

> this is more than a literary device. It is a way of perceiving reality. He (John) saw each story as fully historical, and yet fully eschatological. There operated within his mind a "symbolism of the centre", a perspective which accented simultaneously both the particularity of five cities and their common origin and destiny. For John, space functioned in such a way as to unite Sodom and Rome, not to separate them. Time did not separate the Pharaohs from the Roman emperors but brought them together. He perceived each separate place-time in terms of its content, i.e., that corporate historical action which 'filled it'. He discerned behind this action a "trans-historical model" which linked each story to the others.[175]

Minear's notion of a 'trans-historical' perspective is an excellent way to understand πνευματικῶς. Against those who interpret πνευματικῶς as a figurative expression of the cities' spiritual status, 'spiritually' refers to the divinely given perspective of the witnesses. The church is being called to discern true reality via the assistance of the Spirit. Those who translate πνευματικῶς as 'prophetically'[176] capture the correct connotation but obscure the agent of the prophetic perspective, the Spirit of prophecy.

Indeed, this prophetic perspective is a major (and perhaps the primary) purpose of the book. In the center of the Apocalypse, John places the story of the two witnesses, and in the center of this brief narrative, John describes the spiritual insight of the church discerning the reality of the great city. The Apocalypse is intended to reveal to the church the true identity of Jesus as the king of kings and lord of lords. Despite apparent perceptions, the beast is not the ultimate authority. If a person fears God and gives him glory then there is no

[174] *Contra* the preterist position, which equates a literal apostate Jerusalem with the symbolism of Babylon the great city. See K.L. Gentry, Jr., *Before Jerusalem Fell: Dating the Book of Revelation* (Tyler, TX: Institute for Christian Economics, 1989).

[175] P.S. Minear, 'Ontology and Ecclesiology in the Apocalypse', p. 96. Cf. C.H. Giblin, 'Revelation 11:1-13: Its Form, Function and Contextual Integration', p. 442. Giblin identifies the location in 11:8 as the 'world city'.

[176] Bauckham, *The Climax of Prophecy*, pp. 168-169; Aune, *Revelation 6-16*, p. 620; NRSV.

longer any need to fear the beast. Like John, who was in the Spirit when he saw his visions, the church must also see Spiritually.

Verses 9-10. καὶ βλέπουσιν ἐκ τῶν λαῶν καὶ φυλῶν καὶ γλωσσῶν καὶ ἐθνῶν τὸ πτῶμα αὐτῶν ἡμέρας τρεῖς καὶ ἥμισυ καὶ τὰ πτώματα αὐτῶν οὐκ ἀφίουσιν τεθῆναι εἰς μνῆμα. 10καὶ οἱ κατοικοῦντες ἐπὶ τῆς γῆς χαίρουσιν ἐπ᾽αὐτοῖς καὶ εὐφραίνονται καὶ δῶρα πέμψουσιν ἀλλήλοις, ὅτι οὗτοι οἱ δύο προφῆται ἐβασάνισαν τοὺς κατοικοῦντας ἐπὶ τῆς γῆς ('And those out of the peoples and tribes and tongues and nations see their corpse[177] three days and a half and will not permit their corpses to be laid in a tomb. 10And those who dwell upon the earth rejoice over them and make merry and they will send gifts to one another because these two prophets tormented those who dwell upon the earth').

Several possible interpretations have been offered for the fourfold phrase, ἐκ τῶν λαῶν καὶ φυλῶν καὶ γλωσσῶν καὶ ἐθνῶν.[178] On the one hand, if the great city is understood as a singular location then the phrase suggests that representatives from every group are present in the city to witness the death of the prophets.[179] On the other hand, if the great city represents the 'trans-historical' reality of an anti-God culture, then the fourfold phrase further supports the corporate nature of the witnesses; i.e. the church is visible to the whole world because it is geographically located around the globe.[180]

The witnesses lie dead for three and a half days, an alternative to Daniel's 'a time, times and half a time'. This duration is drastically shorter than the period of three and a half years of the prophecy of the witnesses, suggesting the victory of the beast is only temporary. The time periods in the narrative decrease from forty-two months/1260 days to three and half days and finally a single hour (11:13). The lack of a burial for the witnesses is most likely an echo from Psalm 79,

177 Note again the use of the singular in reference to the witnesses. However, later in this verse, the bodies (plural) are refused burial.

178 This is the second time that the fourfold formula is used to identify those who dwell on the earth. Initially the formula refers to the people of God (5:9; 7:9), but that shifts in 10:11. For an in-depth discussion of John's use of this phrase see Bauckham, *The Climax of Prophecy*, pp. 326-337.

179 Lindsey goes as far as to say that the phrase suggests a global audience via satellite television (H. Lindsey, *There's a New World Coming* [New York: Bantam, 1975], p. 151).

180 Beale, *The Book of Revelation*, p. 574.

which discusses the defilement of the temple, the destruction of Jerusalem as well as the lack of burial for the Israelites.[181]

11:10 begins and ends with the designation 'those who dwell on the earth', 'emphasizing that they live only for the things of this earth and worship the earthly gods' (cf. 3:10; 6:10).[182] They exchange presents to celebrate the death of the prophets (note the explicit reference to the witnesses as 'prophets') who tormented (ἐβασάνισαν) them. Apparently the torment refers to the judgments produced by the witnesses' testimony in 11:5-6 and it also foreshadows discussions of torment later in the Apocalypse (14:10-11; 18:7).

Verse 11. Καὶ μετὰ τὰς τρεῖς ἡμέρας καὶ ἥμισυ πνεῦμα ζωῆς ἐκ τοῦ θεοῦ εἰσῆλθεν ἐν αὐτοῖς, καὶ ἔστησαν[183] ἐπὶ τοὺς πόδας αὐτῶν, καὶ φόβος μέγας ἐπέπεσεν ἐπὶ τοὺς θεωροῦντας αὐτούς ('And after three days and a half,[184] a breath of life out of God entered them and they stood on their feet and great fear fell upon those who were beholding them'). Three and a half days forms a vague parallel with the resurrection of Jesus, who was raised from the dead after three days. The alteration most likely is intended to parallel more clearly the eschatological period of Daniel (cf. the extent of the drought in 11:6 which also extended the time of Elijah's drought to fit the eschatological period of time). The phrase πνεῦμα ζωῆς is probably a double-entendre referring both to the breath of life (cf. Gen. 2:7) and to the Spirit of life. Later in the Apocalypse, John employs πνεῦμα as a reference to 'breath', albeit with a different connotation. The second beast which mimics Christ, possessing two horns like a lamb, yet speaking like a dragon, animates the image of the first beast, giving it breath (πνεῦμα) 'so that the image should even speak' (13:15). This second beast also mimics the signs of the witnesses, making fire come down from heaven to earth. In this latter reference, πνεῦμα lacks the genitive ζωῆς as well as the modifying phrase ἐκ τοῦ θεοῦ, suggesting this to be merely a parody of *the* Spirit.[185]

[181] Aune, *Revelation 6–16,* pp. 621-622; Beale, *The Book of Revelation,* p. 595.

[182] Osborne, *Revelation,* p. 428.

[183] Wall proposes that the shift in the tense from present to aorist (εἰσῆλθεν; ἔστησαν) may suggest John's intent to focus the reader's attention on the resurrection of Jesus (Wall, *Revelation,* p. 147).

[184] The repetition of the comparatively short time of the death of the witnesses (three and a half days) adds emphasis that the victory of the beast is temporary.

[185] The resurrection of the witnesses and the animation of the image of the beast

John's image of resurrection closely parallels Ezek. 37:1-14.[186] The fact that Ezekiel's vision refers to the nation of Israel as a whole supports the interpretation that the witnesses are representative of the church and not two individuals. The vision of the valley of dry bones is commonly understood metaphorically as the restoration of Israel, leading some to interpret Rev. 11:11 not as a literal resurrection but rather a metaphor for the 'decisive deliverance and vindication of God's people at the end of time'.[187] As an intertextual echo from Ezekiel 37, the concept of resurrection may possibly be restricted to a figurative interpretation, yet if the two texts are placed in dialogue another possible reading emerges.

The death of the witnesses (11:7) does not appear to be figurative, though it may be hyperbolic (not every member of the church faces martyrdom). In any case, the resurrection of the saints at the end of time is required if the church as a whole is to be restored. Writing from a perspective that is heavily affected by the resurrection of Jesus, John expands Ezekiel's metaphor of restoration by referring to an actual resurrection of the people of God. Thus, in the light of Revelation, Ezekiel 37 may now be read as a prophecy directed not only toward the Israelites who would return to Jerusalem from Babylon but also the ultimate restoration of the true Israel, namely the church (cf. Rev. 2:9).

A final note on the world's reaction to the resurrection. The 'fear' which the onlookers experienced should not be interpreted as the reverence of the LORD which leads to repentance. Used only three times in the Apocalypse (11:11; 18:10, 15), φόβος refers to the horror associated with the realization of ultimate defeat. Nevertheless, it is interesting that, as Osborne has noted, 'the verb cognate is used for the call to the nations to "fear God and give him glory" in 14:7, and in

may be further contrasted in that the witnesses ἔστησαν ἐπὶ τοὺς πόδας αὐτῶν. According to Aune, "'to stand on one's feet' is an expression used occasionally to underscore the fact that a dead person has come back to life (2 Kgs 13:21)". Conversely, the image of the beast merely speaks which may suggest a case of ventriloquism rather than life.

[186] Beale, *The Book of Revelation,* p. 597. As Beale has noted, one of the variant readings offers εἰσῆλθεν εἰς αὐτοῦς ($\mathfrak{p}^{47}$ ℵ $\mathfrak{M}^{K}$) in place of εἰσῆλθεν ἐν αὐτοῖς, making Revelation 'to conform to the exact wording of Ezekiel 37:10 LXX'.

[187] E.g. Beale, *The Book of Revelation,* p. 597.

11:13 (the cognate ἔμφοβοι) and 15:4 the nations respond, with many converted'.[188]

Verse 12. καὶ ἤκουσαν φωνῆς μεγάλης ἐκ τοῦ οὐρανοῦ λεγούσης αὐτοῖς· 'Ανάβατε ὧδε. καὶ ἀνέβησαν εἰς τὸν οὐρανὸν ἐν τῇ νεφέλῃ, καὶ ἐθεώρησαν αὐτοὺς οἱ ἐχθροὶ αὐτῶν ('And they heard a great voice out of heaven saying to them, "Come up here". And they went up into heaven in the cloud, and their enemies beheld them'). Immediately after their resurrection the witnesses ascend into heaven. The unidentified voice from heaven has not appeared since 10:11. Pinpointing the exact speaker may be impossible, but a close parallel exists with 4:1, where a voice says to John, ἀνάβα ὧδε. On the basis of the parallel with 4:1, Beale concludes that the assumption of the witnesses represents a 'nonliteral rapture in the Spirit', indicating their prophetic commission.[189] However, a commissioning makes little sense at this point after their ministry of prophesying for 1260 days. Aune is right:

> The ascension of the two witnesses narrated in vv 11-12 is essentially a *rapture story,* as distinguished from stories of the heavenly journey of the soul; that is, the two witnesses are physically taken up alive into heaven as the final conclusion of their earthly lives.[190] (italics original)

Unlike the stories of Enoch or Elijah, who are taken into heaven for safe keeping until the time of the eschaton, the witnesses are vindicated fully after their resurrection by ascending in a cloud much like their Lord (cf. Acts 1:9). The articular construction of τῇ νεφέλῃ may refer back to the anarthrous cloud in 10:1 (so Beale) but more likely refers to the cloud of the parousia (Rev. 1:7; 14:14, 15, 16; cf. Matt. 24:30; Mark 14:26; 1 Thess. 4:17).[191]

[188] Osborne, *Revelation,* p. 430.

[189] Beale, *The Book of Revelation,* pp. 598-599.

[190] Aune, *Revelation 6–16,* p. 625.

[191] Osborne rejects a corporate understanding of the witnesses at this juncture owing to an apparent timing difficulty. Although the resurrection of the witnesses follows the three-and-a-half-year period, Osborne questions whether the subsequent earthquake and conversion of the spectators fit with the final events of the end as depicted in 19:11-12 (Osborne, *Revelation,* p. 432). Conversely, the symbols of Revelation seem to be more flexible and resist such literal interpretations of the eschaton.

Verse 13. Καὶ ἐν ἐκείνῃ τῇ ὥρᾳ ἐγένετο σεισμὸς μέγας καὶ τὸ δέκατον τῆς πόλεως ἔπεσεν καὶ ἀπεκτάνθησαν ἐν τῷ σεισμῷ ὀνόματα ἀνθρώπων χιλιάδες ἑπτὰ καὶ οἱ λοιποὶ ἔμφοβοι ἐγένοντο καὶ ἔδωκαν δόξαν τῷ θεῷ τοῦ οὐρανοῦ ('And in that hour came a great earthquake and a tenth of the city fell and seven thousand names of people were killed in the earthquake and the rest were fearful and gave glory to God in heaven'). John employs the symbol of an earthquake on multiple occasions in the Apocalypse. In addition to 11:13, an earthquake is mentioned in the sixth seal opening (6:12) and at the end of each of the series of seven (8:5; 11:19; 16:18).[192] As Bauckham has noted, 'Earthquakes in the Apocalypse of John play no part in the preliminary judgments. Their role ... is the more traditional Old Testament one of heralding the coming of God in judgment.'[193] Beyond the customary warning of judgment, the earthquake in 11:13 also serves as final proof of the divine vindication of the witnesses (cf. Matt. 27:51; 28:2).

The result of the earthquake is that a tenth of the city is destroyed and seven thousand people are killed. Giblin has helpfully pointed out John's inverse numerology of the Old Testament remnant.[194] In the Old Testament the remnant represents the faithful minority that is protected by God, either a tenth of a city (Isa. 6:13; Amos 5:3) or seven thousand (1 Kgs 19:18).[195] However, John turns the imagery on its head so that only a minority perishes, giving the majority an opportunity to repent.

Those who did not die in the earthquake (οἱ λοιποί; cf. 9:20) 'were terrified and gave glory to God in heaven'. Scholars disagree whether the reaction of the survivors constitutes genuine repentance and conversion or rather the forced homage of a defeated foe (cf. Phil. 2:11). Those who support the latter interpretation cite Nebuchadnezzar's

[192] See Bauckham, *The Climax of Prophecy*, pp. 199-209.

[193] Bauckham, *The Climax of Prophecy*, p. 202.

[194] Giblin, 'Structural and Thematic Correlations in the Theology of Revelation 16-22', pp. 445-446, endorsed by Bauckham, *The Climax of Prophecy*, p. 282.

[195] Many commentators attempt to determine the population of the great city on the basis that a tenth of the city equals seven thousand people. For example, Aune concludes that the great city must be Jerusalem since Rome would have far exceeded a population of 70,000 (Aune, *Revelation 6–16*, p. 628). However, this seems unnecessarily mechanical! John does not state that the 7,000 constitute a tenth of the city. The allusions to the Old Testament function as sufficient intertextual echoes leading to the reasonable conclusion of an inverse remnant.

impotent confession, which lacks the evidence of a changed life (Dan. 4:34 LXX).[196] Furthermore, examples exist in the Old Testament of God demanding glory without a hint of conversion (1 Sam. 6:5; Ps. 96:7-8; Isa. 42:12).

In spite of these examples, the majority of commentators see within this verse a reference to true repentance,[197] based primarily on the way John employs identical terminology elsewhere. In 14:7, an angel pronounces the gospel saying, 'Fear God and give him glory', suggesting that John portrays the combination of fear and giving glory as an appropriate response to the gospel (cf. 15:4; 19:5-7). In a related fashion, failure to repent is equated with a refusal to give God glory (16:9).

Granted the stronger argument in favor of true repentance, the question remains whether the phrase οἱ λοιποί supports universalism.[198] Comparison of the use of οἱ λοιποί in 9:20 and 11:13 strongly suggests a universal response since the trumpet judgments engender no repentance from the survivors as opposed to the unanimous repentance generated by the faithful ministry/martyrdom of the witnesses. Bauckham's comment is apt: 'John is not concerned to forecast the proportions of the converted and the finally unrepentant; he simply moves the focus of attention from one to the other.'[199] Thus John employs hyperboles to express different aspects of judgments, namely salvation and damnation. When juxtaposed with the vindication of the church, judgment produces mass conversion far greater than judgment alone (11:13); however, an earthquake for the sole purpose of judgment prompts people to curse God (16:18-21).

[196] E.g. Beale, *The Book of Revelation,* pp. 602-607.

[197] Beckwith, *The Apocalypse of John,* pp. 603-604; Charles, *A Critical and Exegetical Commentary on the Revelation of St. John,* vol. 1, pp. 291-292; Caird, *A Commentary on the Revelation of St. John the Divine,* pp. 139-140; Prigent, *Commentary on the Apocalypse of St. John,* pp. 358-359; J.P.M. Sweet, *Revelation,* pp. 106-109; A.A. Trites, *The New Testament Concept of Witness* (Cambridge: Cambridge University Press, 1977), pp. 169-170; Giblin, 'Structural and Thematic Correlations in the Theology of Revelation 16-22', p. 458; Bauckham, *The Climax of Prophecy,* pp. 278-283; Aune, *Revelation 6–16,* p. 628.

[198] E.g. Caird, *A Commentary on the Revelation of St. John the Divine,* pp. 139-140. A few commentators have argued for a universal conversion of end time Jews (cf. Rom. 11:25-27). So Beckwith, *The Apocalypse of John,* pp. 603-604; Charles, *A Critical and Exegetical Commentary on the Revelation of St. John,* vol. 1, pp. 291-292; A. Feuillet, *Johannine Studies* (trans. T.E. Crane; Staten Island: Alba House, 1964), pp. 249-250.

[199] Bauckham, *The Climax of Prophecy,* p. 208.

3.3. Summary

The role of the Spirit in the Apocalypse is to inspire the prophetic witness of a pneumatic church. The Spirit serves as the presence of God in the church represented as the seven flames which burn before the throne (4:5) and upon each of the seven lampstands. Moreover, the hearing formula at the end of each of the seven prophetic messages suggests that the Spirit speaks the words of Christ. Indeed, the Spirit serves as Christ's representative of power and knowledge symbolized as the seven horns and the seven eyes of the Lamb (5:6). As a prophet who is in the Spirit, John calls the church to be faithful in spite of a hostile world. The church is commissioned by the Spirit to function prophetically in the world (cf. Joel 2; Acts 2). Thus the Spirit in the Apocalypse is the 'Spirit of Prophecy'.[200]

The enigmatic phrase, ἡ γὰρ μαρτυρία Ἰησοῦ ἐστιν τὸ πνεῦμα τῆς προφητείας (19:10c), causes commentators some difficulty. On the one hand, a few commentators understand the phrase to mean, 'the witness to Jesus is the essence of the prophecy'.[201] However, this option fails to convince given John's use of πνεῦμα elsewhere in the Apocalypse. On the other hand, most scholars recognize that πνεῦμα refers to the Spirit.[202] Be that as it may, Mazzaferri highlights an important caveat and resolution:

> It appears impossible to equate an impersonal μαρτυρία with a personal πνεῦμα, as the angelic definition demands. Were the complement ἡ προφητεία τοῦ πνεύματος, the problem would cease. But John's work need not be done for him. The key to this tantalising enigma is the fact, especially apparent in the letters, that Christ's Τάδε λέγει is τί τὸ πνεῦμα λέγει. Μαρτυρία is therefore much less impersonal than it seems. It is equally the personal testimony of Christ and the Spirit.[203]

[200] 'The Spirit of Prophecy' was the most popular designation for the Spirit of God in early Judaism. Cf. Beasley-Murray, *The Book of Revelation,* p. 276.

[201] M.W. Wilson, 'Revelation 19:10 and Contemporary Interpretation', p. 201, see Chapter 1 above for a review of Wilson's argument. Cf. Mounce, *The Book of Revelation,* p. 342. Mounce understands the phrase to say that 'the message attested by Jesus is the essence of prophetic proclamation'.

[202] Beasley-Murray, *The Book of Revelation,* p. 276; A.F. Johnson, 'Revelation', in *Expositor's Bible Commentary,* ed. F.E. Gaebelein, vol. 12 (Grand Rapids: Zondervan, 1983), p. 432, 572.

[203] Mazzaferri, *The Genre of the Book of Revelation,* p. 310.

The identification of πνεῦμα in 19:10 as a reference to the Spirit is not insignificant with regard to the exegesis of the literary parallel in 22:6 ὁ θεὸς τῶν πνευμάτων τῶν προφητῶν ἀπέστειλεν τὸν ἄγγελον αὐτοῦ. Once again commentators are divided. The majority of scholars identify the plural πνευμάτων to be a reference to the human spirits of the prophets.[204] Conversely, Lilje states that, 'God, the Lord, himself, who gave the prophets his Spirit, has made John his messenger!'[205] Mazzaferri supports the latter option on the basis of two observations. 'First, the parallel with 19:9f. is far too close to be ignored, and in each passage there is only the single reference to τὸ πνεῦμα'.[206] Secondly, he cites the use of the plural of πνεῦμα in the symbol of the seven spirits. Perhaps the verse contains a double-entendre, implying that the hearts or minds of the prophets are thoroughly satiated with the Spirit of prophecy.

4. Conclusion

In this chapter the study comes to a climax by integrating biblical studies and literary studies within the context of a Pentecostal community. The intertextual analysis has demonstrated that the double imagery of the two olive trees and the two lampstands, complemented by the use of πνεῦμα and πνευματικῶς, creates a textual fabric that enables John to express richly the role of the Spirit in the prophetic ministry of the church, whose primary task is to bear witness to Jesus in the world.

The theory that 11:1-13 contains the prophecy *in nuce* is supported by the multiple illustrations of phrases and symbols that are enigmatically introduced only to play a more explicit role later in the Apocalypse, e.g. the forty-two months (11:2//13:5); 1260 days (11:3//12:6); the sundry plagues (11:6//16:1-21); the attack of the beast (11:7//13:7); and the resurrection of the church (11:11//20:4-6). Although the essential elements of the Apocalypse may be compressed in 11:1-13, the rest of the vision (12:1–22:5) unpacks them.[207]

[204] E.g. Caird, *A Commentary on the Revelation,* p. 96; Mounce, *The Book of Revelation,* p. 390; Beasley-Murray, *The Book of Revelation,* p. 335; R.J. Bauckham, *The Theology of the Book of Revelation* (Cambridge: Cambridge University Press, 1993), p. 110 n. 1.

[205] H. Lilje, *The Last Book of the Bible,* p. 273.

[206] Mazzaferri, *The Genre of the Book of Revelation,* p. 301.

[207] Bauckham argues that one can 'be sure that the contents of the scroll (the mighty angel) gives to John in chapter 10 extend a (sic) far as 22:5' (Bauckham, *The Climax of*

The role of the Spirit in the Apocalypse is best defined as the Spirit of Prophecy. Closely related to both God and Christ, the Spirit serves as the primary agent of revelation for John and the church. John is in the Spirit when he receives his visionary experience and the churches must hear what the Spirit is saying in order to conquer and receive their reward. Furthermore, the church is anointed by the Spirit to bear a prophetic, faithful witness of Jesus to the world. The Apocalypse serves the church as a prophetic call to respond to the revelation of Jesus Christ which John has received. Only two responses to the Apocalypse seem to be appropriate: worship and witness. On the one hand, worship is directed toward God and the Lamb. Although never depicted as a recipient of worship, it is not insignificant that the Spirit (i.e. the seven spirits) is the only character in the throne room that does not engage in worship. On the other hand, witness is directed toward the world as the church bears witness to the reality of Jesus Christ. In Rev. 11:1-13, John records a prophecy which calls the church to participate in a faithful pneumatic witness.

Prophecy, p. 257).

Conclusion: Contributions and Implications

1. Contributions

This research makes a number of contributions to the study of the Spirit in the Apocalypse as well as scholarly discussions on intertextuality and Pentecostal hermeneutics.

1. Chapter 1 offers the most comprehensive survey to date of the literature concerning the role of the Spirit in the Apocalypse.

2. Chapter 2 critically engages intertextuality in regard to its origin in literary theory. No other treatment of intertextuality in biblical studies has given this level of interdisciplinary attention to the definition of 'text'.[1] The concept of 'text' offered in this study builds on the literary work of S. Fish by answering the critical challenges levied against the theory from a literary perspective. The study also addresses the theological implications of a poststructural definition of text(uality).

3. As one of the most extensive intertextual analysis of a given pericope in the Apocalypse, this study offers the most detailed intertextual reading to date of Rev. 11:1-13, by employing Moyise's theoretical categories of intertextual echo, dialogical intertextuality and postmodern intertextuality. Throughout the analysis, I highlight intertextual echoes from a variety of texts seeking to avoid the pitfall of lapsing into source criticism by listening for a larger span of echoes which often create a double-entendre.

4. Given that responsible employment of postmodern intertextuality requires that the context of the reader be articulated, I construct one of the first Pentecostal strategies of interpretation. This strategy includes: (1) an acknowledgement that revelation is required for proper

[1] Vorster notes that 'the phenomenon text has been redefined' but he does not articulate a new definition of a 'text' (W. Vorster, 'Intertextuality and Redaktionsgeschichte', p. 21).

interpretation; (2) an insistence that scripture is to be followed as well as read; (3) the community via the Spirit plays a primary role in the interpretative process; and (4) the encounter with God through Bible reading necessitates worship.

5. The significance of the Pentecostal community in the intertextual analysis offered in this study is evidenced in part by insights into the text heretofore not seen.[2] The possibility of identifying a Spirit theophany in 10:1-11 is one such example. Although this insight is not exclusively Pentecostal, in Pentecostalism, the Spirit is stressed as the agent of revelation and empowerment. Therefore, a Pentecostal reader who expects to hear that John received the word of God along with the subsequent commissioning from the Spirit, would be open to this interpretative possibility.

6. This study proposes an understanding of the idea of the prophethood of all believers that pushes further than previous discussions.[3] Although most scholars acknowledge the prophetic nature of bearing witness, they stop short of identifying the entire community as prophets.[4] This more fully developed interpretation may be another

[2] The role of the reader has received an increasing amount of attention in biblical studies. As regards intertextual interpretation, E. van Wolde writes, 'The writer assigns meaning to his own context in interaction with the other texts he shapes and forms his own text. The reader, in much the same way, assigns meaning to the generated text in interaction with other texts he knows' (E. van Wolde, 'Trendy Intertextuality', p. 47). Reader-oriented approaches have offered new insights as evidenced by certain feminist, liberation, and other readings from the margins. However, it is important not to limit the value of these contextual readings to their distinctives alone. Employing a criterion of dissimilarity may highlight certain contributions, but it fails to appreciate the connections that different groups share.

[3] The Pentecostal position of the prophethood of all believers is similar to the principle of 'democratization' offered by J.M. Vogelgesang; however, these notions should not be equated. In his Harvard University dissertation, Vogelgesang argues that Revelation does not portray the usual equivocal nature of apocalyptic literature, because John's writing is 'anti-esoteric, universally accessible, and understandable'. Furthermore, he argues that John's experience is obtainable by anyone in the community of faith. Vogelgesang bases his argument on John's experience occurring on the Lord's Day (i.e. during the time of worship). Pentecostals would agree that the experience of John is potentially available to any believer but not because of a principal of democratization. On the contrary, the visionary experience is not brought down to a common level but via the universal activity of the Spirit, God may use whosoever and rapture that one in the Spirit (J.M. Vogelgesang, 'The Interpretation of Ezekiel in the Book of Revelation', Ph.D. study [Harvard University, 1985], p. 282).

[4] E.g. Bauckham writes, 'In chapter 11 it will become clear that the role of prophesying to the nations, which 10:11 gives to John, belongs also to the whole church'

result of placing the Apocalypse and the Pentecostal community of faith into intertextual dialogue. In Pentecostal churches, any member of the community may speak a word of prophecy, whether or not they function in the office of 'prophet'. Each member of the community is understood to be anointed by the Spirit to bear witness in the community of the love and power of God. As demonstrated in the textual analysis, John identifies the church as prophets (Rev. 11:10).

7. This study takes very seriously John's visionary experience, while recognizing that he interprets his visions by utilizing echoes from the Old Testament. Although most scholars wish to reserve a special status for John as a visionary, they depict John in such a way that he appears more like an Old Testament exegete. I argue that he is not simply interpreting Daniel or Ezekiel for his contemporaries. John's literature is similar to the Jewish prophets because he has experienced a similar vision and the same Spirit.

8. This study also contributes to a more nuanced understanding of the structure of the Apocalypse. Guided primarily by the literary marker ἐν πνεύματι, the structure divides the Apocalypse into four major visions with a prologue and an epilogue. However, the four visions are interrupted between the third and the fourth visions to include the intercalation of the parousia, the rewarding of the saints, the final judgment, and eternity. Other outlines that have focused on the marker ἐν πνεύματι have failed to appreciate the way this major watershed in Rev. 19:11–22:8 does not fall within one of the major visions but stands out as the climax of the Apocalypse.

2. Implications for Future Research

First, given the emerging interest in pneumatology among systematic theologians like J. Moltmann[5] or C. Pinnock,[6] one item worthy of future research is a pneumatology that is informed by the findings of this study, allowing the role of the Spirit in the Apocalypse to contribute to the broader theological construction.

(Bauckham, *The Climax of Prophecy*, p. 265). However, Bauckham resists identifying a prophethood of all believers.

[5] J. Moltmann, *The Spirit of Life: A Universal Affirmation* (trans. M. Kohl; Minneapolis: Fortress, 1992).

[6] C.H. Pinnock, *Flame of Love: A Theology of the Holy Spirit* (Downers Grove: InterVarsity Press, 1996).

Secondly, given the close relationship in the Apocalypse between the Spirit and the church, this study also has implications for ecclesiology. Specifically, the church as a community serves as anointed prophetic voice in the world.

Thirdly, in a similar vein, there are also significant implications for missiology. The empowerment of the Spirit is for the sole purpose of bearing witness so that others may believe.

Fourthly, future research may include the history of effects of the Apocalypse with special attention to the effects of its pneumatology in order to broaden the scope of this inquiry and acknowledge the influence which the Apocalypse has enjoyed in Western culture. To date the effects of the Apocalypse on art, music, literature, film, and political critique have received some attention.[7] It would be fruitful to bring this type of investigation to bear on the pneumatology of the Apocalypse. As E. Schüssler Fiorenza writes,

> Exegetes and theologians still have to discover what artists have long understood: the strength of the language and composition of Rev. lies not in its theological argumentation or historical information but in its evocative power inviting imaginative participation... Insofar as exegetes have understood Revelation as a descriptive or predictive account of factual events of

[7] For the influence of the Apocalypse in art see J.M. Ford, 'Visual Art and the Apocalypse', *BibToday* 34:6 (1996), pp. 366-373; F. van der Meer, *Apocalypse;* M.R. James, *The Apocalypse in Art* (London: Oxford University Press, 1931); R. Petraglio *et al., L'Apocalypse de Jean: traditions exégétiques et iconographiques aux III-XIIIe siècles* (Geneva: Librairie Droz, 1979); G. Quispel, *The Secret Book of Revelation* (London: Collins, 1979); N. Grubb, *Revelations: Art of the Apocalypse* (New York: Abbeville, 1997). See the use of the Apocalypse in black American slave spirituals in G. Wilmore, *Last Things First* (Philadelphia: Westminster, 1982), pp. 77-96. A. Boesak, *Comfort and Protest: The Apocalypse from a South African Perspective* (Philadelphia: Westminster, 1987) offers an interpretation of Revelation from the perspective of a black minister living under the oppression of apartheid. For a feminist critique with a psychoanalytical twist see T. Pippin, *Death and Desire: The Rhetoric of Gender in the Apocalypse of John* (Literary Currents in Biblical Interpretation; Louisville: Westminster/John Knox Press, 1992); idem, 'Eros and the End: Reading for Gender in the Apocalypse of John', *Semeia* 59 (1992), pp. 193-210; idem, 'The Heroine and the Whore: Fantasy and the Female in the Apocalypse of John', *Semeia* 60 (1992), pp. 67-82; idem, 'Peering into the Abyss: A Postmodern Reading of the Biblical Bottomless Pit', in *The New Literary Criticism and the New Testament,* ed. E.V. McKnight and E. Struthers Malbon (Sheffield: JSOT Press, 1994), pp. 251-68; S. Moore, 'The Beatific Vision as a Posing Exhibition: Revelation's Hypermasculine Deity', *JSNT* 60 (1995) pp. 27-55, who uses S. Freud as a dialogue partner. See also C. Nessan, 'When Faith Turns Fatal: David Koresh and Tragic Misreadings of Revelation', *CurrTheolMiss* 22:3 (1995), pp. 191-199.

the past and the future or of timeless theological statements and principles, they have tended to reduce the imaginative language of Revelation to a one-to-one meaning.[8]

Finally, perhaps the most fruitful study yet to be done relates to John's use of Zechariah. Extensive attention has been given to all of John's other primary intertexts including Ezekiel,[9] Daniel,[10] and Isaiah.[11] However, a focused work on John's use of Zechariah has yet to be written. As demonstrated in this study, Zechariah serves as the primary intertext as regards the role of the Spirit.

[8] E. Schüssler Fiorenza, *The Book of Revelation, Justice and Judgment* (Philadelphia: Fortress, 1985), pp. 22-23.

[9] J.M. Vogelgesang, 'The Interpretation of Ezekiel in the Book of Revelation', Ph.D. study (Harvard University, 1985); J.-P. Ruiz, *Ezekiel in the Apocalypse: The Transformation of Prophetic Language in Revelation 16,17–19,10* (Frankfurt am Main: Peter Lang, 1989).

[10] G.K. Beale, *The Use of Daniel in Jewish Apocalyptic Literature and the Revelation of St John* (Lanham, MD: University Press of America, 1984).

[11] J. Fekkes, *Isaiah and Prophetic Traditions in the Book of Revelation; Visionary Antecedents and their Development* (Sheffield: Sheffield Academic Press, 1994).

Bibliography

Abbott, N.A., ed. *The Documents of Vatican II.* New York: Guild Press, 1966.

Aichele, G. and G.A. Phillips. 'Introduction: Exegesis, Eisegesis, Intergesis', *Semeia* 69/70 (1995), pp. 7-18.

Alexander, L. 'The Living Voice: Scepticism towards the Written Word in Early Christianity and in Graeco-Roman Texts'. In *The Bible in Three Dimensions: Essays in Celebration of Forty Years of Biblical Studies in the University of Sheffield*, ed. D.J.A. Clines *et al.* Sheffield: Sheffield Academic Press, 1990, pp. 221-247.

Alexander, L., ed. *Images of Empire.* Sheffield: Sheffield Academic Press, 1991.

Allo, E.B. *Saint Jean: L'Apocalypse.* Paris: Lecoffe, 1921.

Anderson, R.M. *Vision of the Disinherited: The Making of American Pentecostalism.* Peabody: Hendrickson, 1972.

Archer, K.J. *Forging a New Path, A Contemporary Pentecostal Hermeneutical Strategy for the 21st Century.* London: T. & T. Clark, 2004.

———. 'Pentecostal Hermeneutics: Retrospect and Prospect', *JPT* 8 (1996), pp. 63-81.

Arrington, F.L. 'Hermeneutics', *DPCM,* pp. 376-389.

Aune, D. 'The Apocalypse of John and the Problem of Genre', *Semeia* 36 (1986), pp. 65-96.

———. 'Intertextuality and the Genre of the Apocalypse'. In *Society of Biblical Literature Seminar Papers*, 30, ed. E.H. Lovering, Jr. Atlanta: Scholars Press, 1991, pp. 142-160.

———. *The New Testament in its Literary Environment.* Philadelphia: Westminster, 1987.

———. *Prophecy in Early Christianity and the Ancient Mediterranean World.* Grand Rapids: Eerdmans, 1983.

———. *Revelation 1-5.* vol. 1. Waco: Word, 1997.

———. *Revelation 6-16.* vol. 2. Waco: Word, 1998.

Austin, J.L. *How to Do Things with Words.* Cambridge, MA: Harvard University Press, 1975.

Baker, R.O. 'Pentecostal Bible Reading: Toward a Model of Reading for the Formation of Christian Affections', *JPT* 7 (1995), pp. 34-48.

Barr, D.L. 'The Apocalypse as a Symbolic Transformation of the World: A Literary Analysis', *Int* 38 (1984), pp. 39-50.

———. 'The Apocalypse of John as Oral Enactment', *Int* 38 (1984), pp. 243-256.
———. *New Testament Story: An Introduction*. Belmont: Wadsworth, 1987.
Barrett, C.K. *The Gospel According to St John*. London: SPCK, 1978.
Barrett, D.B. 'Statistics, Global', *DPCM,* pp. 810-830.
Barthes, R. *Image Music Text*. Trans. S. Heath. New York: Hill and Wang, 1977.
———. *The Pleasure of the Text*. Trans. R. Miller; New York: Hill and Wang, 1975.
Bauckham, R.J. 'The Book of Revelation as a Christian War Scroll', *Neot* 22 (1988), pp. 17-40.
———. *The Climax of Prophecy: Studies in the Book of Revelation*. Edinburgh: T. & T. Clark, 1993.
———. 'Enoch and Elijah in the Coptic Apocalypse of Elijah', *StudP* 16 (1985), pp. 66-76.
———. 'The Role of the Spirit in the Apocalypse', *EQ* 52 (1980), pp. 66-83.
———. 'Synoptic Parousia Parables and the Apocalypse', *NTS* 23 (1977), pp. 162-176.
Beal, T.K. 'Ideology and Intertextuality: Surplus of Meaning and Controlling the Means of Production'. In *Reading Between Texts: Intertextuality and the Hebrew Bible,* ed. D.N. Fewell. Louisville: Westminster, 1992, pp. 27-40.
Beale, G.K. *The Book of Revelation*. Grand Rapids: Eerdmans, 1999.
———. 'The Danielic Background for Revelation 13:18 and 17:9', *TynBul* 31 (1980), pp. 163-170.
———. 'Did Jesus and His Followers Preach the Right Doctrine from the Wrong Texts? An Examination of the Presuppositions of Jesus' and the Apostles' Exegetical Method', *Themelios* 14 (1989), pp. 89-96.
———. 'The Problem of the Man from the Sea in IV Ezra 13 and its Relation to the Messianic Concept in John's Apocalypse', *NovT* 25 (1983), pp. 182-188.
———. *The Use of Daniel in Jewish Apocalyptic Literature and the Revelation of St John*. Lanham, MD: University Press of America, 1984.
Beasley-Murray, G.R. *The Book of Revelation*. London: Marshall, Morgan & Scott, 1974.
Beckwith, I.T. *The Apocalypse of John*. Grand Rapids: Baker Book House, 1967, reprint of 1919 edition.
Bergmeier, R. 'Die Buchrolle und das Lamm (Apk 5 und 10)', *ZNW* 76 (1985), pp. 230-241.
Bittlinger, A., ed. *The Church Is Charismatic*. Geneva: Renewal and Congregational Life, World Council of Churches, 1981.
Black, M. 'The "Two Witnesses" of Rev. 11:3f in Jewish and Christian Apocalyptic Tradition'. In *Donum Gentilicum: New Testament Studies in Honour of David Daube,* ed. E. Bammel, *et al.* Oxford: Clarendon Press, 1978, pp. 227-237.
Blevins, J.L. *Revelation as Drama*. Nashville: Broadman, 1984.

Bloom, H. *The Breaking of the Vessels.* Chicago & London: University of Chicago Press, 1982.

———. *The Revelation of St John the Divine.* Modern Critical Interpretations, NY: Chelsea House, 1988.

Boesak, A. *Comfort and Protest: The Apocalypse from a South African Perspective.* Philadelphia: Westminster, 1987.

Bogaert, P.-M. 'Les apocalypses contemporaines de Baruch, d'Esdras et de Jean'. In *L'Apocalypse johannique et l'apocalyptique dans le Nouveau Testament,* ed. J. Lambrecht. Leuven: Leuven University Press, 1980, pp. 47-68.

Boismard, M.-E. 'Notes sur L'Apocalypse', *RB* 59 (1952), pp. 161-181.

Boring, M.E. 'The Apocalypse as Christian Prophecy'. In *Society of Biblical Literature Seminar Papers,* ed. G. MacRae. Missoula, MT: Scholars Press, pp. 43-62.

———. 'The Theology of Revelation: "The Lord Our God the Almighty Reigns"', *Int* 40 (1986), pp. 257-269.

Bornkamm, G. 'Die Komposition der apokalyptischen Visionen in der Offenbarung Johannes', *ZNW* 36 (1937), pp. 132-149.

Bousset, W. *Die Offenbarung Johannes.* Göttingen: Vandenhoeck & Ruprecht, 1906.

Bowman, J.W. 'The Revelation to John: Its Dramatic Structure and Message', *Int* 9 (1955), pp. 436-453.

Brett, M.G. 'Four or Five Things to Do with Texts: A Taxonomy of Interpretative Interests'. In *The Bible in Three Dimensions: Essays in Celebration of Forty Years of Biblical Studies in the University of Sheffield,* ed. D.J.A. Clines *et al.* Sheffield: Sheffield Academic Press, 1990, pp. 356-377.

Brewer, D.I. *Techniques and Assumptions in Jewish Exegesis before 70 C.E.* Tübingen: Mohr, 1992.

Brewer, R.R. 'The Influence of Greek Drama on the Apocalypse of John', *Anglican Theological Review* 71 (1936), pp. 74-92.

Bridges Johns, C. 'The Adolescence of Pentecostalism: In Search of a Legitimate Sectarian Identity', *Pneuma* 17 (1995), pp. 3-17.

———. 'Meeting God in the Margins, Ministry among Modernity's Refugees'. In *The Papers of the Henry Luce III Fellows in Theology,* ed. M. Zyniewicz. Atlanta: Scholars Press, 1999, pp. 7-31.

———. *Pentecostal Formation: A Pedagogy among the Oppressed.* Sheffield: Sheffield Academic Press, 1993.

Brown, R. *The Gospel According to John.* 2 vols. Garden City, NY: Doubleday, 1966.

Bruce, F.F. 'The Spirit in the Apocalypse'. In *Christ and Spirit in the New Testament: In Honour of Charles Francis Digby Moule,* ed. B. Lindars and S.S. Smalley. Cambridge: Cambridge University Press, 1973, pp. 333-344.

Brueggemann, W. 'II Kings 18-19: The Legitimacy of a Sectarian Hermeneutic', *HBT* 8 (1985), pp. 1-42.

———. *Texts under Negotiation: The Bible and Postmodern Imagination.* Minneapolis: Fortress, 1993.

Brütsch, C. *Die Offenbarung Jesu Christi: Johannes-Apokalypse.* vol. 1. Zürich: Zwingli Verlag, 1970.

Buchanan, G. *Introduction to Intertextuality.* Lewiston, NY: Edwin Mellen Press, 1994.

Burge, G. *The Anointed Community.* Grand Rapids: Eerdmans, 1987.

Burgess, S.M. *et al. Dictionary of Pentecostal and Charismatic Movements.* Grand Rapids: Zondervan, 1988.

Burnett, F. 'Postmodern Biblical Exegesis: The Eve of Historical Criticism', *Semeia* 51 (1990), pp. 51-80.

Byrd, J. 'Paul Ricoeur's Hermeneutical Theory and Pentecostal Proclamation', *Pneuma* 15:2 (1993), pp. 203-214.

Caird, G.B. *A Commentary on the Revelation of St. John the Divine.* London: A. & C. Black, 1966.

Cargal, T.B. 'Beyond the Fundamentalist-Modernist Controversy: Pentecostals and Hermeneutics in a Postmodern Age', *Pneuma* 15:2 (1993), pp. 163-187.

Carson, D.A. *The Gagging of God.* Grand Rapids: Eerdmans, 1996.

Cartledge, M. 'Empirical Theology: Towards an Evangelical–Charismatic Hermeneutic', *JPT* 9 (1996), pp. 115-126.

Charles, R.H. *A Critical and Exegetical Commentary on the Revelation of St John.* 2 vols. Edinburgh: T. & T. Clark, 1920.

———. *Studies in the Apocalypse.* Edinburgh: T & T Clark, 1913.

Childs, B.S. 'Interpretation in Faith', *Int* 18 (1964), pp. 432-449.

———. *Introduction to the Old Testament as Scripture.* London: SCM Press, 1979.

———. 'Midrash and the Old Testament'. In *Understanding the Sacred Text: Essays in Honor of Morton S. Enslin on the Hebrew Bible and Christian Beginnings,* ed. J. Reumann. Valley Forge: Judson, 1972, pp. 45-49.

———. *The New Testament as Canon: An Introduction.* London: SCM Press, 1984

Cimpean, F. 'From Margins to Center: Pentecostal and Orthodox Readings of Romans 8 in Romania', *JPT* (forthcoming).

Clayton, J. and E. Rothstein, 'Figures in Corpus: Theories of Influence and Intertextuality'. In *Influence and Intertextuality in Literary History,* eds. J. Clayton and E. Rothstein. Madison, WI: University of Wisconsin Press, 1991, pp. 3-36.

Clayton, J. and E. Rothstein, eds. *Influence and Intertextuality in Literary History.* Madison, WI: University of Wisconsin Press, 1991.

Clines, D.J.A. *I, He, We, They.* Sheffield: Sheffield Academic Press, 1976.

Coe, S. 'In Search of Renewal in Theological Education', *Theo Ed* 9 (1973), pp. 233-243.

Collins, J.J. ed., 'Apocalypse: The Morphology of a Genre', *Semeia* 14 (1979), pp.1-214.

Considine, J.S. 'The Two Witnesses, Apoc. 11:3-13', *CBQ* 8 (1946), pp. 377-392.

Court, J.M. *Myth and History in the Book of Revelation.* London: SPCK, 1979.

Cox, H. *Fire from Heaven: The Rise of Pentecostal Spirituality and the Reshaping of Religion in the Twenty-first Century*. Reading, MA: Addison-Wesley, 1995.

Culler, J. *On Deconstruction: Theory and Criticism After Structuralism*. Ithaca, NY: Cornell University Press, 1982.

———. *The Pursuit of Signs: Semiotics, Literature, Deconstruction*. London: Routledge & Kegan Paul, 1981.

Cullmann, O. *Salvation in History*. London: SCM, 1967.

Davies, P. *Whose Bible is it Anyway?* Sheffield: Sheffield Academic Press, 1995.

Dayton, D.W. *Theological Roots of Pentecostalism*. Metuchen: Scarecrow Press, 1987.

Deere, J. *Surprised by the Power of the Spirit*. Grand Rapids: Zondervan, 1993.

Dempster, M.W. 'Paradigm Shifts and Hermeneutics: Confronting Issues Old and New', *Pneuma* 15:2 (1993), pp. 129-135.

Derrida, J. 'Living On'/'Border Lines'. In *Deconstruction and Criticism,* ed. H. Bloom *et al.* London: Routledge & Kegan Paul, 1979.

———. 'Signature Event Context', *Glyph* 1 (1977), pp. 172-197.

de Smidt, J.C. 'Die Oë van die Gees in die boek Openbaring - 'n teologiese perspektief', *Scriptura* 54 (1995), pp. 159-176.

———. 'Hermeneutical Perspectives on the Spirit in the Book of Revelation', *JPT* 14 (1999), pp. 27-47.

———. 'The Holy Spirit in the Book of Revelation-Nomenclature', *Neot* 28 (1, 1994), pp. 229-244.

Devillers, L. 'L'Apocalypse', *RevThom* 95 (4, 95), pp. 689-699.

Dilthey, W. *The Essence of Philosophy*. Trans. S.A. Emery. New York: AMS, 1969.

Dix, G. 'The Seven Archangels and the Seven Spirits', *JTS* 28 (1926), pp. 233-250.

Dunn, J. *Jesus and the Spirit, A Study of the Religious and Charismatic Experience of Jesus and the First Christians as Reflected in the New Testament*. Philadelphia: Westminster, 1975.

Eagleton, T. *Literary Theory: An Introduction*. Minneapolis: University of Minneapolis Press, 1983.

Eco, U. *Interpretation and Overinterpretation*. Cambridge: Cambridge University Press, 1992.

Eliot, T.S. *Selected Essays*. London: Faber, 3rd edn, 1951.

Ellington, S.A. 'Pentecostalism and the Authority of Scripture', *JPT* 9 (1996), pp. 16-38.

Elliott, K. 'Nouns with Diminutive Endings in the New Testament', *NovT* 12 (1970), pp. 391-398.

Enroth, A.M. 'The Hearing Formula in the Book of Revelation', *NTS* 36 (1990), pp. 598-608.

Farrer, A.M. *A Rebirth of Images: The Making of St. John's Apocalypse*. Westminster: Dacre Press, 1949.

———. *The Revelation of St. John the Divine*. Oxford: Clarendon, 1964.

Faupel, D.W. *The Everlasting Gospel: The Significance of Eschatology in the Development of Pentecostal Thought.* Sheffield: Sheffield Academic Press, 1996.
Fee, G. *Gospel and Spirit: Issues in New Testament Hermeneutics.* Peabody, MA: Hendrickson, 1991.
Fekkes, J. *Isaiah and Prophetic Tradition in the Book of Revelation. Visionary Antecedents and their Development.* Sheffield: Sheffield Academic Press, 1994.
Feuillet, A. *Johannine Studies.* Trans. T.E. Crane. Staten Island: Alba House, 1964.
———. 'Les 144,000 Israelites marques d'un sceau', *NovT* 9 (1967), pp. 191-224.
Fewell, D.N., ed. *Reading between Texts: Intertextuality and the Hebrew Bible.* Louisville, KY: John Knox Press, 1992.
Fish, S. *Doing What Comes Naturally: Change, Rhetoric, and the Practice of Theory in Literary and Legal Studies.* Oxford: Oxford University Press, 1989.
———. 'Interpreting the *Variorum*', *Critical Inquiry* 2 (1976), pp. 465-485.
———. *Is There A Text in This Class? The Authority of Interpretative Communities.* Cambridge, MA: Harvard University Press, 1980.
———. 'Literature in the Reader: Affective Stylistics', *New Literary History* 2 (1970), pp. 123-62.
———. *Self-Consuming Artifacts: The Experience of Seventeenth-Century Literature.* Berkeley: University of California Press, 1972.
———. *Surprised by Sin: The Reader in Paradise Lost.* Berkeley: University of California Press, 1967.
———. *There is No Such Thing as Free Speech: And It's a Good Thing Too.* Oxford: Oxford University Press, 1994.
Ford, J.M. 'For the Testimony of Jesus is the Spirit of Prophecy', *ITQ* 42.4 (October 1975), pp. 285-292.
———. *Revelation.* Garden City, New York: Doubleday, 1975.
———. 'Visual Art and the Apocalypse', *BibToday* 34, 6 (1996), pp. 366-373.
Fowl, S.E. 'The New Testament, Theology and Ethics'. In *Hearing the New Testament,* ed. J.B. Green and M. Turner. Grand Rapids: Eerdmans, 1995, pp. 394-410.
Fowl, S.E. ed. *The Theological Interpretation of Scripture: Classic and Contemporary Readings.* Cambridge: Blackwell, 1997.
Fowl, S.E. and L.G. Jones. *Reading in Communion: Scripture & Ethics in the Christian Life.* Grand Rapids: Eerdmans, 1991.
Frantz, N.P. 'The (Inter)Textuality of Our Lives: An Anabaptist Feminist Hermeneutic', *CGR* 14 (1996), pp. 131-144.
Frei, H.W. *The Eclipse of Biblical Narrative: A Study in Eighteenth and Nineteenth Century Hermeneutics.* New Haven: Yale University Press, 1974.
Freund, E. *The Return of the Reader: Reader-Response Criticism.* New York: Methuen, 1987.
Freyne, S. 'Reading Hebrews and Revelation Intertextually'. In *Intertextuality in Biblical Writings,* ed. S. Draisma. Festschrift for B. van Iersel; Kampen: Kok, 1989, pp. 83-93.

Frow, J. *Marxism and Literary Theory*. Oxford: Blackwell, 1986.

Gadamer, H.-G. *Truth and Method*. Trans. A. Lingis. Pittsburg: Duquesne Press, 1969.

Gangemi, A. 'L'utilizazione del Deutero-Isaia nell' Apocalipse di Giovanni', *Euntes Docete* 27 (1974), pp. 109-144.

Garrow, A.J.P. *Revelation*. New York: Routledge, 1997.

Gause, R.H. *Revelation: God's Stamp of Sovereignty on History*. Cleveland, TN: Pathway Press, 1983.

Genette, G. *Narrative Discourse*. Ithaca: Cornell University Press, 1980.

———. *Narrative Discourse Revisited*. Ithaca: Cornell University Press, 1988.

Giblin, C.H. *The Book of Revelation: The Open Book of Prophecy*. Collegeville, MN: Liturgical Press, 1991.

———. 'Recapitulation and the Literary Coherence of John's Apocalypse', *CBQ* 56 (1994), pp. 94-95.

———. 'Revelation 11:1-13: Its Form, Function and Contextual Integration', *NTS* 30 (1984), pp. 458.

———. 'Structural and Thematic Correlations in the Theology of Revelation 16-22', *NTS* 30 (1984), pp. 433-459.

Gentry, K.L., Jr. *Before Jerusalem Fell: Dating the Book of Revelation*. Tyler, TX: Institute for Christian Economics, 1989.

Giesen, H. *Die Offenbarung des Johannes*. Regensburg: Pustet, 1997.

Goldingay, J. *Models for the Interpretation of Scripture*. Grand Rapids: Eerdmans, 1995.

Gonzalez, G. *A Theology of Liberation: History, Politics and Salvation*. Maryknoll, NY: Orbis, 1973.

Goppelt, L. *Typos: The Typological Interpretation of the Old Testament in the New*. Grand Rapids: Eerdmans, 1982.

Goulder, M.D. 'The Apocalypse as an Annual Cycle of Prophecies', *NTS* 27 (1981), pp. 342-367.

Gray, A.F. *Christian Theology*. vol. 1. Anderson, IN: Warner Press, 1944.

Greene, T.M. *The Light of Troy: Imitation and Discovery in Renaissance Poetry*. New Haven: Yale University Press, 1982.

Grubb, N. *Revelations: Art of the Apocalypse*. New York: Abbeville, 1997.

Guthrie, D. *New Testament Introduction*. 4th edition. Downers Grove: Inter-Varsity Press, 1990.

Habermas, J. 'On Hermeneutics' Claim to Universality'. In *The Hermeneutics Reader,* ed. K. Mueller-Vollmer. New York: Continuum, 1985.

Hailey, H. *Revelation*. Grand Rapids: Baker, 1979.

Hanson, A.T. *Studies on Paul's Technique and Theology*. Grand Rapids: Eerdmans, 1974.

Hanson, P.D. 'Scripture, Community and Spirit: Biblical Theology's Contribution to a Contextualized Christian Theology', *JPT* 6 (1995), pp. 3-12.

Hatina, T.R. 'Intertextuality and Historical Criticism', *Bib Int* 7 (1999), pp. 28-43.

Hauerwas, S. *Unleashing the Scriptures: Freeing the Bible from Captivity to America.* Nashville: Abingdon Press, 1993.

Haussleiter, J. *Vicorinus Episcopi Petavionensis Opera.* Leipzig: Feytag, 1916.

Hays, R.B. *Echoes of Scripture in the Letters of Paul.* New Haven: Yale University Press, 1989.

Heidegger, M. *Being and Time.* Trans. J. Macquarrie and E. Robinson. New York: Harper and Row, 1962.

Hemer, C.J. *The Letters to the Seven Churches of Asia in their Local Setting.* Sheffield: Sheffield Academic Press, 1986.

Hendricksen, W. *More than Conquerors: An Interpretation of the Book of Revelation.* 2nd edition. Grand Rapids: Baker, 1967.

Hill, D. *Greek Words and Hebrew Meanings.* Cambridge: Cambridge University Press, 1967.

———. *New Testament Prophecy.* London: Marshall, Morgan & Scott, 1979.

———. 'Prophecy and Prophets in the Revelation of St John', *NTS* 18 (1972), pp. 401-414.

Hirsch, E.D. *Aims of Interpretation.* Chicago: University of Chicago Press, 1976.

———. *Validity in Interpretation.* New Haven: Yale University Press, 1967.

Hocken, P.D. 'The Charismatic Movement', *DPCM,* pp. 130-160.

Hollander, J. *The Figure of Echo: A Mode of Allusion in Milton and After.* Berkeley: University of California Press, 1981.

Hollenweger, W.J. 'The Critical Tradition of Pentecostalism', *JPT* 1 (1992), pp. 7-17.

———. 'Intellectual Honesty and Healing the Wounds of Division', keynote address presented to the 28th Annual Meeting of the Society for Pentecostal Studies, 1999.

———. *Pentecostalism: Origins and Developments Worldwide.* Peabody: Hendrickson, 1997.

———. *The Pentecostals.* Peabody: Hendrickson, 1972.

Hooker, M.D. 'Beyond the Things That Are Written? St. Paul's Use of Scripture', *NTS* 27 (1981-82), pp. 295-309.

Horton, S.M. *What the Bible Says About the Holy Spirit.* Springfield: Gospel Publishing House, 1976.

Hühn, E. *Die alttestamentlichen Citate und Reminiscenzen im Neuen Testament.* Tübingen: J.C.B. Mohr, 1900.

Hurtado, L.W. 'Revelation 4-5 in the Light of Jewish Apocalyptic Analogies', *JSNT* 25 (1985), pp. 105-124.

Irvin, D.T. 'Contextualization and Catholicity: Looking Anew for the Unity of the Faith', *Stud Theo* 48 (1994), pp. 83-96.

———. '"Drawing All Together in One Bond of Love": The Ecumenical Vision of William J. Seymour and the Azusa Street Revival', *JPT* 6 (1995), pp. 25-53.

Israel, R.D., D.E. Albrecht and R.G. McNally. 'Pentecostals and Hermeneutics: Texts, Rituals and Community', *Pneuma* 15:2 (1993), pp. 137-161.

James, M.R. *The Apocalypse in Art.* London: Oxford University Press, 1931.

Jeske, R.L. 'Spirit and Community in the Johannine Apocalypse', *NTS* 31 (1985), pp. 452-466.

Jefferson, A. 'Autobiography as Intertext: Barthes, Sarraute, Robbe-Grillet'. In *Intertextuality: Theories and Practices,* ed. M. Worton and J. Still. pp. 108-129.

Jenkins, F. *The Old Testament in the Book of Revelation.* Marion, IN: Cogdill Foundation, 1972.

Johnson, L.T. *Religious Experience in Earliest Christianity: A Missing Dimension in New Testament Studies.* Minneapolis: Fortress, 1998.

Joüon, P. 'Apocalypse, 1.4', *RSR* 21 (1931), pp. 486-487.

Kempson, W.R. 'Theology in the Revelation of John'. Unpublished Ph.D. dissertation. Louisville: Southern Baptist Theological Seminary, 1982.

Kitzberger, I.R., ed. *The Personal Voice in Biblical Interpretation.* London: Routledge, 1999.

Kline, M.G. *Images of the Spirit.* Grand Rapids: Baker, 1980.

Klien, W.W., C.L. Blomberg and R.L. Hubbard. *Introduction to Biblical Interpretation.* Dallas: Word Books, 1993.

Knight, H. *A Future for Truth: Evangelical Theology in a Postmodern World.* Nashville: Abingdon Press, 1997.

Koivisto, R. *One Lord, One Faith: A Theology for Cross-Denominational Renewal.* Wheaton, IL: Bridgepoint/Victor, 1993.

Kraft, H. *Die Offenbarung des Johannes.* Tübingen: Mohr, 1974.

Kristeva, J. 'Bakhtine, le mot, le dialogue et le roman', *Critique* 33 (1967), pp. 438-465.

———. *Desire in Language: A Semiotic Approach to Literature and Art.* Trans. L.S. Roudiez; New York: Columbia University Press, 1980.

———. 'A New Type of Intellectual: the Dissident'. In *The Kristeva Reader,* ed. T. Moi. New York: Columbia University Press, 1986, pp. 292-300.

———. *Revolution in Poetic Language.* Trans. Margret Waller; New York: Columbia University Press, 1984.

Kuhn, T.S. *The Structure of Scientific Revolutions.* 2nd rev. ed. Chicago: Chicago University Press, 1970.

Lancellotti, A. 'L'Antico Testamento nell' Apocallise', *Rivista Biblica* 14 (1966), pp. 369-384.

Ladd, G.E. *A Commentary on the Revelation of John.* Grand Rapids: Eerdmans, 1972.

Lampe, W.H. 'The Testimony of Jesus is the Spirit of Prophecy (Rev 19:10)'. In *The New Testament Age: Essays in Honor of Bo Reicke,* ed. W.C. Weinrich. Macon: Mercer University Press, 1984, pp. 245-258.

Land, S.J. 'A Passion for the Kingdom: Revisioning Pentecostal Spirituality', *JPT* 1 (1992), pp. 19-46.

———. *Pentecostal Spirituality: A Passion for the Kingdom.* Sheffield: Sheffield Academic Press, 1993.

———. 'The Triune Center: Wesleyans and Pentecostals Together in Mission', *WTJ* 34:1 (1999), pp. 83-100.

Lee, M.V. 'A Call to Martyrdom: Function as Method and Message in Revelation', *NovT* 40 (1998), pp. 174-175.
Levison, J. and P. Pope-Levison. 'Global Perspectives on New Testament Interpretation'. In *Hearing the New Testament,* ed. J.B. Green, pp. 329-348.
Lewis, W.H., ed. *Letters of C.S. Lewis.* New York: Harcourt, Brace and World, 1966.
Lindars, B. 'The Place of the Old Testament in the Formation of New Testament Theology', *NTS* 23 (1977), pp. 59-66.
Lindsey, H. *There's a New World Coming.* New York: Bantam, 1975.
Lints, R. *The Fabric of Theology: A Prolegomenon to Evangelical Theology.* Grand Rapids: Eerdmans, 1993.
Lohmeyer, E. *Die Offenbarung des Johannes.* Tübingen: Mohr, 1926.
Lohse, E. *Die Offenbarung des Johannes.* Göttingen: Vandenhoek & Ruprecht, 1960.
Loisy, A. *L'Apocalypse de Jean.* Paris: Nourry, 1923.
Longenecker, R. 'Can We Reproduce the Exegesis of the New Testament?', *TynBul* 21 (1970), pp. 3-38.
———. 'Who Is the Prophet Talking About? Some Reflections on the New Testament's Use of the Old', *Them* 13 (1987), pp. 4-8.
Lund, N.W. *Chiasmus in the New Testament.* Chapel Hill: University of North Carolina, 1942.
———. *Studies in the Book of Revelation.* Chicago: Covenant, 1955.
Lupieri, E. 'The Seventh Night: Visions of History in the Revelation of John and the Contemporary Apocalyptic', *Henoch* 14 (1992), pp. 113-32.
Luz, U. *Matthew in History: Interpretation, Influence, and Effects.* Minneapolis: Fortress Press, 1994.
———. 'A Response to Emerson B. Powery', *JPT* 14 (1999), pp. 19-26.
Lyons, W.J. *Canon and Exegesis: Canonical Praxis and the Sodom Narrative.* Sheffield: Sheffield Academic Press, 2002.
Macchia, F.D. 'A Reply to Rickie Moore', *JPT* 17 (2000), pp. 15-19.
———. 'Guest Editorial: 'The Toronto Blessing': No Laughing Matter', *JPT* 8 (1996), pp. 3-6.
Marconcini, B. 'L'utilazione del T.M. nelle citazioni isaiane dell' Apocalipse', *Rivista Biblica* 24 (1976), pp. 113-136.
Martin, R.F. 'Apocalypse, Book of the', *DPCM,* pp. 11-13.
———. *The Spirit and the Church: A Personal and Documentary Record of the Charismatic Renewal and the Ways it is Bursting to Life in the Catholic Church.* New York: Paulist Press, 1976.
Martínez, F.G. and E.J.C. Tigchelaar, eds. *The Dead Sea Scrolls: Study Edition.* vol. 1. Leiden: Brill, 1997.
Mazzaferri, F.D. *The Genre of the Book of Revelation from a Source-Critical Perspective.* New York: de Gruyter, 1989.
McDonnell, K. *Charismatic Renewal in the Churches.* New York: Seabury Press, 1976.

McDonnell, K., ed. *Presence, Power, and Praise: Documents on the Charismatic Movement.* Collegeville: Liturgical Press, 1980.

McGee, G. 'Review of *Fire from Heaven: The Rise of Pentecostal Spirituality and the Reshaping of Religion in the Twenty-first Century,* by H. Cox', *Missiology* 24 (1996), p. 421.

McKay, J. 'When the Veil is Taken Away: The Impact of Prophetic Experience on Biblical Interpretation', *JPT* 5 (1994), pp. 17-40.

McKnight, E.V. *Post-Modern Use of the Bible: The Emergence of Reader-Oriented Criticism.* Nashville: Abingdon, 1988.

McQueen, L.R. *Joel and the Spirit: The Cry of a Prophetic Hermeneutic.* Sheffield: Sheffield Academic Press, 1995.

Menzies, R.P. 'Jumping Off the Postmodern Bandwagon', *Pneuma* 16:1 (1994), pp. 115-120.

Michaels, J.R. *Interpreting the Book of Revelation.* Grand Rapids: Baker Books, 1992.

Michaels, W.B. 'The Interpreter's Self: Pierce on the Cartesian "Subject"', *Georgia Review* 31 (1977), pp. 383-402.

Míguez Bonino, J. 'Changing Paradigms: A Response'. In *The Globalization of Pentecostalism: A Religion Made to Travel,* ed. M.W. Dempster *et al.* Oxford: Renum, 1999.

Minear, P.S. 'Ontology and Ecclesiology in the Apocalypse', *NTS* 12 (1966), pp. 96-97.

Miscall, P.D. 'Isaiah: New Heavens, New Earth, New Book'. In *Reading between Texts: Intertextuality and the Hebrew Bible,* ed. D.N. Fewell. Louisville, KY: Westminster/John Knox Press, 1992.

Moffatt, J. 'The Revelation of St. John the Divine', vol. 5 in *The Expositor's Greek Testament.* Grand Rapids: Eerdmans, 1983, pp. 279-494.

Moi, T. ed. *The Kristeva Reader.* Oxford: Basil Blackwell, 1986.

Moltmann, J. *The Way of Jesus Christ: Christology in Messianic Dimensions.* Trans. M. Kohl. Minneapolis: Fortress, 1990.

Moore, R.D. 'A Letter to Frank Macchia', *JPT* 17 (2000), pp. 12-14.

———. '"And Also Much Cattle?!": Prophetic Passions and the End of Jonah', *JPT* 11 (1997), pp. 35-48.

———. 'Canon and Charisma in the Book of Deuteronomy', *JPT* 1 (1993), pp. 75-92.

———. 'Deuteronomy and the Fire of God: A Critical Charismatic Interpretation', *JPT* 7 (1995), pp. 11-33.

———. 'The Integrity of Job', *CBQ* 45:1 (1983), pp. 17-31.

———. 'Pentecostal Approach to Scripture', *The Seminary Viewpoint* 8:1 (1987), pp. 4-5.

Moore, R.D., J.C. Thomas and S.J. Land. 'Editorial', *JPT* 1 (1992), pp. 3-5.

Moore, S. 'The Beatific Vision as a Posing Exhibition: Revelation's Hypermasculine Deity', *JSNT* 60 (1995) pp. 27-55.

———. *Literary Criticism and the Gospels: The Theoretical Challenge,* New Haven, CN: Yale University Press, 1989.

———. *Mark and Luke in Poststructuralist Perspectives: Jesus Begins to Write.* New Haven: Yale University Press, 1989.
———. 'Negative Hermeneutics, Insubstantial Texts: Stanley Fish and the Biblical Interpreter', *JAAR* 4 (1988), pp. 707-719.
Moore, S., ed. *Derrida and Biblical Studies.* SBL Semeia Studies 23. Decatur: Scholars Press, 1982.
Morgan, R. with J. Barton. *Biblical Interpretation.* Oxford: Oxford University Press, 1988.
Moulton, J.H. *Early Religious Poetry of Persia.* Cambridge: Cambridge University Press, 1911.
Mounce, R.H. *The Book of Revelation.* Grand Rapids: Eerdmans, 1977.
Moyise, S. 'Does the New Testament Quote the Old Testament Out of Context', *Anvil* 11 (1994), pp. 133-143.
———. 'Intertextuality and the Book of Revelation', *ExpTim* 104 (1993), pp. 295-298.
———. 'Intertextuality and the Study of the Old Testament in the New Testament'. In *The Old Testament in the New Testament: Essays in Honour of J.L. North,* ed. S. Moyise. Sheffield: Sheffield Academic Press, 2000, pp. 25-32.
———. *The Old Testament in the Book of Revelation.* Sheffield: Sheffield Academic Press, 1995.
———. 'The Old Testament in the New: A Reply to Greg Beale', *IBS* 21 (1999), pp. 54-58.
Mulholland, M.R. *Revelation: Holy Living in an Unholy World.* Grand Rapids: Zondervan, 1990.
Muller, R.A. *The Study of Theology: From Biblical Interpretation to Contemporary Formulation.* Grand Rapids: Zondervan, 1991.
Murphy, F.J. 'The Book of Revelation', *CR:BS* 2 (1994), pp. 181-205.
Nessan, C. 'When Faith Turns Fatal: David Koresh and Tragic Misreadings of Revelation', *CurrTheolMiss* 22 (3, 1995), pp. 191-199.
Nielsen, K. 'Intertextuality and Biblical Scholarship', *Scandinavian Journal of the Old Testament* 2 (1990), pp. 89-95.
O'Connor, E.D. *The Pentecostal Movement in the Catholic Church.* Notre Dame: Ave Maria Press, 1971.
O'Connor, E.D., ed. *Perspectives on Charismatic Renewal.* Notre Dame: University of Notre Dame Press, 1974.
O'Rourke, J.J. 'The Hymns of the Apocalypse', *CBQ* 30 (1968), pp. 399-409.
Osborne, G.R. *The Hermeneutical Spiral: A Comprehensive Introduction to Biblical Interpretation.* Downers Grove: InterVarsity Press, 1991.
———. *Revelation.* Grand Rapids: Baker Academic, 2002.
Panagopoulos, J. *Prophetic Vocation in the New Testament and Today.* Leiden: Brill, 1977.
Pannenberg, W. *Metaphysics and the Idea of God.* Trans. P. Clayton. Grand Rapids: Eerdmans, 1990.

Paul, I. 'The Value of Paul Ricoeur's Hermeneutic of Metaphor in Interpreting the Symbolism of Revelation Chapters 12 and 13'. Ph.D. thesis. The Nottingham Trent University, 1998.

Paulien, J. *Decoding Revelation's Trumpets: Literary Allusions and Interpretation of Revelation 8:7-12*. Andrews University Seminary Doctoral Dissertation Series, 21; Berrien Springs, MI: Andrews University Press, 1987.

———. 'Elusive Allusions: The Problematic Use of the Old Testament in Revelation', *BR* 33 (1988), pp. 40-48.

Peterson, N.R. *Literary Criticism for New Testament Critics*. Philadelphia: Fortress, 1978.

Petraglio, R. *et al. L'Apocalypse Jean: traditions exégétiques et iconographiques aux III-XIIIe siècles*. Geneva: Librairie Droz, 1979.

Pietersen, L., ed. *The Mark of the Spirit? A Charismatic Critique of the Toronto Blessing*. Carlisle: Paternoster, 1998.

Pinnock, C.H. 'The Work of the Holy Spirit in Hermeneutics', *JPT* 2 (1995), pp. 3-23.

Pippin, T. *Death and Desire: The Rhetoric of Gender in the Apocalypse of John*. Literary Currents in Biblical Interpretation; Louisville: Westminster/John Knox Press, 1992.

———. 'Eros and the End: Reading for Gender in the Apocalypse of John', *Semeia* 59 (1992), pp. 193-210.

———. 'The Heroine and the Whore: Fantasy and the Female in the Apocalypse of John', *Semeia* 60 (1992), pp. 67-82.

———. 'Peering into the Abyss: A Postmodern Reading of the Biblical Bottomless Pit'. In *The New Literary Criticism and the New Testament,* ed. E.V. McKnight and E. Struthers Malbon. Sheffield: Sheffield Academic Press, 1994, pp. 251-68.

Plett, H.F., ed. *Intertextuality*. Berlin: de Gruyter, 1991.

Plüss, J-D. 'Azusa and Other Myths: The Long and Winding Road from Experience to Stated Belief and Back Again', *Pneuma* 15:2 (1993), pp. 189-201.

Poloma, M.M. 'The Spirit Movement in North America at the Millennium: From Azusa Street to Toronto, Pensacola and Beyond', *JPT* 12 (1998), pp. 83-107.

Pope, L. *Mill Hands and Preachers: A Study of Gastonia*. New Haven: Yale University Press, 1965.

Porter, S.E. 'The Use of the Old Testament in the New Testament: A Brief Comment on Method and Terminology'. In *Early Christian Interpretation of the Scriptures of Israel: Investigations and Proposals,* ed. C.A. Evans and J.A. Sanders. Sheffield: Sheffield Academic Press, 1997, pp. 79-96.

Powell, M.A. *What is Narrative Criticism?* Minneapolis, Fortress, 1990.

Powery, E.B. 'Ulrich Luz's *Matthew in History:* A Contribution to Pentecostal Hermeneutics?' *JPT* 14 (1999), pp. 3-17.

Prigent, P. *Apocalypse et Liturgie*. Paris: Delachaux et Niestlé, 1964.

———. *Commentary on the Apocalypse of St. John*. Trans. W. Pradels. Tübingen: Mohr Siebeck, 2001.

Quebedeaux, R. *The Charismatics II*. San Francisco: Harper & Row, 1983.

Quispel, G. *The Secret Book of Revelation*. London: Collins, 1979.

Ranaghan, K. and D. Ranaghan. *Catholic Pentecostals*. Paramus: Paulist Press, 1969.

———. *As the Spirit Leads Us*. Paramus: Paulist Press, 1971.

Ramsay, W.M. *The Letters to the Seven Churches of Asia and their Place in the Plan of the Apocalypse*. London: Hodder & Stoughton, 1904.

Reiling, J. 'Prophecy, the Spirit and the Church'. In *Prophetic Vocation in the New Testament and Today*, ed. J. Panagopoulos. Leiden: Brill, 1977.

Ricoeur, P. *Hermeneutics and the Human Sciences*. Cambridge: Cambridge University Press 1981.

Rissi, M. *Zeit und Geschichte in der Offenbarung der Johannesapokalypse*. Zürich: Zwingli, 1965.

Robertson, A.T. *A Grammar of the Greek New Testament in the Light of Historical Research*. Nashville: Broadman Press, 1934.

Roloff, J. *Revelation*. Trans. J.E. Alsup. Minneapolis: Fortress, 1993.

Rorty, R. 'Texts and Lumps', *New Literary History* 17 (1985), pp. 1-16.

———. *Philosophy and the Mirror of Nature*. Princeton: Princeton University Press, 1980.

Rosenswig, B. 'The Hermeneutic Principles and Their Application', *Tradition* 13 (1972), pp. 49-76.

Rowland, C. *The Open Heaven: A Study of Apocalyptic in Judaism and Early Christianity*. New York: Crossland, 1982.

Rowland, C. and M. Corner, *Liberating Exegesis: The Challenge of Liberation Theology to Biblical Studies*. Louisville: John Knox Press, 1989.

Ruiz, J.-P. *Ezekiel in the Apocalypse: The Transformation of Prophetic Language in Revelation 16,17-19,10*. Frankfurt am Main: Peter Lang, 1989.

Russell, L., ed. *Changing Contexts of Our Faith*. Philadelphia: Fortress, 1985.

Sandmel, S. 'Parallelomania', *JBL* 81 (1962), pp. 1-13.

Satake, A. *Die Gemeindeordnung in der Johannesapokalypse*. Neukirchen: Neukirchener Verlag, 1966.

Schlatter, A. *Das Alte Testament in der johanneischen Apokalypse*. Gütersloh: Bertelsmann, 1912.

Schüssler Fiorenza, E. *The Book of Revelation, Justice and Judgment*. Philadelphia: Fortress, 1985.

———. *Revelation: Vision of a Just World*. Edinburgh: T. & T. Clark, new edn, 1993.

Schweizer, E. 'Die sieben Geister in der Apokalypse', *EvT* 6 (1951-52), pp. 502-512.

———. 'Πνεῦμα, [NT]', *TDNT* 6 (1968), pp. 389-455.

Seiss, J.A. *The Apocalypse: A Series of Special Lectures on the Revelation of Jesus Christ*. Grand Rapids, Eerdmans, 1966.

Shelton, J.B. 'Epistemology and Authority in the Acts of the Apostles: An Analysis and Test Case of Acts 15:1-29', a paper presented to the 28th annual meeting of the SPS, March 1998.

Shepherd, M.H. *The Pascal Liturgy and the Apocalypse.* Richmond: John Knox, 1960.

Skrinjar, A. 'Les sept Esprits (Apoc. 1.4; 3.1; 4.5; 5.6)', *Bib* 16 (1935), pp. 1-25, 113-140.

Sjöberg, E. 'רוח in Palestinian Judaism', *TDNT* 6 (1968), pp. 375-389.

Smith, C.R. 'The Structure of the Book of Revelation in Light of Apocalyptic Literary Conventions', *NovT* 36 (1994), pp. 373-393.

Smith, J.K.A. 'The Closing of the Book: Pentecostals, Evangelicals, and the Sacred Writings', *JPT* 11 (1997), pp. 49-71.

———. *The Fall of Interpretation: Philosophical Foundations for a Creational Hermeneutic.* Downers Grove: InterVarsity Press, 2000.

———. 'How to Avoid Not Speaking: Attestations'. In *Knowing Other-wise: Philosophy on the Threshold of Spirituality,* ed. J.H. Olthuis, Perspectives in Continental Philosophy. Bronx: Fordham University Press, 1997.

———. 'Originary Violence: The Fallenness of Interpretation in Derrida', *Concept* 19 (1996), pp. 27-41.

———. 'The Art of Christian Atheism: Faith and Philosophy in Early Heidegger', *Faith and Philosophy* 14:1 (1997), pp. 71-81.

Snyman, G. 'Who is Speaking? Intertextuality and Textual Influence', *Neot* 30:2 (1996), pp. 427-449.

Sommer, B.D. 'Exegesis, Allusion and Intertextuality in the Hebrew Bible: A Response to Lyle Eslinger', *Vetus Testamentum* 44:4 (1996), pp. 479-489.

Spinks, L.C. 'A Critical Examination of J.W. Bowman's Proposed Structure of the Revelation', *EQ* 50 (1978), pp. 211-222.

Spitta, F. *Die Offenbarung des Johannes.* Halle: Waisenhaus, 1889.

Stanley, J.E. 'Elements of a Postmodern Holiness Hermeneutic Illustrated by the Way of the Book of Revelation', *WTJ* 28 (1993), pp. 23-43.

Steinmetz, D.C. 'The Superiority of Pre-Critical Exegesis', *Theology Today,* 37, 1 (1980), pp. 27-38.

Stephanou, E.A. *The Charismatic Renewal in the Orthodox Church: 100 questions most frequently asked about the Orthodox Charismatic Renewal.* Fort Wayne: Logos Ministry for Orthodox Renewal, 1976.

Strand, K.A. 'Chiastic Structure and Some Motifs in the Book of Revelation', *AUSS* 16 (1978), pp. 401-408.

———. 'An Overlooked Old Testament Background to Revelation 11:1', *AUSS* 22 (1984), pp. 322-324.

———. 'The Two Witnesses of Rev. 11:3-12', *AUSS* 19 (1981), pp. 127-135.

Strathmann, H. 'μάρτυς, μαρτυρέω, μαρτυρία, *TDNT* 4 (1967), pp. 474-514.

Stronstad, R. *The Charismatic Theology of St. Luke.* Peabody: Hendrickson, 1984.

———. 'The Dynamics of a Pentecostal Pneumatology: Essays in Hermeneutics and Theology.' Unpublished monograph.

———. *The Prophethood of All Believers.* Sheffield: Sheffield Academic Press, 1999.

Sugirtharajah, R.S., ed. *Voices from the Margin: Interpreting the Bible in the Third World.* Maryknoll: Orbis, 1991.

Sullivan, F.A. 'Catholic Charismatic Renewal', *DPCM,* pp. 110-126.

Sweet, J.P.M. *Revelation.* London: SCM Press, 1979.

Swete, H.B. *The Apocalypse of St John.* London: Macmillan, 1907.

Synan, V., ed. *The Holiness-Pentecostal Movement in the United States.* Grand Rapids: Eerdmans, 1971.

Tate, W.R. *Biblical Interpretation: An Integrated Approach.* Peabody: Hendrickson, 1991.

Tenney, M.C. *Interpreting Revelation.* Grand Rapids: Eerdmans, 1958.

Thiselton, A.C. *New Horizons in Hermeneutics: The Theory and Practice of Transforming Biblical Reading.* London: HarperCollins, 1992.

———. 'On Models and Methods: A Conversation with Robert Morgan'. In *The Bible in Three Dimensions: Essays in Celebration of Forty Years of Biblical Studies in the University of Sheffield,* ed. D.J.A. Clines *et al.* Sheffield: Sheffield Academic Press, 1990, pp. 337-356.

Thomas, J.C. *Footwashing in John 13 and the Johannine Community.* Sheffield: Sheffield Academic Press, 1991.

———. *Ministry & Theology. Studies for the Church and Its Leaders.* Cleveland: Pathway Press, 1996.

———. 'Pentecostal Theology in the Twenty-First Century', *Pneuma* 20 (1998), pp. 3-19.

———. 'Reading the Bible from within Our Traditions: A Pentecostal Hermeneutic'. In *Between Two Horizons:Spanning New Testament Studies & Systematic Theology,* eds. J.B. Green and M. Turner. Grand Rapids: Eerdmans, 2000, pp. 108-122.

———. 'Women, Pentecostals and the Bible: An Experiment in Pentecostal Hermeneutics', *JPT* 5 (1994), pp. 41-56.

Thomas, R.L. 'John's Apocalyptic Outline', *Bibliotheca Sacra* 126 (1969), pp. 334-341.

———. *Revelation 1-7: An Exegetical Commentary.* Chicago: Moody, 1992.

———. *Revelation 8-22: An Exegetical Commentary.* Chicago: Moody, 1995.

Todorov, T. *Grammaire du Décaméron.* The Hague: Mouton, 1969.

Tompkins, J.P., ed. *Reader-Response Criticism: From Formalism to Post-Structuralism.* Baltimore: Johns Hopkins University Press, 1980.

Trites, A.A. *The New Testament Concept of Witness.* Cambridge: Cambridge University Press, 1977.

Trudinger, L.P. 'Some Observations Concerning the Text of the Old Testament in the Book of Revelation', *JTS* 17 (1966), pp. 82-88.

Ukpong, J. 'What is Contextualization?', *NZM* 43 (1987), pp. 161-168.

van der Meer, F. *Apocalypse, Visions from the Book of Revelation in Western Art.* New York: Alpine Fine Arts Collection, Ltd, 1978.

van Ruiten, J. 'The Intertextual Relationship between Isaiah 65:17-20 and Revelation 21:1-5b', *Estudios Bíblicos* 51 (1993), pp. 473-510.

van Wolde, E. 'Trendy Intertextuality'. In *Intertextuality in Biblical Writings,* ed. S. Draisma. Festschrift for B. van Iersel; Kampen: Kok, 1989, pp. 43-49.

Vanhooser, K. *Is There a Meaning in This Text? The Bible, the Reader and the Morality of Literary Knowledge.* Grand Rapids, MI: Zondervan, 1998.

Vanhoye, A. 'L'utilisation du livre d'Ezéchiel dans l'Apocalypse', *Bib* 43 (1962), pp. 436-476.

Vanni, U. 'L'Apocalypse johannique: Etat de la question'. In *L'Apocalypse johannique et l'Apocalyptique dans le Nouveau Testament,* ed. J. Lambrecht, Leuven: Leuven University Press, 1980, pp. 21-46.

Victorinus. *Commentary in Apocalypsin,* ed. J. Haussleiter, Vienna, 1916.

Vischer, E. *Die Offenbarung Johannis: Eine jüdische Apokalypse in christlicher Bearbeitung.* Leipzig: Hinrichs, 1886.

Vogelgesang, J.M. 'The Interpretation of Ezekiel in the Book of Revelation'. Ph.D. thesis. Harvard University, 1985.

Vorster, W.S. '"Genre" and the Revelation of John: A Study in Text, Context and Intertext', *Neot* 22 (1988), pp. 103-123.

———. 'Intertextuality and Redaktionsgeschichte'. In *Intertextuality in Biblical Writings,* ed. S. Draisma. Festschrift B. van Iersel. Kampen: Kok, 1989.

Vos, L.A. *The Synoptic Traditions in the Apocalypse.* Kampen: Kok, 1965.

Wacker, G. 'Bibliography and Historiography of Pentecostalism (U.S.)', *DPCM,* pp. 65-76.

Waddell, R. 'Hearing What the Spirit Says to the Churches: A Profile of a Pentecostal Reader of the Apocalypse', a paper presented to the 28th annual meeting of the SPS, March 1998.

Waechter, S.L. 'An Analysis of the Literary Structure of the Book of Revelation according to Textlinguistic Methods'. Ph.D. thesis. Mid-America Baptist Theological Seminary, 1994.

Wainwright, A.W. *Mysterious Apocalypse. Interpreting the Book of Revelation.* Nashville: Abingdon Press, 1993.

Wall, R. *Revelation.* Peabody, MA: Hendrickson, 1991.

Walvoord, J.F. *The Revelation of Jesus Christ.* London: Marshall, Morgan, & Scott, 1966.

Wagner, C.P. 'Third Wave', *DPCM,* pp. 843-844.

Watson, F. *Text Church and World: Biblical Interpretation in Theological Perspective.* Grand Rapids: Eerdmans, 1994.

Weiner, A.D. 'Sidney/Spencer/Shakespeare: Influence/Intertextuality/Intention'. In *Influence and Intertextuality in Literary History,* ed. J. Clayton and E. Rothstein. Madison, WI: University of Wisconsin Press, 1991, pp. 245-270.

Weingreen, J. 'The Rabbinic Approach to the Study of the Old Testament', *BJRLM* 34 (1951-52), pp. 166-190.

Weiss, B. *Die Johannes-Apocalypse: Textkritische Untersuchungen und Textherstellung.* Leipzig: Hinrichs, 1892.

Weiss, J. *Die Offenbarung des Johannes*. Göttingen: Vandenhoeck & Ruprecht, 1904.
Wesley, J. *Explanatory Notes upon the New Testament*. 1755, repr. London: Epworth 1950.
West, G. *Biblical Hermeneutics of Liberation*. Pietermaritzburg: Cluster, 1991.
———. 'Reading the Bible and Doing Theology in the New South Africa'. In *The Bible and Human Society,* ed. D. Carroll, D. Clines and P. Davies. Sheffield: Sheffield Academic Press, 1995, pp. 445-58.
Weyland, W.G.J. *Omwerkings en Compilatie-Hypothesen toegepast op de Apokalypse van Johannes*. Groningen: Wolters, 1888.
Whealen, J.F. 'New Patches of an Old Garment: The Book of Revelation', *BTB* 11 (1981), pp. 54-59.
Williams, J.R. 'Harvey Cox and Pentecostalism: A Review of *Fire form Heaven'*, *APS* 1 (1998), pp. 23-26.
Wilcock, M. *I Saw Heaven Opened*. London: InterVarsity Press, 1975.
Wilmore, G. *Last Things First*. Philadelphia: Westminster, 1982.
Wilson, M.W. 'A Pie in a Very Bleak Sky: Analysis and Appropriation of the Promise Sayings in the Seven Letters to the Churches in Revelation 2-3'. Ph.D. thesis. University of South Africa.
———. 'Revelation 19:10 and Contemporary Interpretation'. In *Spirit and Renewal: Essays in Honor of J. Rodman Williams,* ed. M.W. Wilson. Sheffield: Sheffield Academic Press, 1994.
Worton, M. and J. Still, eds. *Intertextuality: Theories and Practices*. Manchester: Manchester University Press, 1990.
Wright, N.T. *The New Testament and the People of God*. Minneapolis: Fortress, 1992.
Yarbro Collins, A. *The Combat Myth in the Book of Revelation*. Missoula: Scholars Press, 1976.
———. *Crisis and Catharsis: The Power of the Apocalypse*. Philadelphia: Westminster, 1984.
Yong, A. *Discerning the Spirit(s): A Pentecostal-Charismatic Contribution to Christian Theology of Religions*. Sheffield: Sheffield Academic Press, 2000.
Zahn, T. *Die Offenbarung des Johannes*. Leipzig: Deichert, 1924.

Index of Authors

Index of Scripture References

Extra-canonical Writings

Journal of Pentecostal Theology Supplement Series

1. Steven J. Land, *Pentecostal Spirituality: A Passion for the Kingdom*. ISBN 1 85075 442 X.
2. Cheryl Bridges Johns, *Pentecostal Formation: A Pedagogy among the Oppressed*. ISBN 1 85075 438 1.
3. Jon Ruthven, *On the Cessation of the Charismata: The Protestant Polemic on Miracles*. ISBN 1 85075 405 5.
4. Harold D. Hunter & Peter D. Hocken (eds.), *All Together in One Place: Theological Papers from the Brighton Conference on World Evangelization*. ISBN 1 85075 406 3.
5. Mark Wilson (ed.), *Spirit and Renewal: Essays in Honor of J. Rodman Williams*. ISBN 1 85075 471 3.
6. Robert P. Menzies, *Empowered for Witness: The Spirit in Luke-Acts*. ISBN 1 85075 721 6.
7. Stephen E. Parker, *Led by the Spirit: Toward a Practical Theology of Pentecostal Discernment and Decision Making*. ISBN 1 85075 746 1.
8. Larry R. McQueen, *Joel and the Spirit: The Cry of a Prophetic Hermeneutic*. ISBN 1 85075 736 4.
9. Max Turner, *Power from on High: The Spirit in Israel's Restoration and Witness in Luke-Acts*. ISBN 1 85075 756 9.
10. D. William Faupel, *The Everlasting Gospel: The Significance of Eschatology in the Development of Pentecostal Thought*. ISBN 1 85075 761 5.
11. Wonsuk Ma & Robert P. Menzies, *Pentecostalism in Context: Essays in Honor of William W. Menzies*. ISBN 1 85075 803 4.
12. John Michael Penny, *The Missionary Emphasis of Lukan Pneumatology*. ISBN 1 85075 800 X.
13. John Christopher Thomas, *The Devil, Disease, and Deliverance: Origins of Illness in New Testament Thought*. ISBN 1 85075 869 7.
14. Samuel Solivan, *The Spirit, Pathos and Liberation: Toward an Hispanic Pentecostal Theology*. ISBN 1 85075 942 1.
15. Allan H. Anderson & Walter J. Hollenweger, *Pentecostals after a Century: Global Perspectives on a Movement in Transition*. ISBN 1 84127 006 7.
16. Roger Stronstad, *The Prophethood of All Believers: A Study in Luke's Charismatic Theology*. ISBN 1 84127 005 9.
17. Daniel E. Albrecht, *Rites in the Spirit: A Ritual Approach to Pentecostal/Charismatic Spirituality*. ISBN 1 84127 017 2.
18. Blaine Charette, *Restoring Presence: The Spirit in Matthew's Gospel*. ISBN 1 84127 059 8.
19. Matthias Wenk, *Community Forming Power: The Socio-Ethical Role of the Spirit in Luke-Acts*. ISBN 1 84127 125 X.

20. Amos Yong, *Discerning the Spirit(s): A Pentecostal-Charismatic Contribution to Christian Theology of Religions*. ISBN 1 84127 133 0.
21. Simon Chan, *Pentecostal Theology and the Christian Spiritual Tradition*. ISBN 1 84127 144 6.
22. Gerald Hovenden, *Speaking in Tongues: The New Testament Evidence in Context*. ISBN 1 84127 307 6.
23. Lynne Price, *Theology out of Place: A Theological Biography of Walter J. Hollenweger*. ISBN 0 82646 028 3.
24. Wonsuk Ma & Robert P. Menzies, *The Spirit and Spirituality: Essays in Honour of Russell P. Spittler*. ISBN 0 56708 167 2.
25. Peter Althouse, *Spirit of the Last Days: Pentecostal Eschatology in Conversation with Jürgen Moltmann*. ISBN 0 82647 162 5.
26. Martin William Mittelstadt, *The Spirit and Suffering in Luke-Acts: Implications for a Pentecostal Pneumatology*. ISBN 0 82647 164 1.
27. S. David Moore, *The Shepherding Movement: Controversy and Charismatic Ecclesiology*. ISBN 0 82647 160 9.
28. Kenneth J. Archer, *A Pentecostal Hermeneutic for the Twenty-First Century: Spirit, Scripture and Community*. ISBN 0 56708 367 5.

Volumes 1-28 were originally published by Sheffield Academic Press/Continuum. Subsequent titles are published by Deo Publishing under ISSN 0966 7393:

29. Kimberly Ervin Alexander, *Pentecostal Healing: Models in Theology and Practice*. ISBN 90 5854 031 6.
30. Robby Waddell, *The Spirit of Revelation*. ISBN 90 5854 030 8.
31. David Reed, *"In Jesus' Name": The History and Beliefs of Oneness Pentecostals*. ISBN 1 905679 01 7 / 978 1 905679 01 0.

Also published by Deo Publishing:
John Christopher Thomas, *The Spirit of the New Testament*. ISBN 90 5854 029 4.